Stefanie Sievers

Liberating Narratives

FORECAAST

(Forum for European Contributions
to African American Studies)

Volume 2

LIT

Stefanie Sievers

Liberating Narratives

The Authorization of Black Female Voices
in African American Women Writers' Novels of Slavery

LIT

Die Deutsche Bibliothek – CIP-Einheitsaufnahme

Sievers, Stefanie
Liberating Narratives : The Authorization of Black Female Voices in African
American Women Writers' Novels of Slavery / Stefanie Sievers. – Hamburg :
LIT, 1999
   (FORECAAST ; 2.)
   Zugl.: Kassel, Univ., Diss., 1996
   ISBN 3-8258-3919-2

NE: GT

© LIT VERLAG
   Grindelberg 15a 20144 Hamburg Tel. 040–44 64 46 Fax 040–44 14 22

Distributed in North America by:

Transaction Publishers
New Brunswick (U.S.A.) and London (U.K.)

Transaction Publishers   Tel.: (732) 445 – 2280
Rutgers University   Fax: (732) 445 – 3138
35 Berrue Circle   for orders (U.S. only):
Piscataway, NJ 08854   toll free 888-999-6778

ACKNOWLEDGEMENTS

"Books are not solitary births"—especially a critical study draws its *raison d'être* from books that have come before. And although the writing itself creates many solitary moments, these moments are embedded in conversations and the sharing of ideas with others. This is the place and the time, then, to show my appreciation for the generous support I have received in the course of my work on this project.

This study started as a Ph.D.-thesis at the Universität-Gesamthochschule Kassel. It was Martin Schulze who offered me the opportunity to pursue my Ph.D.-work in Kassel, and who accompanied this project as my advisor. Financial support came from an International Student Exchange Service-Scholarship to spend the academic year 1990/91 at the University of Wisconsin-Madison and a doctoral fellowship from the State of Hessen, 1991 to 1993.

My thanks go to my family and all friends and colleagues on both sides of the Atlantic who have—over the last decade—provided support through inspiring discussions and helpful suggestions, and especially through their continuing reassurances that I could do it: Karin and Manfred Sievers, who never doubted that I would make the right decisions; Corinna Heipcke, Sabine Meyer, Heike Hartrath, Karin Wenz and Kerstin Wolff, who took the time to listen, think about, and (proof-)read parts or all of the manuscript at different times and at different stages; Justine Tally and Winfried Nöth, who carefully read the complete manuscript and made helpful editorial suggestions; Sid Bremer, Maria Diedrich, Susan Friedman and Peter Kellogg, whose dedication to their students and their work continues to be an inspiration. I am especially indebted to Estella Lauter. She has, in the course of this project, shown me the true meaning of intellectual and personal generosity, and has become both mentor and most trusted friend.

This book is for Yasha.

Minnepolis, March 1999   Stefanie Sievers

CONTENTS

"Moving history beyond nightmare into structures for the future"—
African American Women Writers' Historical Narratives

> It's not that we haven't always been here, since
> there was a here. It is that the letters of our names
> have been scrambled when they were not totally
> erased, and our fingerprints upon the handles of
> history have been called the random brushings of
> birds.
>
> —Audre Lorde, "Forword"

A deep concern with history and its consequences for the present is a shared point of emphasis in many otherwise widely differing novels by contemporary African American women writers. In some, the main focus is on late 20th-century people and events—as in Paule Marshall's *The Chosen Place, the Timeless People* (1969) and *Daughters* (1991), Alice Walker's *The Temple of My Familiar* (1988), or Gayl Jones's *Corregidora* (1975). Others are set one or more generations in the past—for example Toni Morrison's *Sula* (1973) or Walker's *The Color Purple* (1983). Almost always, however, black cultural traditions, family genealogies, and the impact of the historical experiences of slavery and racism on the characters' everyday lives play important roles. "The use of history in the novels of contemporary African-American women writers . . . is constant and consistent," critic Barbara Christian affirms ("Somebody Forgot to Tell" 328). To come to an understanding of the African American past is often shown as a precondition for 20th-century characters' attempts to develop and give voice to confident, self-defined perspectives.

Within a more general context of exploring the complexities of black life in the United States, a number of African American women writers have recently expanded the time frames of their stories and turned to the 19th-century past in their explicitly historical narratives.[1] Margaret Walker's *Jubilee* was, at the time of its publication in 1966, the first novel by a black woman writer with a temporal setting outside of what immediate memory could recall. Other texts that are completely or in substantial part set before the twentieth century include Barbara Chase-Riboud's *Sally Hemings* (1979), a text that shares with *Jubilee* its strong reliance on verifiable historical data and traditional conventions of realistic novel writing. Octavia Butler's *Kindred* (1979) and Jewelle Gomez's *The Gilda Stories* (1991) explore—through their protagonists' abilities to travel through space and time—how context-bound perceptions of historical events invariably are. Sherley Anne Williams's *Dessa Rose* (1986) challenges the uncritical acceptance of white-authored historical accounts of black lives as "facts." In *Family* (1991), J. California Cooper further extends the possibilities of narrative perspective: telling the life stories of her enslaved children, the narrative voice is a dead mother's who is speaking from a place somewhere between life and death, where she can watch but no longer get in touch with her family. And Toni Morrison offers *Beloved* (1987) as a memorial to the ancestors, creating a space for active remembrance through the recognition that slavery constitutes a collective trauma that still demands our attention today.[2]

The following study will present detailed analyses of Walker's *Jubilee*, Williams's *Dessa Rose*, and Morrison's *Beloved*. This selection of texts is neither meant to suggest a clearly definable sub-genre within African American women's writing, nor a clear-cut distinction between narratives with historical and those with contemporary settings. Rather, the three texts occupy, along with those mentioned above and many others, different positions on a continuum of fictional texts that all negotiate the implications of historical understanding for contemporary black and female identities. What connects *Jubilee, Dessa Rose* and *Beloved* in a very general thematic sense is that all three tell—on the basis of verifiable historical data—stories about the past by imaginatively recreating the lives of historical 19th-century black women and their extended families in clearly defined temporal and spatial settings.[3] In contrast to writers whose novels deal explicitly with a 20th-century person's engagement with history and historiography—like Butler's *Kindred* or Bradley's *The Chaneysville Incident*—Walker, Williams and Morrison do not emphasize today's interest in the processes of confronting the past as explicit thematic concerns within the fictional texts.

Within the specific thematic and structural choices that they do make, however, their novels also lead attention to present concerns and preoccupations, albeit in more indirect ways. As one small selection of a steadily growing number of late 20th-century narratives of slavery, they, too, prompt us to ask with Deborah McDowell,

> [w]hy the compulsion to repeat the massive story of slavery in the contemporary Afro-American novel, especially so long after the empirical event itself? ... What personal need, what expressive

function, does re-presenting slavery in narrative serve the twentieth-century black American writer? ("Negotiating between Tenses" 144)

In the most general sense, the writers' turning to the past for subject matter asserts the importance of a historically grounded concept of identity within contemporary African American and feminist thinking. As their novels embrace three decades of black women writers' reconceptualizations of the experience of enslavement, Walker, Williams and Morrison are deeply involved in political and philosophical questions: How can the past be "known" at all in a meaningful way? Which theories of historical knowledge have so far shaped public consciousness? What kind of historical information is available at any given time? Can novelistic discourse express an understanding of history that differs from the kind of understanding supported by traditional historiography, and thus help to change perceptions? Which historical and literary pre-texts does each writer choose to engage in? How do these choices relate to her (self-)positioning within and vis-à-vis various socio-cultural groups? How does she authorize her revisionary narrative?

The very choice of subject matter is already a critical comment on some seemingly basic assumptions. The writers' insistence on the explanatory power of fiction calls into question truth claims of a supposedly objective historiographic discourse; their novels also strongly suggest a reassessment of literary art as politically invested and ethically responsible. Within the framework of fictional prose, Walker, Williams and Morrison critically investigate traditional parameters of historiography and of novel writing; they "re-vision"—in Adrienne Rich's sense of the term—issues of historical knowledge, of the generation of meaning through narrative, of the correlations between knowledge of the past and contemporary definitions of "self," "experience" and "identity."[4] The three texts share an outspokenly revisionist impulse in addressing lack and distortion in previous public discourses on African American historical experiences, and all three claim the public space and the concomitant authority to write about these experiences from perspectives that reflect their specific concerns as women of African descent.

The three literary projects central to this study are thus explicitly and self-reflexively intertextual.[5] First, the novels engage thematically in earlier historiographic and literary interpretations of slavery—both the institution and its ideological bases—and its deep and long-lasting effects on 19th and 20th-century American society. The authors' very choice of discipline—literature rather than historiography—is one expression of this engagement. Morrison's assertion that "art can do what other things cannot do" (Byatt) points to the writers' critical reflection of the various possible modes of historical narrative. It raises the question how "fiction" as a conceptual frame impacts on the ways in which the texts are meant to function, and how it enables readers to come to a kind of understanding that other forms of presentation preclude. Secondly, within the context of literature, the novels discuss the adequacy of established literary conventions, investigate possible intersections of African(-American) and European forms of cultural expression, and explore how revisionary shifts in thematic emphases demand careful reconsiderations of formal organization. Thirdly, because of the socio-political and cultural developments that have taken place since the publication of *Jubilee* in 1966, the novels not only refer to other texts as a group, but also stand in signifying relations to each other.[6] In this sense, *Jubilee* in particular has to be regarded as an important pre-text for *Dessa Rose* and *Beloved.*

All three novels are, albeit in significantly different ways, "disruptions" and "revisions" of conventional ways of historical representation, as well as spaces for "remembrance"—"sites of memory"[7] that shift the conceptual ground on which readings of "the past" are based. They offer a variety of approaches to question and redefine earlier narrative models—like 19th-century historical novels and the original slave narratives—in order to develop discourses that are able to accommodate more adequately the complexity of African American women's experiences. Within their respective contexts, the novels are elaborate manifestations of their authors' self-reflexive positionings in late-20th-century social and cultural configurations. The diversity of approaches with which Walker, Williams and Morrison engage in the issues outlined above reflect not only individual interests, but also the far-reaching social and political changes that have occurred over the last thirty years. Despite some shared concerns, they bring substantially different ideas, questions and assumptions to their individual literary projects. This includes addressing different groups of readers, and consequently employing different textual strategies to render their revisionary historical narratives plausible for their respective primary audiences. And although not explicitly part of the stories that the novels tell, the writers' personal answers to all of these issues nevertheless become part of their texts, as they influence and find expression in thematic choices and narrative structures.

Jubilee, composed over a period of several decades before it was finally completed and published in 1965/66, plays a special role among contemporary historical narratives as the very first novel of slavery by a 20th-century black woman writer. In addition, Walker was also breaking new thematic ground with her intention to place the unspectacular life of a slave woman at the center of a popular novel. This was as yet without model—the only earlier 20th-century black novel of slavery, Arna Bontemps's *Black Thunder* (1936), had a decidedly different focus in its depiction of the widely known Gabriel Prosser rebellion. Moreover, the fact that *Jubilee* is based on the life-history of Walker's own great-grandmother adds another demanding facet to her project. Even with only a brief look at the circumstances, it becomes obvious that to conceptualize and to write this fictional portrayal of Walker's own family history was no easy task in the 1940s and 1950s. The long time it took to complete the book, as well as Walker's thematic, generic and structural choices support this impression.

When Walker began to conceptualize the "Jubilee"-project, general knowledge about slavery was limited at best and today's recognition and appreciation of the 19th-century slave narratives was not yet to be anticipated (cf. Christian "Somebody Forgot to Tell," 334). Had texts like Harriet Jacobs's *Incidents in the Life of a Slave Girl* been known to her at the time, they might have become models to adopt and modify in order to fit the changed circumstances of the mid-20th century. Walker did have access to former slaves' accounts, though, in the form of interviews with former slaves that were conducted and collected as part of the Federal Writers' Project of the WPA in the 1930s. Knowing these narratives helped to consolidate her perception that her grandmother's story was "the most valuable slave narrative of all" ("How I Wrote *Jubilee*" 56). They could not, however, provide a viable formal alternative at the time. As Ashraf Rushdy explains, oral slave testimony was—in the 1930s and 1940s—still frowned upon as a serious subject of historical study ("I Write in Tongues" 101-4). In this context, it can indeed be regarded as a remarkable achievement that Walker was at all able to recognize the relevance of her grandmother's stories.[8]

In contrast to Williams and Morrison, Walker did not have a support group of other black women writers. She repeatedly stated that she saw herself primarily as a poet, and she emphasized the important influence of some of the Harlem Renaissance poets—especially of Langston Hughes—on the development of her lyrical voice (Rowell 6-7). About any influence that her friendship with Richard Wright in the years 1936-1939 might have had she was noticeably silent, both in her biography of Wright and in her autobiographical texts (*Richard Wright* 71-94, 103-4). Walker's comments in "How I Wrote *Jubilee*" in the early 1970s suggest, however, that her political shift to the left while she was working for the WPA in

Chicago encouraged her to see connections between analyses of the situation of industrial workers and the living conditions of poor southern blacks.

With Sir Walter Scott and Tolstoy as explicitly mentioned models for her prose writing, Walker finally decided to work in a literary genre that seemed best suited to her goal of presenting a "true-to-life" account of her great-grandmother's experiences during and after slavery: the realist historical novel as she had come to know it particularly through these 19th-century European authors ("How I Wrote *Jubilee*" 63-64). Black cultural forms found their way into the text literally "from the margins": in the chapter headings, the epigraphs, the dialogues, the exact descriptions of slave life on the fringes of the "big house." Considerations of reader expectations certainly also played a role in making these decisions. Having to situate herself in relation to mainstream historiographic and literary conventions in order to create a public forum for her revisionary narrative, Walker chose to rely on a well-known genre and conventional form in order to make her still unconventional thematic choices more easily acceptable for the general audience she intended to address. *Jubilee* can thus be described as an attempt to bridge the chasm between "official"—both southern and northern—interpretations of history and the orally transmitted version told by Walker's grandmother. It is an attempt to mediate between public and private, literary and oral, credible and discredited information, in order to reach a broad audience and teach her readers a history lesson with a difference.

This strategy of telling an unconventional story while "borrowing authority"[9] from traditional literary forms is only partially successful, however: there is a notable discrepancy between alleged thematic priorities—the positioning of a black enslaved woman as central character—and the discursive representation of that character which fails to support her thematic centrality. The central character Vyry is given a body but not a voice; for the longest time, she remains at the mercy of others' "readings," still not a subject in her own right but, until the very end, the object of other people's definitions. I will also consider how this discrepancy between story and discourse might have influenced the critical reception of *Jubilee* in such a way that the novel's significance as part of a black women's literary tradition has been underestimated.

In the 1970s, when Sherley Anne Williams was extending her earlier story "Meditations on History" into *Dessa Rose*, her first novel, she could already look back to texts like *Jubilee* and Ernest Gaines's *The Autobiography of Miss Jane Pittman* (1971); in addition, the cultural climate in general was in a process of change as a result of the socio-political and cultural movements of the sixties. In contrast to

Walker, Williams could also draw from a significantly changed critical landscape: her material no longer fell exclusively into the seemingly opposite categories of "private" (i.e. family history, oral tradition, black female experience) and "public" (i.e. historiography, written documents, white male perception). In the Civil Rights and Black Aesthetics movements, as well as in the historical research of Herbert Aptheker and the cultural criticism of Angela Davis, Williams found alternative sites of knowledge validation that were no longer confined to the privatized realm of family traditions. And she herself was actively engaged in the theorizing of "the black experience" with her nonfictional study *Give Birth to Brightness: A Thematic Study in Neo-Black Literature* (1972).

Williams's work with the material that finally became *Dessa Rose* was partly motivated by her anger and indignation at William Styron's novel *The Confessions of Nat Turner* (1967) and the heated discussion that followed the book's being awarded the Pulitzer Prize for fiction in 1968. Rather than directly entering the public debate about the political and moral dimensions of Styron's appropriation of the black slave leader's voice, however, Williams set out to investigate the politics of "speaking for" in fictional form, by making the struggle over authority her explicit thematic and structural focus. In the course of both story and novel, the most prominent white male character discredits himself, while the black, female, and initially still enslaved protagonist emerges as the indisputable authority on her life and experiences.

Whereas Walker relied largely on the accuracy of external evidence, and tried to convince through the presentation of seemingly unrefutable historical facts, Williams chose a different strategy of legitimation in shifting the locus of authorization into the text. Despite the novel's historical sources, the main emphasis does not lie on a close-to-the-facts depiction of an enslaved woman's life, but on the question of how knowledge about this life was created and passed on. Although the shift from the white man's authority-demanding (written) "voice" to the black woman's communally validated spoken voice is rendered plausible and coherent within the text, and *Dessa Rose* has been positively reviewed, the history of the novel's composition and publication speaks a different language: it clearly shows Williams's need to authorize her narrative about matters of authorization as a legitimate artistic and historiographic concern. First it took ten years to find a publisher for the story "Meditations on History," then the editors of the novel requested that Williams hide the factual basis of her narrative: the text obviously appeared to be less threatening if perceived of as purely imaginary, as "just fiction" ("Lion's History" 257-58). Nevertheless, Williams has also commented on the positive developments between the initial conceptualization of "Meditations on History" and the completion of *Dessa Rose*: numerous reprints of both original slave narratives and early black novels were put on the market, and black feminist criticism came into its own. To learn more about the wide variety of texts on the African American historical experience was, according to Williams, an important background for her work with the "Dessa"-material, and the substantial changes from the short story to the novel testify to the relevance of the socio-political developments between 1970 and 1986 ("Lion's History" 255).

Beloved, finally, has to be looked at not only in relation to earlier texts in general, but also needs to be situated within Morrison's oeuvre as a whole and the growth of her reputation as one of America's great writers. *Beloved's* position as Morrison's fifth novel published within a seventeen-year period has to bear on any discussion of how authority gets established in and for the text. Morrison's reputation as one of the most prolific and successful African American woman writers was basically in place before the publication of *Beloved*; it was further consolidated by *Beloved's* immediate success. What this novel therefore did not have to accomplish—in contrast to Walker's and Williams's first novels—was to attract an audience. Morrison could rely on getting a receptive hearing, and therefore did not need to employ the same authorizing devices in the text that a first novel might require.

Since its publication more than a decade ago, *Beloved* has established so much public authority that it appears to be turning more and more into the prototypical "black female text" that is used in every critical context imaginable.[10] Morrison's ability to deconstruct western patriarchal epistemology takes a strong stance in making "conventional" ways of thinking—ways of thinking that adhere to and privilege dominant concerns—unacceptable within the fictional world and, by implication, outside of it. Morrison is thus carrying the project of constructing a historical black female subject significantly further than either Walker or Williams. She asserts that the very foundations of western patriarchal epistemology make it difficult, if not impossible, for black women to step out of constructions of center and margin, in which they are always already defined as "other." Ironically, it is the widespread public recognition that her writing is enjoying today that makes it possible for Morrison to launch ever sharper critiques of western forms of self-definition that still rely heavily on ideological constructions of "difference" and, as a consequence, political and cultural practices of exclusion.

In *Beloved*, Morrison establishes new conceptual categories for creating images of "the past"—especially the black historical experience—that clearly reject the authority traditionally bestowed on hegemonic interpretations of slavery. She explicitly locates her own authority as a writer and storyteller in contexts of knowledge validation that cannot be contained in constructions of (white/male) authoritative center and (black/female) authorization-seeking margin. Within this critical space that is explicitly not committed to fulfilling dominant cultural expectations, she sets out to imagine how the material reality of slavery can be recreated and represented today to acknowledge its continuing influence on individual lives as well as communities. This includes the recognition that seemingly "forgotten" aspects of black history constitute a subconscious collective memory that not only contains information willfully disregarded by white culture, but also traumatic experiences that the black community has had to repress. As long as the ideology and the social practices responsible for the initial trauma are still in place—which is evident in continuing racism—there is also the continuing need to repress memories—individual or communal—of the traumatic event(s). If confrontation and "working-through" are, however, the only way out of the circle of repetition compulsion inherent in repression, then the oppressive ideology itself has to be dislocated to create a space safe enough for this process to be successful. *Beloved*, I claim, is such a space.

Chapter 1 outlines the critical concepts that inform my discussion of *Jubilee*, *Dessa Rose* and *Beloved*. Drawing particularly from recent African American and European American feminist studies that are specifically concerned with questions of narrative theory, I develop a theoretical framework with three main points of emphasis: 'authority/ authorization,' '(self-)positioning,' and 'disruption, revision, and remembrance.' Definitions of social and discursive authority intersect with considerations of how writers are situated and situate themselves and their texts within the larger matrix of socio-cultural relations. These (self-) positionings affect the conceptual spaces in which it becomes possible to disrupt conventional historical narratives, imaginatively revision historical material, and re-member aspects of black historical experience that have been severed from the body of cultural memory.

Chapters 2 to 4 open with analyses of Walker's, Williams's and Morrison's public statements about their work in general and the novels to be discussed in particular. Each of the three writers has deliberately taken advantage of extra-fictional, public spaces like articles and interviews to explain her personal approach to writing and to define her authorial role in larger social and cultural contexts. Although these comments cannot be considered transparent statements but need to be contextualized in their respective moments and places of genesis, they provide the contours of self-defined public personae that contribute to the critical reception of their fiction. A focus on the novels' paratexts[11]—titles, prefaces, epigraphs, tables of contents, etc.—leads into the textual discussions. Extending the writers' extratextual statements, these textual "thresholds" (Genette 2) anticipate and prepare for the respective conceptual orientations of the novels. The central parts of the chapters then consist of detailed textual analyses, in which the definitions and distributions of narrative "voices" and the structural organizations of plot are most important points of emphasis. The central question is how each writer conceptualizes and represents social relations within her text, and within these relations endows her black female protagonist with a privileged voice. Finally, the concluding sections of each chapter reconnect textual and contextual concerns by examining the novels' implications for broader discussions of historical and socio-cultural engagement.

CHAPTER 1

Critical Concepts

> Speech needs to be authorized only where silence is the rule.
>
> —Bat-Ami Bar On, "Marginality"

> It is in the belief that our narratives can be transformational that we begin.
>
> —Abena Busia, "Words Whispered Over Voids"

It is one of the major premises of much recent feminist theory that each literary text is rooted in, reflects, and comments on the cultural moment out of which it is written—a rootedness not only observable in the chosen thematic focus, but also in the treatment and uses of genre, narrative perspectives, and claims to thematic and aesthetic integrity and sincerity. "[T]he writing of fiction," cultural critic Michele Wallace explains, "inevitably addresses the material conditions, the cultural context and the psychological terms of its own production" ("Slaves of History" 226). And narrative theorist Susan Sniader Lanser specifies that "[t]he important point is to recognize that textual structures manifest a reaction—whether of similarity or contrast—to their genesis" (*Narrative Act* 103).[1] My study takes this assertion of what literary critic Karla Holloway calls "cultural mooring place[s]" (*Moorings* 1) as one point of departure: the critical discussion of the novels cannot stand disconnected from attention to their respective contexts, and especially to the ways in which these contexts manifest themselves thematically and structurally within the texts. In such an approach, a feminist interest in the connections between the material conditions and literary representations of women's lives and poststructuralist insights into the discursive construction of "reality" meet.

As a basis for the analyses to come, this approach suggests—in connection with the critical premise that the perspective each critic brings to an interpretive project also always impacts on the direction and the result of the reading process—the following understanding of "interpretation": every act of reading is an attempt and an effort to "make meaning" out of the complexly intersecting coordinates of texts and the critic's standpoint, to tell a new "meaningful" story of dichotomous split between text and context in which no attention is given to audience; it makes it necessary to include both the texts' implied readers as well as their actual receiving communities—including academic critical voices—in any analysis.

Working with such a definition of "text" that no longer allows a clear-cut separation of text and context, but instead sees each literary text as a verbal expression in which context is always contained, I am going to focus on ways in which the "verbal text[s]" of the three chosen novels show traces of the complex "social text[s]" of black women's historical experiences (Wall 9). Which stories could get told by a particular author at a particular historical moment? How did these stories get told? One goal is to explore the intricate webs of possible influences—(self-)imposed restrictions as well as licences—on the novels. Another is to locate the texts' acts of subversion, and describe the different strategies of "re-vision" with which they redefine traditional (mis)representations of African American women within their respective conceptual frameworks. A third goal is to analyze the different strategies of (self-)authorization with which the authors claim the necessary public spaces for the expression of their revisionary narratives.

Additionally, every engagement in a historical topic raises issues of historical knowledge and memory: how is the temporal gap bridged, how is the process of remembering structured? What is included, what is left out—deliberately or undeliberately? How does the dominant western ideology with its race and gender stratification influence what is thinkable and sayable today? How does the "political unconscious" of both dominant and subjugated groups influence authorial decisions—a question that touches on different kinds of forgetting and repressing?

With these questions and the critical focus they suggest, this study is situated at an intersection of African American and European American feminist theorizing. Especially Mae Gwendolyn Henderson's model for reading black women's texts within a framework of "disruption and revision"—outlined in her 1989 essay "Speaking in Tongues: Dialogics, Dialectics, and the Black Woman Writer's Literary Tradition"[3]—and Karla Holloway's investigations into the processes of "revision and (re)membrance"—developed in her 1992 book-length study *Moorings and Metaphors: Figures of Culture and Gender in Black Women's Literature*[4]—provide important critical orientation for the following analyses of *Jubilee*, *Dessa Rose*, and *Beloved*. In addition, my explicit interest in discursive strategies of positioning and authorization makes it necessary also to engage in theoretical approaches that focus more specifically on questions of narrative authority. The questions formulated by Lanser in her feminist narratological study *Fictions of Authority: Women Writers and Narrative Voice* have proved especially useful in this regard.[5]

Authority, (self-)positioning, and revision are three critical points of focus that are central to critics' and writers' projects of cultural self-definition and socio-political critique. These concepts continuously intersect with and impact on each other; although they are treated separately here for the sake of clarity, it is the complex connections among them that shape the critical framework on which my textual analyses rely.

AUTHORITY AND AUTHORIZATION

As a working definition of "authority" in the context of literary analysis, I adopt Lanser's explanation of "discursive authority" as "the intellectual credibility, ideological validity, and aesthetic value claimed by or conferred upon a work, author, narrator, character, or textual practice" (*Fictions of Authority* 6). This very general definition immediately raises questions about the conditions under which a writer or text can achieve such high esteem. Lanser elaborates:

> Novelistic authority is more than an individual circumstance; it is conventionalized behavior which varies with time and place. Each moment in literary history produces a specific framework for the writer-reader-text relationship and shapes the possibilities by which this relationship can be aesthetically structured and expressed. Not only the linguistic and literary conventions of the time, but the cultural norms and values and the very concept of authority itself provide a variable context for the novelist's relationship to the writing act. (*Narrative Act* 98-99)

A description like this explicitly presents narrative authority as the result of complex processes of negotiation. "Authority" is thus understood as a dynamic concept that needs to be contextualized and historicized in order to maintain its explanatory potential.

This understanding of a writer's or a text's "authority" as the result of negotiation in a heterogeneous socio-cultural field—as it has been presented by narrative theorists, e.g. Ross Chambers and Rachel Blau DuPlessis—departs from conventional definitions of "authority" in political discourse. The "standard view" in political theory, according to Kathleen B. Jones, is of authority "as a distinctive type of social control or influence. . . . [R]ecognition of authority is [considered] sufficient for acceptance produced by authority systems" (122-123). And Richard B. Friedman defines authority as a "mutually recognized normative relationship giving the one the right to command or speak and the other the duty to obey" (134). These short descriptions correspond to sociological definitions of the concept; according to G. Duncan Mitchell,

> [a]uthority is that form of power which orders or articulates the actions of other actors through commands which are effective because those who are commanded regard the commands as *legitimate*. Authority differs from coercive control, since the latter elicits conformity with its commands and prescriptions through its capacity to reward or punish. (13; emphasis in original)[6]

These definitions of public authority preclude negotiation as a possible strategy of engagement, because in this understanding, "authority" would be lost as soon as it is questioned.[7] They are also based on a hierarchical concept of social relations in which a dominant center claims authoritative status for itself, while relegating all "others" to marginal—de-authorized—positions. Such a center-margin construction makes it difficult, if not impossible, within a racialized and gendered society such as the United States to even envision the possibility that black women could ascertain such authority for themselves.

In contrast, the notion of authority as a relational concept that is subject to constant negotiation is, *qua* definition, more accommodating for processes of social change, including the possible dismantling of traditional hierarchies. In order to be at all applicable, however, it requires contextualization within a different model of society. I concur with Linda Alcoff and Elizabeth Potter that simplifying center-margin constructions need to be replaced with an image of society as a "complicated social grid . . . [in which] the notion of a single center becomes displaced" (6). This approach also intersects with a Foucauldian definition of power as "relational, something that is exercised from a variety of points in the social body" (Smart 122).

Such a more complex notion of social dynamics is also more conducive to the social and literary analyses presented by African American feminists, in which marginalization has been described as a systematic process of invalidating—and thus de-authorizing—the experiences of racial and sexual "others." As one result of these dominant political and cultural practices, Henderson explains, "the absence of black female voices has allowed others to inscribe, or write, and ascribe to, or read them" ("Speaking in Tongues" 24). However, this imposed silencing in and being defined by the dominant culture has often been misinterpreted as actual silence; it also does not connote black women's absence from the dominant culture's consciousness. African American feminist thinkers have repeatedly commented on how black women have been made to function as white America's literal and metaphorical "other" while being denied the opportunity to make their own standpoints known.[8]

Texts by writers of marginalized groups are thus always inherently political in that their very existence disturbs and destabilizes hegemonic interpretations of the socio-political whole; in addition, they are also always potential challenges to the dominant society's claims to universality and "objective," authoritative knowledge by bringing in alternative perspectives and interpretations.[9] It has therefore been one important concern of oppositional discourses to insist on the necessity for self-description and self-definition in order to reveal how context-bound, subjective and particular the dominant culture's perceptions of itself and of "others" really are, and to investigate the dynamics of dominant ideology to mask these particularities (cf. Bhabha; Collins, *Black Feminist Thought* 91-114).

The above considerations reveal two qualitatively different approaches to authority—one inherently hierarchical and static, the other potentially nonhierarchical and dynamic. It is particularly relevant for the theoretical frame of this study that the dynamic approach to discursive authority suggested by narrative theorists intersects in many ways with the socio-cultural and literary analyses by black feminist critics. What is also apparent in studies that explicitly deal with questions of authority in literature is the difficulty of consistently sustaining a notion of negotiation in the practical work with literary texts. Lanser's study *Fictions of Authority* is a case in point here: in the introduction, Lanser clearly affiliates herself with the relational, dynamic approach, stating that "discursive authority . . . [must be] characterized with respect to specific receiving communities" (6). In the course of the study, however, it becomes apparent that despite these theoretical disclaimers, Lanser still limits herself and the writers she discusses to a framework in which a white male dominant socio-cultural center continues to set the terms with which women writers—black and white—ultimately have to contend.

For the purposes of this study, I take Lanser's definition of narrative authority to be more open than her own application suggests. It will be one of my major premises that although the dominant culture is always in some way present in the making of a literary text, it is not warranted to automatically equate "specific receiving communit[y]" with "mainstream/dominant audience."[10] Even if we agree with Lanser's argument that "the act of writing a novel and seeking to publish it . . . is implicitly a quest for discursive authority: a quest to be heard, respected and believed, a hope of influence" (*Fictions of Authority* 7), the question needs to be asked who is addressed here. Who hears, respects and believes, and thus sets the terms for the writing? Lanser's passive construction implicitly locates the power to authorize a writer and her text in the group that claims a central socio-cultural space. As a basic definition of the writing situation, however, this is too narrow. Despite the apparent pervasiveness of an ideology of white male privilege that continues to set the terms for what is considered acceptable within mainstream cultural institutions—including universities and publishing houses—it would grant this mainstream too much power to reduce the literary production of African American women writers to being merely a response to it.[11] The quest to be given a public hearing raises more complex questions than could possibly be encompassed in an inherently static binary concept of a white/male center as authorizing instance, and a black/female margin that is either authorized or denied legitimation.[12]

(SELF-)POSITIONING

The concept of society as a "matrix" or "grid," in which "authority" is perceived as the result of a process of negotiation, makes it necessary to examine who the participants in this process are, and how much influence each one has in shaping its outcome. What thus needs to be looked at are the ways in which African American women define and situate themselves within the complex socio-cultural matrix of U.S.-American society. This includes, but is by no means limited to, the relationship to the dominant culture; it also recognizes the influence and importance of other groups, especially the community of other black women. How does each writer situate herself within various social and cultural communities? Which literary traditions does she adopt as her own, and which does she criticize or circumvent? Which audiences does she address and feel accountable to, and whose expectations does she refuse to fulfill? It is as part of this general process of self-positioning, I argue, that writers—and by extension, critics—deal with questions of authority and authorization.[13]

In turn, what readers consider worthy of attention is also influenced by their location in the socio-cultural matrix. Whether, for example, a mimetic depiction is considered plausible depends on the historical moment when a text is published and read, and on readers who have learned to read "realism" as a viable mode of narration and who have some belief in the linguistic representability of "the real." Whether historical "certainties" (McDowell, "Negotiating between Tenses" 145) are considered authoritative depends to some extent on the kind of historical discourse readers have learned to accept as normal. And if readers are willing to suspend disbelief and accept a mysterious young woman as a dead child returned, this is also contingent on the ways in which they have learned to read.

The writer's position vis-à-vis any audience—however this audience is composed and defined—is thus extremely complex. I therefore suggest paying special attention to the ways in which each of the three writers chosen for this study describes how she situates herself and her novel, and how much attention in this process of self-positioning is given to considerations of authority and the need to authorize one's voice. Such a focus on the public persona that each writer creates in interviews and articles can give important clues as to whom she addresses and how she wants her text to be read. This public image then needs to be read against issues of representation as they are inscribed in the fictional texts themselves.

Assertions that their primary intended readers are other black women are part and parcel of many black women writers' authorial self-definitions. In turn, black feminist critics' explicit emphasis on the literature by African American women is also, as I have outlined above, an instance of self-positioning in which a communal context of mutual support and empathetic attention is formulated. The development of an explicitly black and feminist literary criticism over the last thirty years would have been unthinkable without the simultaneous emergence of a large body of fictional texts by African American women writers. The mutual importance and influence that each body of texts has had on the other is therefore well encapsuled in Spillers's description of a "community of black women writing," a formulation that reflects the close link between creative writers and critics by deliberately blurring genre boundaries:

> [T]he community of black women writing in the United States now can be regarded as a vivid new fact of national life. I deliberately substitute the participle for the noun to suggest not only the palpable and continuing urgency of black women writing themselves into history, but also to convey the variety of aims that accompanies their project. ("Crosscurrents" 249)

Spillers's formulation emphasizes that creative writers and critics form a supportive network as well as authorize each others' concerns as legitimate and worthy of critical attention: if the existence of fiction and poetry by African American women writers is the *raison d'être* for black feminist criticism, the public presence of black feminist readers has also provided writers with the assurance of a responsive and empathetic audience in the face of what Valerie Smith has characterized as mainstream literary study's "legacy of oversight and condescension" (40).

DISRUPTION, REVISION, AND REMEMBRANCE

In her 1972 essay "When We Dead Awaken," Adrienne Rich proposes a "radical critique of literature, feminist in impulse" and based on projects of "re-vision." "Re-vision," she explains, is

> the act of looking back, of seeing with fresh eyes, of entering an old text from a new critical direction. ... [This] is for women more than a chapter in cultural history: it is an act of survival. Until we can under-stand the assumptions in which we are drenched we cannot know ourselves. ... We need to know the writing of the past, and know it differently than we have ever known it; not to pass on a tradition, but to break its hold over us. (35)

While Rich initially used the concept of "re-vision" to formulate a feminist critique of writing by men in order to describe and challenge dominant assumptions about women and literature, the concept has since been broadened and applied in various contexts of oppositional writing. It has generally retained the idea of bringing a new perspective to seemingly well-known texts, in order to locate the ideological underpinnings of these texts, and to envision alternative ways of representation.

In an African American critical context, the necessity to revision—both in the sense of "looking at something again" and of "revising"—not just individual literary texts, but the dominant "culture text" as a whole has long been a funda-mental critical assumption.[14] Recently, the concept of "revision" has been considered a particularly appropriate way of theoretically framing black women writers' texts. Black feminist theories of "revision" start with a concept of African American female identity in which the existence of black and female support structures as well as the unavoidability of a critical confrontation with the dominant—eurocentric and patriarchal—culture is recognized. Black women's cultural engagement thus negotiates between "affiliative" and "antagonistic" (2) impulses—to use Homi Bhabha's formulation.

One critical approach that has as its explicit focus black women writers' responses to a potentially hostile cultural script is developed in Henderson's by now widely anthologized article "Speaking in Tongues." Henderson describes African American women as being positioned in society in such a way that in order to "function" and survive, they have had to learn the language(s) of the dominating culture(s), in addition to interacting in the affirmative and supportive context of a black and female community. This ability to "speak[ ] in tongues"—a metaphor taken from a black church context and reminiscent of Mikhail Bakhtin's concept of "heteroglossia"—comes to stand for the various ways in which black women discursively engage in their environment and arrive at self-knowledge and self-definition.

Concurring with a wider concern in African American literary studies that "Afro-American literature has so often been misread as mimetic representation or sociology" (Wall 9), Henderson states explicitly that her primary interest is not so much an analysis of the material conditions of black women's lives, but of the ways in which these conditions inform black women's writing. In accordance with the Bakhtinian notion that "consciousness, like language, is shaped by the social environment" ("Speaking in Tongues" 18), Henderson takes Barbara Smith's concept of the "simultaneity of oppressions" ("Introduction" xxxii) and investigates how black women writers have made these oppressive conditions, as well as the complex communicative issues they entail, the focus of their literary projects: "In their works, black women writers have encoded oppression as a discursive dilemma, that is, their works have consistently raised the problem of the black woman's relationship to power and discourse" ("Speaking in Tongues" 24). Henderson's choice of literary examples poignantly supports this thesis: the scenes chosen from Morrison's *Sula,* Williams's *Dessa Rose* and Zora Neale Hurston's *Their Eyes Were Watching God* all illustrate black women's conflicting and confirming engagements with "others"; they all show how the female protagonists go through periods of intense crisis that are reflected in verbal fights and sharp arguments and emerge bruised, maybe, but ultimately successful and more sure of themselves than before.

Henderson's presentation of what she regards as African American women writers' privileged vision is important as a strategy that deliberately contradicts stereotypical notions of black women's subordinated and powerless status. As critic, she creates a "best case-scenario" in describing a cultural space in which African American women's voices are endowed with greater authority than white men's, white women's, or black men's. She bases this authority on black women's

African American women's voices are endowed with greater authority than white men's, white women's, or black men's. She bases this authority on black women's ability to communicate with a wide variety of "others"—to be able to hear/understand other perspectives and engage in them is presented as a value that elicits respect and acknowledgement. "[I]t is black women writers who are the modern day apostles, empowered by experience to speak as poets and prophets in many tongues," she proposes (24).

Explicitly presenting this proposition as an "enabling critical fiction" (24), Henderson situates herself in various ways in a black feminist critical context. First, her model has the specific goal of creating a conceptual framework in which black women's writing occupies an authoritative position on its own terms, in contrast to the status it still has in mainstream critical contexts. Secondly, by describing her approach as a critical *fiction* she draws attention to the constructedness of her explanatory narrative; this is an implicit comment on the constructedness of any critical project, and it emphasizes that critical practice always reflects the context in which it is developed.

In comparison, Holloway's model—as she develops it in *Moorings and Metaphors*—especially emphasizes affirmative cultural relations by identifying symbolic and structural similarities of texts by African American and African women writers. Her "primary argument is that black women's literature reflects its community—the cultural ways of knowing as well as ways of framing that knowledge in language," and the specific goal of the study is to "trace figures of language that testify to that cultural mooring place" (1). These opening statements mark the affinity of Holloway's inquiry with Patricia Hill Collins's assertion of a black female community with a distinctive epistemology that manifests itself especially in black women's approaches to language (cf. *Black Feminist Thought* 201-20). Mapping the contours of her inquiry, Holloway also implicitly addresses possible objections by asserting that the textual structures she is setting out to examine add "a dimension [to the black text that is] only accessible when its cultural context is acknowledged" (1).

Holloway's usage of "revision" approximates most closely the intertextual engagement in adversarial traditions and cultural scripts, whereas "(re)membrance" connotes the deliberate identification with a black and female group (*Moorings* 13-14). She thus also integrates both processes—critical/revisionary and affirmative/identificatory intertextuality—into her theoretical considerations. In this context, it is significant that Holloway chooses *Beloved* as one of the major texts to illustrate her argument. Her focus on identifiably black cultural links conventions, but also of the ideological underpinnings that these conventions carry. In order to genuinely make a conceptual space for and affirm black women's perspectives, both Holloway and Morrison suggest, much more attention has to be given to forms of representation that do not rely on traditionally western ways of conceptualizing social relations.

Henderson's and Holloway's theoretical models actively engage in the process of tradition building, and in doing so necessarily have to use what Henderson herself calls "strategies of containment" ("Response" 162). Both critics emphasize that they are aware of the dangers of exclusiveness, but both are nevertheless exclusive to a certain extent. What they presuppose is a basically clear-cut political choice on the part of the writers: to identify with and actively integrate into their work those aspects of the African American experience that have been marginalized and silenced in the mainstream traditions. They additionally assume that on a conceptual level, black women's historical experiences of marginalization and the concomitant development of a distinctly black and female culture have placed them in an epistemically privileged position to describe and interpret their own lives.

Without usually being spelled out explicitly, this specific "black female standpoint" is often posited as a moment of originary identity, and identified as one of the basic conceptual premises of "representative" texts by black women writers. The shared experience of multiple forms of oppression, as well as social and political practices that still exclude and marginalize black women has led—according to a sizeable number of theorists—to the constitution of a black female culture that provides coherence, identification, and support. This "society of sister outsiders" is distinguished from other socially marginalized groups through an epistemically unique position that allows them to understand and enter the discourses of both hegemonic and "ambiguously (non)hegemonic"[15] groups, while retaining a space that is accessible only to themselves.

In a critique of this concept, Bat-Ami Bar On argues that the notion of an epistemologically privileged space is a strategy of authorizing marginalized voices that does not, however, depart from the notion of a ubiquitous dominant center. "The claim of epistemic privilege in the realm of sociopolitical theory mostly justifies claims for authority, specifically the authority of socially marginalized groups to speak for themselves," she states (89). What connects the various uses of the notion of "epistemic privilege" is the retention of a model of social relations based on a center-margin construction. With reference to oppositional discourses, Bar On explains further: "Epistemic privilege . . . becomes a function of the distance from the center. . . . Presumably the more distant one is from the center, the more advantageous is one's point of view" (89). This conceptual set-up constitutes a clear reversal of the usual construction in which the center is endowed with the greatest authority—the construction that Lanser's discussion ultimately also remains bound to. This reversal is understandable as a critical response to the workings of the dominant ideology to prevent the so-called "margins" from becoming self-defined spaces of agency. It is problematic, however, in that it does not fundamentally alter the categories of the discussion; it continues to work with a dualistic split between center and margin that make efforts to mediate, or to go even beyond the very notion of opposites, impossible. If the authority of a literary text is dependent on the extent to which it rejects dominant conventions and expectations, texts that are less obviously critical cannot easily be accounted for.

While retaining Henderson's and Holloway's emphasis on the polyvocality of black women's texts and their complex investigations into the intersections of identity, voice, and literary representation, I want to allow for a broader spectrum of texts. Some cautionary remarks by DuPlessis open a critical space to recognize texts by writers who—for whatever reason—choose to adapt to the dominant culture's expectations rather than critique them:

> [M]arginality in two arenas . . . [either] compels the person to negate any possibility for a critical stance, seeking instead "conformity and inclusion" because the idea of an authoritative center is defensively affirmed, or it enlivens the potential for critique. (*Writing beyond the Ending* 33)

The notion of a multi-layered, polyphonic text—one that addresses the concerns and expectations of a variety of readers, both sympathetic and resistant—gains special relevance in those novels in which the various discourses seem to be at odds with each other and create tensions rather than workable communication. My choice of *Jubilee* as one major text for this study is the result of this observation: because the novel is missing from most recent theoretical accounts of black women's writing, an analysis of this text can point out some blindspots in these theories. Although *Jubilee* has not often been mentioned by younger writers as a relevant influence on their own work, I take it to be widely read and known; it might well have figured as a model, albeit a problematic one, for later texts. *Jubilee* is—for this very reason—an important text to start with.

CHAPTER 2

"We are climbing Jacob's ladder"—
Margaret Walker's *Jubilee*

> [M]y novel is a canvas on which I paint my vision
> of the world.
>
> Margaret Walker, "How I Wrote *Jubilee*"

Margaret Walker's *Jubilee* is a novel of epic proportions—a historical novel that for the first time in literary history describes the life of a black enslaved woman in the context of both black and white 19th-century southern cultures from the vantage point of a 20th-century black woman writer. The outcome of Walker's early resolution to write down her great-grandmother's life and of decades of historical study, the novel is indeed an impressive document. As a "first" in a now steadily growing body of texts that fictionalize 19th-century black female characters within the political and social developments of the time, *Jubilee* raises questions of genre and literary traditions, of writer intentions and reader expectations. With its objective to portray 19th-century black life in the South as comprehensively as possible, the novel contains an unprecedented wealth of cultural information. However, the relationship between "fact" and "fiction"—as Walker herself has repeatedly stated in the early 1970s ("How I Wrote *Jubilee*" 64)—is a complex and potentially problematic issue. *Jubilee's* insistence on being as "truthful" as possible to her material—both the orally transmitted family genealogy and the recorded historical data—needs to be examined with regard to its implications for the text as a whole. What is involved in the process of combining "public" and "private" information, especially if the "private" material has been systematically devalued and excluded from the "public" record? How does the writer's engaging in her own family history and the need to recognize the significance of that history create additional psychological complications within the writing?

It is one assumption of the following discussion that *Jubilee* is on the one hand notable for its thematic achievements, but on the other hand also problematic because of the intricacies of its narrative structure. I agree in this regard with Maryemma Graham that "*Jubilee* presents an interesting challenge for the scholarship on discourse theory and narrative composition" ("Margaret Walker" 23). In the following discussion, I am going to argue that Walker's novel can be described as the site of an intense struggle over narrative authority—a struggle in which the protagonist Vyry's apparently central position is always contested. The conflicts and tensions apparent in the text—between silence and voice, privileged perspective and distribution of power—reverberate with some of the contextual difficulties that Walker as author was faced with. Not only did she have to deal with the task of conceptualizing a way of inserting the life-story of a 19th-century black woman into the mid-20th-century historical and literary discourses of slavery and Reconstruction; she also had to establish authority for herself and prove the legitimacy of her revisionary narrative.

After a brief survey of the critical attention to *Jubilee*, I will outline how Walker positions herself and her literary project within historical, biographical, and literary frames of reference. The central part of this chapter will then cover the textual analysis; I will first examine the overall organization and its implications for the representation of black (female) life and culture, and then focus on individual scenes in which questions of (discursive) power are raised. This will finally lead to an evaluation of Vyry's perspective as the privileged moral vision of the novel—a moral vision that is shaped as significantly by gender as it is motivated by race and class.

Critical Attention

Early reviewers call *Jubilee* a "good book, in a dual sense of the word" (Buckmaster 11), which offers a "wealth of knowledge and information" (Maroney 493) by "faithfully render[ing] the everyday lives of slaves in the old South" (Rev. of *Jubilee* 76). Although there is some disagreement as to the novel's literary merit—especially in regard to the "realiz[ation] of characters"—reviewers largely agree on the "recreation of the past [as] the strong point of [the] novel" (76). In the years immediately following the novel's publication, academic critical attention was scant, however; only since the late 1970s—several years after Walker's 1972 publication of her essay "How I Wrote Jubilee"—has a sizeable number of articles finally appeared. Most early critics follow the reviews in strongly emphasizing the novel's thematic achievements. With rare exceptions, *Jubilee* is in the 1970s praised as a milestone in black literature, as a successful attempt—in Margaret Walker's own words—to "set the record straight where Black people are concerned" (Rowell 10).

In her 1977 article "'Oh Freedom'—Women and History in Margaret Walker's *Jubilee*," Phyllis Klotman examines the roles of black women in the transmission of historical knowledge. Connecting Walker's novel with Arna Bontemps' *Black Thunder*—rather than with Margaret Mitchell's *Gone With the Wind*—and associating it with the slave narratives both in structure and in intent, Klotman describes the book as "history told from the perspective of the women folk who lived it" (145). Focusing specifically on Walker's use of folklore, James E. Spears outlines the contours of the black "folk" community on the Dutton plantation, emphasizing the importance of song, language, religion, and folk customs. Charlotte Goodman highlights the specifically female contributions to black rural culture—needlework, cooking, medicinal knowledge—by situating *Jubilee* next to *Uncle Tom's Cabin* and describing the two texts as complementary.

What is noticeably missing in these thematically focused analyses, however, is attention to the ways in which fiction and history intersect—to the implications of narrative organization for the representation of historical "reality." It is only in very recent criticism—starting in the late 1980s—that some scholars take on the novel's complexity, including its problems and contradictions, while at the same time still being quick to acknowledge Walker's thematic achievements. Reflecting on the "relation between history and historical fiction," Hazel Carby sees *Jubilee* as a response to the mythology of the antebellum South created in Margaret Mitchell's *Gone With the Wind*, and additionally relates it to *Black Thunder*. Within the context of her critical stance toward an apparent romanticization of the black rural South in recent African American criticism, Carby evaluates Walker's reticence about using her folk material more prominently in the text as positive: "[S]he deliberately avoids a romantic evocation of an undifferentiated rural folk." As part of her "social commitment to realism," Carby argues, Walker's "ideology of a black folk forged from the social system of slavery is a fictional representation of Lukács's formulation of historical necessity" ("Ideologies of Black Folk" 133-34).

In her critique of recent attempts to delineate a tradition of black women's writing, Hortense Spillers includes *Jubilee* as a study in contrast to Hurston's *Their Eyes Were Watching God* and Morrison's *Sula*: "This novel of historical content has no immediate precedent in Afro-American literary tradition ... [and] assumes a special place in the canon" ("Hateful Passion" 186). Spillers's interpretation of *Jubilee* as not only historical, but "Historical"—as a "metaphor for the unfolding of the Divine Will" (186) goes beyond any other analysis and will be included in more detail in the discussion below.

Especially in the light of the largely positive responses to *Jubilee* in the articles mentioned above, it is notable that Spillers's inclusion of the novel in her discussion of the concept of "tradition" is an exceptional move—in most recent book-length studies that attempt to outline the parameters of a black women writers' tradition, Walker's text is conspicuously absent.[1] This silence could be a deliberate choice in order to "protect" a text that is considered important but sits uneasily with contemporary critics. The lack of attention to *Jubilee* within a critical framework that is otherwise very interested in the relationships among novels by contemporary African American women writers strengthens Spillers's argument that *Jubilee* demands a special place in the African American canon. It also raises questions about the underlying premises of theories of African American women's writing, if such a well-known text is often not even considered worth mentioning.

Two recent studies focus specifically on the narrative complexity and the ensuing thematic and structural ambiguities of Walker's novel. In "Margaret Walker and the Vision of Afro-American Life," Graham comments on the contrast between the scarcity of critical attention given to *Jubilee* and the discussion "that surrounds the historical novels of Gore Vidal, William Styron, Alex Haley, or Mary Lee Settle" ("Margaret Walker" 22). Graham is particularly interested in the "issue[s] of historical representation" that the novel raises. She interprets some of the text's apparent incongruities as Walker's deliberate attempt to show "slavery as a culture of contradictions," by creating "a dialogue between historical narrative (facts) and the historical fiction (story)" (24). Finally, Sabine Bröck-Sallah's "Women Writing: Plotting against HIStory" examines the ideological implications of narrative discourse and the distribution of voices within in the text. Her discussion of the function of Vyry's whip scars has spurned my own thinking about the politics of discourse in *Jubilee*. Attention to matters of discourse and its difficult and complex relationship to plot can provide a link between Walker's novel and the critical concerns raised by later texts like *Dessa Rose* and *Beloved*.

AUTHORIAL POSITIONING:
THE NOVELIST AS BIOGRAPHER AND SOCIAL HISTORIAN

Margaret Walker repeatedly commented on her early decision to document her great-grandmother's life-story in writing, as well as on the decades of historical research that preceded the eventual completion of *Jubilee* in 1965. If the predominant impulse was initially to preserve her grandmother's oral account of her great-grandmother's experiences for the family record—and Walker stressed the importance of the book for herself, regardless of public recognition[2]—the project later took on a more "public" purpose in her attempt to present an encompassing picture of 19th-century southern life. The task that Walker had mapped out for herself was thus to be both literary biographer and social historian.

In "How I Wrote *Jubilee*," Walker's most extensive comment on the genesis of her novel, she explains how the study of Civil War history and literature made her even more determined to go ahead with her project. The almost complete lack of a black perspective as well as the obvious distortions in the existing representations of 19th-century African Americans needed to be addressed:

> [H]istory books were divided into three classes, according to their viewpoints: (1) history from the southern white point of view, (2) history from the northern white viewpoint, and (3) history from the Negro viewpoint. . . . It was amazing to discover how widely these history books differed. . . .
>
> Faced with these three conflicting viewpoints, a novelist in the role of social historian finds it difficult to maintain an "objective" point of view. Obviously she must choose one or the other—or create her own. (52-53)

To add information that had so far been critically neglected—information she had had the privilege to learn about first hand from her grandmother—was therefore a strong motivating force in the planning and writing of *Jubilee*. And this concern about adequate historical representation was, as many of Walker's critical statements indicate, implicitly linked with didactic considerations: what kind of information had so far been available to the general public? Whose perspective had been presented as the most valid? How could the distortions and omissions be redressed?

Walker saw her own situation as comparatively privileged: as a writer interested in history, she not only had access to material preserved in archives and history books,[3] but she also had her grandmother's account, the "most valuable slave narrative of all, . . . a precious, almost priceless document" ("How I Wrote *Jubilee*" 56). Within the philosophical and educational framework that she described as "new humanism"—the "preoccupation toward providing a full measure of human dignity for everyone" ("Religion, Poetry, and History" 288)—*Jubilee* became her contribution to the urgent and overdue project of re-education. In a speech delivered at the National Urban League Conference in 1968, Walker explained her vision of a "new educational system":

> White America has educated black and white children with a set of
> monstrous lies—half truths and twisted facts—about Race. Both black
> and white children, as a result, have been stunted in the mental growth
> and poisoned in their world outlook.
>
> . . . The appreciation of other people and their cultures is predicated
> upon an understanding of them and *understanding is predicated purely upon
> genuine knowledge.* (286/288; emphasis added)

Walker's perception of the ideological biases of historiography—as she outlines
but does not explain them in "How I Wrote *Jubilee*"—in connection with this
genuine belief in the power of education provides a strong rationale for addressing
this information deficit and sharing her insights with a large audience of both
black and white readers. Although she recognizes that all knowledge, including her
own, is necessarily situated in specific historical contexts, she argues that one can
at least strive toward comprehensiveness by taking into account all kinds of
available material. The most inclusive presentation will then produce the most
thorough understanding—and will, at the same time, also be the most convincing.

One potential problem of this additive approach—despite its less racist and
less exclusionary agenda—is that it does not deal with, and in the long run cannot
account for, the structural aspects of oppression inherent any philosophical
and/or social system that depends on universalizing definitions—definitions that
not only make it difficult to deal with internal differences, but also the various
ways in which the existence of "others" is politically and socially functional. As
sociologists Jack and William Levin state, "discrimination and prejudice persist
because they have some extremely important system-maintaining, or positive
functions, especially for the most powerful segments of our society" (115).[4] In
developing her concept of a modified, "new" humanism, Walker emphasizes the
need for changes in the individual, but does not challenge the connections
between individual consciousness and socio-political structures. Her critique
moves within the accepted parameters of European American culture and society,
with the basically optimistic outlook that it must be possible to remedy its
shortcomings in a joint effort of all its members.

However, it is an extremely difficult task to change—even on a personal
level, for example between teacher and student, or writer and reader—
stereotypical beliefs about the "other" that are as deeply engrained in the culture's
self-definition as racial prejudice. For many white students and/or readers, to be
able to "understand"—to recognize and acknowledge the validity of a hitherto
systematically devalued perspective—demands a degree of open engagement with

unfamiliar ideas that is not likely to be supported by society at large. For a black educator and writer like Margaret Walker, then, the belief that positive changes can only be achieved by a joint effort of black *and* white leaves the work cut out for her to find ways of establishing such a basis for communication—across the rifts of segregation and racist discrimination. *Jubilee*, I argue, is such an outstretched hand—the attempt to make people listen who might not have any apparent interest in doing so, and to create a fruitful dialogue.

Especially for a writer from a marginalized group, however, to establish authority for what s/he has to say involves more than just adding information and then hoping for the persuasive power of good arguments. Walker, with her explicitly didactic intention to introduce the life-experiences of her great-grandmother into the historical and fictional discourses of the mid-20th century, on some level must have confronted this issue of legitimation. Although she repeatedly mentions the importance of her very supportive and reaffirming family background for her own self-confidence and inner strength ("Willing to Pay the Price"), to write as a southern black woman in the 1940s and 50s with the goal to reach out to and educate a broad audience of female and male, black and white readers must have been an uphill struggle, despite the advantages of family encouragement and university training.

How aware Walker was of moving into difficult terrain can only be deduced from some statements in "How I Wrote *Jubilee*." She briefly mentions, for example, the pressures she felt to authenticate her orally transmitted family narrative with undisputable historical data. This obligation not to leave any doubts as to the "truthfulness" of her story permeates the novel:

> What was I trying to prove through this search among the old documents? I was simply determined to substantiate my material, to authenticate the story I had heard from my grandmother's lips. I was using literary documents to undergird the oral tradition. (56)

The fact that it took her several decades before she finally felt knowledgeable enough to write the book is an additional indication of the anxieties that might have been involved in her project. At a time when conservative historians like Stanley Elkins were seriously arguing the non-existence of a specifically black culture and Marxist historian Herbert Aptheker's research was discredited not on academic grounds but for political reasons, Walker's claim to portray a functional black community under the conditions of slavery obviously needed careful substantiation.[5]

Additionally, the conservative attitudes concerning women's roles that pervaded the 1950s complicated the presentation of a strong black woman as central character. Cultural stereotypes that regarded African American women as "emasculating," and "explained" the difficult situation of the black community with its "matriarchal" structure must have been widely shared before they resulted in the infamous Moynihan-report of 1965. The redefinition of (white) women's roles after the end of World War II, with the renewed emphasis on their "natural vocation" as wives and mothers contradicted black women's historical experience of always having had to work outside the home. In an interview with Lucy Freibert, Walker interprets these differences positively in the context of the evolving women's movement:

> The white woman in the past fifty years has sought to be liberated from her husband and from a patriarchal bond. The black woman never felt that kind of pressure. The black woman was always a working woman from the days of slavery. . . . We do not have the same kind of conflict between marriage and career that white women have. . . . [B]lack women have always been very strong women, but not necessarily taking the places of men. (Freibert 54)

Nevertheless, in the framework of the dominant society's role expectations—as the Moynihan report clearly demonstrates—black women were likely to be seen as deviant: "A fundamental fact of Negro American family life is the often reversed roles of husband and wife [,. . . which leads to] a tangle of pathology" (Rainwater/ Yancey 77). The reason for worsening conditions within the black community thus no longer had to be sought in the "external machinery of racism and discrimination," as historian Paula Giddings explains, but could be blamed on the "internal problems of the Black family" (325). This matrix of racial and sexual tensions, conflicts over definitions, and discussions about adequate interpretations of historical and contemporary phenomena provides one contextual frame in which *Jubilee* was written and published.

Considerations of Genre

In "How I Wrote *Jubilee*," Walker explains that her goal to give a detailed description of her great-grandmother's life within the broader context of 19th-century historical events suggested following the conventions of the European historical novel. Commenting on early literary influences in a 1987 interview,

Walker explains that "most of us in the South grew up on . . . the King James version of the Bible, as much as on reading Dickens and Sir Walter Scott" (Freibert 52). For her own sense of technique—especially in regard to *Jubilee*—she found Georg Lukács's *The Historical Novel* "indispensable for philosophy and point of view" (52). Acknowledging these literary and critical voices as important for her own perceptions, Walker deliberately places her historical project within the framework of a widely recognized literary tradition—a tradition that especially values detailed, realistic descriptions of everyday life and its intersections with larger historical events and developments. Walker might have been particularly taken by Lukács's emphasis on the significance of what he calls "mittlere Helden"—"mediocre heroes" (*Historical Novel* 35). In his chapter on Sir Walter Scott, Lukács explains some of the assumptions of traditional historical fiction: "For the being of an age can only appear as broad and many-sided picture if the everyday life of the people, the joys and sorrows, crises and confusions of average human beings are being portrayed (39).[6] This privileging of "the folk" corresponds well to Walker's belief that African Americans played a pivotal role in the events leading to the Civil War and the abolition of slavery—a role that, as her extensive research showed, was largely ignored or at least underestimated in 20th-century historical accounts.

There are no obvious indications that Walker doubted the feasibility of using the traditional form of the historical novel. According to later statements, she chose what she thought to be the most adequate formal structure for what she wanted to say.[7] Selecting realism as a mode of literary representation that allowed her to present much of her research as detailed background information for the account of her great-grandmother's life, Walker could be sure that almost any audience would be well-acquainted with the narrative style of her text. As part of her didactic intentions, this deliberate combination of factual material and fictional form promised to be successful, as Walker

> believe[d] that the role of the novelist can be . . . the role of a historian. More people will read fiction than will history, and history is slanted just as fiction may seem to be. People will learn about a time and a place through a historical novel. (Rowell 10)

Especially in connection with an unconventional thematic focus that lacked public recognition, a well-known and recognizable literary form seemed to offer definite advantages. Situating herself in the tradition of historical novel writing, Walker therefore borrowed authority from that genre for her own bio-historical project.

Michele Wallace presents a carefully formulated evaluation of the conceptual difficulties inherent in Walker's project when she states that

> [l]ittle of this [historical] fiction [about the American South] has been written from the perspective of the black woman slave. Her narrow access to the world, which effectively erased her from the historical record, also impeded her conceptualization in fiction; for how is the author to give the story in which she is the center of intelligence a broad enough perspective to support the omniscient tone so characteristic of the historical novel? ("Slaves of History" 141)

Wallace understands *Jubilee* as the starting point of a larger cultural endeavor to find adequate means of representing the black and female experience of enslavement. She points to Walker's usage of folk material as a first attempt to de-center conventional narrative structures: "Margaret Walker in *Jubilee* begins the process of substitution by using Afro-American folk culture . . . to provide the substance and insights of the world of Vyry, her house-slave protagonist" (141).

Other critics have remarked that *Jubilee*—mainly because of its specific temporal setting—follows a typical slave narrative pattern: bondage, transition, and freedom (e.g. Klotman 142-43). Such a categorization, however, glosses over significant differences without trying to account for them. The obvious similarities are partly due to the demands of chronology that are implied in both the realist project and the original slave narratives, and partly to the givens of the life of Walker's great-grandmother. In her comments on the book, Walker deliberately connects her learning about her own family history with slave narratives that she read in the 1950s ("How I Wrote *Jubilee*" 56). What is at stake here—rather than the similiarities of chronologically told narratives—are the implications of Walker's decision to combine the slave narrative content with the structural and stylistic conventions of the 19th-century historical novel. This includes a necessary shift from a first-person autobiographical narrative voice—with its specific claim to credibility based on first-hand experience—to a third-person omniscient narrator who no longer coincides with the author. Accordingly, strategies of authorization also have to change. Instead of being able to draw from lived experience, Walker combines factual information with a point of view that presents the narrative as an unmediated representation of "reality." The third-person omniscient narrator claims authoritative knowledge by giving the impression of mimesis, or—to borrow a formulation from DuPlessis—by "mask[ing interpretation] as representation" (*Writing beyond the Ending* 106).

The shift to a third-person narrative voice might be positive in terms of a possible broadening of the textual scope; it also raises questions, however, about the ways in which a traditionally omniscient narrator is part and parcel of a hegemonic cultural practice like realism, which makes it difficult to adequately represent ideas and experiences that the dominant culture defines as "other." A number of African American and/or feminist critics have analyzed the ways in which realism and its ideological underpinnings have contributed to consolidate the dominant position of an assumedly "typical" subject by implicitly denying white women as well as women and men of color representational authority. In particular, these arguments address claims to universality based on (mainly) white, male, middle-class experience.[8] Lanser, for example, argues that "[w]ithin the hierarchical structures of the realist novel, any project to authorize characters outside the social hegemony is already undermined by the conventions of narrative form" (*Fictions of Authority* 125). And Joanne Frye, in her analysis of the adequacy of conventional literary models to accommodate the specificities of women's lives and stories, adds that in the realist novel, "reality is seen to be manifest in the material world as if selection were not determinant of how that reality is seen" (39). These critical voices focus explicitly on the discursive aspects of literary narrative.

Emphasizing characterization and plot rather than discursive structures, Barbara Foley argues for the positive potential of an "untypical" (i.e. black) hero to lead to a redefinition of the function of realism in narrative (*Telling the Truth* 234). Rather than supporting and stabilizing the dominant system, such a main character might in fact successfully challenge and disrupt conventionally accepted truth claims, because a black and/or female protagonist can—according to white patriarchal ideology—never be really "typical" in a European or Euro-American framework. Accordingly, "the postulation of typicality assumes a subversive quality: instead of confirming, analogous configuration disputes deep-seated assumptions about the nature of the social totality and who is eligible to represent it" (244). This approach comes closer to Walker's optimistic assumptions about the flexibility of genres. It is an important hypothesis that such a subtle expansion of the boundaries of genre can undermine from within some of its conventional implications by disappointing reader expectations and thus provoking a critical reflection of what is considered "typical."

As one effect of this complex writing situation, a coherent, unambivalent and unambiguously convincing narrative that moves straightforwardly toward conflict resolution and closure is no longer possible.[9] The difficult historical and cultural circumstances in which Walker was conceptualizing and writing the book as well as the complexities inherent in her material left their traces in the text, observable in various disruptive undercurrents beneath the seemingly smooth narrative surface. These additional narrative levels both expand Walker's stated intentions to write a black female slave into history and introduce aspects that implicitly contradict these intentions. A critical emphasis on this complexity challenges the notion that the novel presents an unambiguously jubilant portrayal of Walker's great-grandmother. Not only did she have to adhere closely to the facts of her family history as well as to the known historical data about the era at large, but she also had to find a narrative strategy in which a positive, celebratory portrayal of a black woman could be presented at all to a general reading public more used to negative narrative clichés, and in a literary climate still very much insisting on the irrelevance of "women's issues" and/or "black issues" for so-called serious fiction.

If we assume that Walker in general managed to address a widespread information deficit and not to alienate potentially hostile readers, the questions then remain if and how it is possible to effectively displace the dominant culture's oppressive discourses without drawing too much attention to the fact that they are oppressive. Can the black female slave's and the white male planter's points of view really stand side by side? Is Vyry's physical presence enough to value her and devalue the white man's perceptions of her? Is it possible to conceive of a third-person narrator who does not devalue the black female character in this configuration of discursive and social power inequities? Or does Walker's narrator have to approximate a white male angle of vision in order to make the inclusion of Vyry possible at all? Is it possible to strike the delicate balance of criticizing without risking alienation?

In marked contrast to younger writers like Morrison and Williams, who doubt the possibility of telling new stories without fundamentally critiquing and revising traditional forms, Walker does not explicitly call into question the role of language and dominant forms of cultural expression in the historical denial of a specifically black and female point of view. Nevertheless, the politics of genre as well as the cultural and political tensions that form the context of *Jubilee* are present in the text and influence our reading of it. It will be the task of the following analysis to examine these controversial undercurrents and to see whether they support or undermine Walker's stated intentions.

JUBILEE: AMBIVALENT VALIDATIONS OF THE BLACK FEMALE PERSPECTIVE

In *Jubilee*, the reader's attention is first directed to a "Dedication" to Walker's own family. It characterizes Walker as an author who is very aware of her own social connections that reach from the past into the future, as her mentioning of her grandmothers, mother, same generation-kin, and children shows; it thus underlines the "communal" genesis of the text. The lyrics of the spiritual "Jubilee" then function as an epigraph, expanding not only the focus on oral transmission already implied in the "Dedication," but also creating a direct link with the novel's title. Setting up necessary improvement as one of its basic tenets, the spiritual sets the tone and atmosphere for the text proper and anticipates the novel's teleological thrust.

The epigraph is followed by an extended "Acknowledgments"-page, which contains references to the "real," historical persons Vyry and Randall Ware. Unlike the "Dedication," however, these references are no longer embedded in a context of oral storytelling, but they are presented as factual information, based on material data like a photograph and an entry in the Terrell County Courthouse. Already at this early stage, Walker's intention to "undergird the oral tradition . . . with literary documents" ("How I Wrote *Jubilee*" 56) is thus clearly apparent; the extrafictional framework anticipates the novel's later reliance on "hard data." Walker's historiographic approach is further supported by the mere existence of an "Acknowledgments" page—a rather unusual addendum to a novel.

The following "Contents" pages show a very detailed subdivision not only into three main parts, but also into numbered chapters that all have individual titles. This also supports the impression of a well-researched project. The titles given to the individual parts express the basic combination of family/folk material and "straight" history: they connect "private" expression ("Sis Hetta's Child," "Mine Eyes Have Seen the Glory," "Forty Years in the Wilderness") with a chronological outline of historical periods ("The Ante-Bellum Years," "The Civil War Years" and "Reconstruction and Reaction"). The chapter headings continue this strategy: they are mostly lines, sayings, or quotes that are lifted directly out of chapters and thus additionally emphasize a vernacular, or folk, context.

The last of the paratexts that precede the text proper is a map of Alabama and Georgia that show the locations important for family history (e.g., "Abbeville: Vyry's first free home, log cabin") as well for national history (e.g., "Atlanta: Post Civil War capital"). The whole group of paratexts, then, already conveys a strong sense of some of the priorities set in the novel: an emphasis on historical verifiability within a conceptual framework that attempts to combine oral and written, marginalized and centralized, black and white knowledge and traditions.

How much Walker's approach to writing *Jubilee* was shaped by the (historian's) desire to educate readers by documenting a wealth of neglected information is also apparent in the way she conceptualized the basic structure of the novel: "I anticipated about two hundred fifty . . . incidents and then reduced them to about one hundred. In essence, I never deviated from that outline" ("How I Wrote *Jubilee*" 54). The larger subdivision of the text into three major parts corresponding to the antebellum, the Civil War, and the Reconstruction periods supports the novel's emphasis on historical progress. The use of dates and events as structuring devices allows Walker to situate her detailed descriptions of 19th-century life within a verifiable context, and thus—in Lukács's words—"to *demonstrate* by *artistic* means that historical circumstances and characters existed in precisely such and such a way" (43; original emphasis). The novel's plot line parallels Vyry's life from early childhood to her thirties, although there are—especially in part II—lengthy excursions into areas outside of Vyry's reach and vision.

This chronological, largely event-oriented approach supports Walker's intentions to inform readers as comprehensively and completely as possible about important historical developments. Moreover, it allows her to include a wealth of information about life in the slave quarters before the Civil War, and the daily struggles of a black family during Reconstruction—information largely unknown before, especially for white readers. However, the deviations from the trajectory of Vyry's life that this also entails point to a paradox in Walker's conceptualization of the novel: the plot makes it clear that there is a disparity between Vyry's experiences and what has usually been considered the decisive events of the time (cf. Christian, *Black Women Novelists* 71). Because this obvious divergence is not used to question the adequacy of traditional historical explanations, Vyry's central position is—on this structural level—implicitly challenged.

Walker's decision to use spirituals and folksongs to lead into individual chapters emphasizes the plot's simultaneous embeddedness in a predominantly, though not exclusively, black folk context. Within this framework, the connection to Vyry's life is more readily apparent. As an extension of Graham's argument that the chapter headings—based mainly on oral information—provide an alternative frame of reference that disrupts any reading which takes the primacy of the written for granted, I want to suggest that Walker's references to oral cultural forms function as a counterstance to an unchallenged privileging of historiographic data (Graham, "Margaret Walker" 23-24). Furthermore, they support the respective thematic emphases of each of the three main parts.

While we find mainly spirituals and black folk songs in part I, part II shows a mixture of black and white folk songs mainly related to the war experience; part III again returns to African American forms. This sequence directly parallels the shifting thematic emphases within the plot. Thus, these folk expressions serve as additional authorizing devices for the larger narrative. They show that "ordinary" people, too, were actively engaged in the historical process of which they were a part and that this engagement found expression in, for example, song. Drawing from written records as well as predominantly oral "folk-lore," Walker thus explicitly situates herself in both traditions. Because of the structural separation, however, the oral material still appears largely as an addendum that can supplement, but not really challenge the primacy of the traditional (European) realist approach. As such, it remains a cautious gesture to include hitherto neglected sources of information.

Within the context of this attempt to combine written and oral historical concepts, the shifting thematic focus of the plot introduces an additional complication that challenges the coherence of the novel at its surface. The correspondence between the novel's three parts and the historical periods of antebellum South, Civil War, and Reconstruction makes it necessary for the author to consider the particularities of each period, including the perceptions and evaluations of her own time. The three parts appear to be attempts to counter three different sets of stereotypes about the cultural and political position of 19th-century African Americans current in the 1940s and 50s. From what is highlighted in each part, it seems that Walker was deliberately trying to counter the stereotypical assumptions that

(a) during slavery, slaves did not have a distinct culture;

(b) during the Civil War, Blacks were only marginally involved in the fight for their emancipation, and

(c) Reconstruction failed because former slaves were incapable of leading a "free" life based on self-motivated industriousness.[10]

The novel's trajectory from life on the plantation to the "larger" events of the war, and finally back to the struggles of Vyry's small family takes into account all of these different aspects. In addition, it situates Vyry's life in a clearly teleological framework, progressing as it does from Sis' Hetta's death at the beginning to a vision of (relatively) peaceful family life at the very end. Within this underlying notion of the unavoidability of progress, however, *Jubilee* shows that the improvement of living conditions was nevertheless extremely difficult and sometimes obviously contingent on factors beyond individual influence. Highlighting Vyry's pragmatism, growing sense of responsibility, and sheer staying power especially toward the end, the novel pays tribute to the contributions of black women like her to the difficult process of redefining African American existence after slavery.

Walker herself recognized the difficulties inherent in the development and representation of fictional(ized) characters within such a complex starting position. In "How I Wrote *Jubilee*," she comments on her own struggle to create "muscle and flesh for the real and living bones of history":

> [Verlin Cassill] showed me how to dramatize my material and make it come alive. I had never had any trouble with dialogue, but now under his tutelage I was learning how to . . . make character charts, establish relationships, and control the language more powerfully and effectively. (58)

Despite Walker's stylistic efforts, the final version of the text still shows the episodic initial structure, often shifting from scene to scene—or chapter to chapter—almost without transition. This causes a sense of rupture, especially when an event is emotionally charged for one or more of the characters, but the plot still moves on without dealing with or solving the psychological and/or emotional disturbances. The impression remains that it is the progression of events, rather than the characters' personal development, that ultimately moves the plot forward.

Narrative Perspectives: Partial Decisions

In agreement with the conventions of the realist historical novel, this event-oriented organization of plot is linked with a narrative structure based on the mediating functions of a third-person omniscient narrative voice. It is one characteristic commonly associated with such a narrator, according to Lanser, that s/he claims an authoritative position as "sole mediator of the fictional world, who occupies a 'higher' discursive plane than the characters" (*Fictions of Authority* 85-86). Within a narrative context in which the "narrator is the highest authority and the characters' positions are contingent upon their relationship to that authority" (125), it is especially important to examine how the fictional characters are discursively situated, both in relation to each other and to the narrator.

Above, I have described the novel as the site of an intense struggle over narrative authority—a struggle which I consider at least partly the result of the difficult constellation of black female author and white/male-oriented "general" intended audience, in which Walker has to legitimize her own claim to an authoritative position. It is the underlying thesis of the following textual analysis that Walker deals with her own contested status by creating a narrative voice whose attitude to the fictional characters approximates that of the mainstream audience that the novel addresses. The struggle over whose perspective holds more authority is carried out on the discursive level; the prevalent narrative perspective, represented especially by the third-person omniscient narrator, often does not support the thematic emphasis on the black woman's importance.

This ambivalent attitude finds expression especially in the way the text handles issues of voice. Although much of the novel is arranged around Vyry's physical presence, this presence does not, at first, include the right to speak—the right to claim at least verbal agency in a situation in which her physical agency is severely restricted. For a long time she remains silent, her personal perspective repeatedly challenged or completely suppressed both by other characters and by the narrator. In several instances, her physical presence is used merely as a catalyst to keep the narrative going: she is seen, described, defined by others, but she is hardly ever given the chance—especially in part I—to present her own view of things. This impression of Vyry's silence is intensified by the narrator's decision to be very reserved about providing insights into her thoughts.

What makes these decisions about Vyry's textual representation invite closer inspection is that the strategies used to present her are not consistently applied to other characters as well. The narrator displays a partial attitude toward the fictional characters that manifests itself in the distribution of textual spaces. The event-oriented plot structure of the novel is—especially in connection with a focus on historically verifiable information—often more conducive to male experiences; this is particularly noticeable in the Civil War section. In addition, the discursive attitude toward the characters also challenges the claim to a conceptual centrality of the black female protagonist. In order to substantiate this claim, I will examine some of the narrator's choices about what to say about whom, and what these choices imply for the reading of the text.

How the narrator's bias is prepared for and presented as the prevalent perspective is especially obvious in chapter 1, in which not only significant thematic issues but also the general style of presentation are introduced. The following textual analysis will therefore start with a close reading of this introductory chapter. I will examine in detail the thematic and stylistic decisions involved and their implications for the novel as a whole. I will then move on to analyze selected scenes in which some of the concerns that are raised at the very beginning are either validated or modified in response to the changing historical circumstances. The tensions between the novel's thematic trajectory from slavery to freedom and its reticence to grant the black female protagonist the status of a "free" and—at least discursively—"equal" subject are most apparent in the encounter between the pregnant Vyry and her master/father, the circumstances surrounding her attempted flight and the following auction, and the final argument among Vyry, Randall Ware, and Innis Brown, in which Vyry is finally granted the textual space to speak her mind and, in a deliberate discursive act, demonstrate her moral integrity.

Individual Silences

Jubilee opens with the impressive account of the death of Vyry's mother, Sis' Hetta. This decision to begin the novel with the death of a black woman worn out by fifteen pregnancies in as many years indicates an overall interest in the point of view of slavery's victims. The deathbed scene is clearly intended as the first fundamental statement about slavery: Hetta's fate of being forced into a sexual relationship with her owner, and of having more babies than she could literally bear, is one poignant example for the lack of control enslaved women had over themselves and their bodies. Beginning this fictional biography with the death of the mother, and not with Vyry's birth, Walker thus immediately defines Vyry's existence within a framework of violence—violence that includes the habitual disruption of families and the commodification of black women as sexual objects and "breeders." In connection with the novel's title and the reader's knowledge that Vyry will grow up to have children herself, this first scene establishes the teleological thrust of the novel: things will have to get better, and this general improvement will be tied in crucial ways to the improvement of the situation of black women.

In addition to this thematic contextualization, however, the first chapter also prepares the stage for narrative privileges that are to run through the remainder of the text. Placing an enslaved woman in a position in which she is not only psychologically, but physically prevented from speaking her own mind, the first chapter replicates the conceptual set-up of the novel as a whole: her physical presence is clearly central for the development of plot, but this does not necessarily entail a corresponding centrality on the discursive level. Unable to raise her voice above a raspy whisper, Hetta is not just represented as a quiet person, but as literally silenced by her condition. Barely alive and unable to communicate much to the people around her, she is read and defined by those who observe her dying. Significantly, not even the otherwise omniscient narrative voice seems to have access to her thoughts, but has to deduce from external clues what might be going on inside her:

> After having given birth to fifteen children, all single births, she was waiting for death in childbirth. . . . Evidently her mind wandered back over happier and earlier days, for her quick, beady eyes, glittering with fever, sometimes lighted up. (*J* 5)

Thus the only information we get about Hetta are the thoughts of others: the other black women who tend her dying, her slave husband, Jake, and—most extensively—her white master and the father of most of her children, John Morris Dutton. Although certainly a lot more extreme than Vyry's situation, Hetta's condition allows Walker to establish an overall narrative perspective in which (black) women are shown as predominantly voiceless—objects of the narrator's and of other, mostly male characters' observations and thoughts.

Within the set-up of the first chapter, it is especially illuminating to examine the portrayal of John Dutton. Much space is given to his incriminating musings about Hetta, after he himself has been introduced in a startlingly positive way through the focalizing perspective of Granny Ticey:

> John Morris Dutton scarcely looked like the Marster. He still looked like a boy to Granny Ticey, but a big husky boy, whose sandy hair fell in his face and whose gray-blue eyes always twinkled in fun. . . . He never seemed to take anything too seriously, and his every other word was a swearing, cursing song. . . . He was a young man with hot blood in his veins. (*J* 6)

This is scarcely the expected description of "a rich man with two plantations and sixty slaves on this one" (*J* 6). Significantly, however, it is the first description of Dutton in the book, and thus prepares the ground for the role he is to play—immediately afterwards as well as later in the text.

Whereas the black women who attend Hetta's dying reflect on her present condition, Dutton quickly displaces the uncomfortable present—which he is, after all, largely responsible for—with reminiscences of Hetta as a young woman:

> He remembered how she had looked growing up, long legged like a wild
> colt and just that temperamental. She looked like some African queen
> from the Congo. She had a long thin neck and she held her head high.
> *She must have imagined herself,* he thought, in an African jungle among
> palms and waterfalls with gold rings coiled around her neck. (*J* 7,
> emphasis added)

The insidiousness of this passage is not only Hetta's objectification through the
white male gaze, but Dutton's attempt to appropriate her thoughts in order to
justify the relationship he has forced upon her. The romanticized notion of an
Africa full of palms, waterfalls and pretty women negates the harsh reality of
North American slavery and allows Dutton to gloss over and thus negate his own
responsibility for Hetta's terrible present condition. Significantly, he himself is
granted the textual space to explain and excuse his own behavior by describing his
marriage to his wife Salina and his disappointed expectations that make it seem
"natural" for him to "satisf[y] his lust" (*J* 8) with Hetta.

Not only does this narrative strategy consciously employ stereotypical
notions about the frigidity of white women and the sexual availability of black
women, it also does not explicitly challenge the legitimacy of Dutton's
assumptions. He literally gets away with pulling himself out of all responsibility,
displaying no moral scruples for his actions. This stance is additionally supported
by the narrator, who offhandedly remarks that "[m]iscegenation was no sin to
Marse John" (*J* 9). How much any possible concern with Hetta's well-being is
overshadowed by Dutton's own egotistical motifs is particularly obvious in the
matter-of-factness with which he views the present situation: "Now, Hetta was
dying. He would miss her. Perhaps Salina will be pleased, he thought" (*J* 9). The
white master is thus not only granted the privileged space to introduce readers to
the history of his "relationship" with Hetta—and thereby Vyry's family history; he
is also allowed to legitimize his own actions, and as a consequence define the
terms of both his and Hetta's textual representations.

This distribution of narrative voices turns Hetta into a symbol of suffering; it
does not leave room for any examination of what that suffering might mean for
her. The "institutionalized rape of black women" (Carby, *Reconstructing Womanhood*
39) is here presented as a normal part of plantation life. It is described as so
customary, in fact, that we are even expected to accept the master's attempts to
think/talk himself out of his responsibility with the statement that "[i]t was all his
father's fault" (*J* 7).

A second detailed description of Hetta is offered by Jake, the slave who was given to her as a husband by Dutton. Fearing immediate sale after her death, Jake reflects on how this initially forced relationship with Hetta has affected his own life, and how her death will in turn affect his and his children's future. His reminiscences also include a description of Hetta as a young woman, but in contrast to Dutton, Jake is not turning away from the gradual changes in her that he has been able to observe:

> When their children were sold away and some babies never cried she would cry and grieve over their helplessness. She was a sullen-looking woman with a pouting lip who rarely smiled and almost never talked and who kept her hair wrapped in endless clean little rags. Once, when she was young and shapely, she was proud and she walked like she owned the earth. . . . Now she was no longer young and slender and lovely. . . . Only her face was still the same, serene, dignified, sullen, and quiet by turns. (*J* 12)

Jake's account is certainly a corrective for Dutton's in many ways; it lets us imagine some of *his* pain and frustration of being given "Marster's woman" (*J* 12), but the image of Hetta that emerges here is still shaped mainly by his own struggle for a positive self-image. His particular role in the triangular relationship Dutton-Hetta-Jake is clearly a threat to his sense of manhood: "Jake hated Marster and despised himself and looked at Hetta and got mad and evil. But that was the end of it. He never dared say anything or do anything about it" (*J* 12). His aversion to the whole situation is only lessened because "Hetta had been a good wife to him. . . . She never showed him her nakedness, but she never refused him either" (*J* 12). Significantly, his virility also becomes a source of pride—in a corrupted way, because it reduces him to his sexual function: "Guess in a way I am glad to get away from here. Marster's always said he'll get a fair price for a good stud like me" (*J* 13). The only "positive" self-definition available to him is the one that results from his commodity status; as property, his personal "value" is directly related to the amount of money he can be sold for.

Neither John Dutton's nor Jake's reminiscences are motivated by the genuine desire to understand the woman with whom they are both so intimately connected. The closest we can come to insights into Hetta's specific situation is to imagine her through the thoughts of the other black women who care for her during her final hours, and who are clearly more empathetic than the two men. In the context of generally insufficient medical care, the almost unbearable hardship of too many pregnancies is presented through the thoughts of Caline, Aunt Sally and Granny Ticey:

> It wasn't the first time this heavy breeding woman, whose babies came too fast, tearing her flesh in shreds, had had a hard and complicated time. . . . Hetta was sick every day this last time. Toward the end she rarely left her bed. She was bloated and swollen beyond recognition. But Jake said nothing, as usual, and Marster only laughed. (J 5)

Hetta's retreat into a silent bearing of her lot corresponds to Caline's conviction that there is nothing else one could possibly do. In this context of sexual violence it can literally appear to be a woman's saving grace not to be able to have children: "Caline had no children. She had never known why. . . . Slaves were better off, like herself, when they had no children to be sold away, to die, and to keep on having till they killed you" (J 4).

In addition to the sympathetic attitude toward John Dutton shown by the narrator, the first chapter presents—thematically as well as discursively—an understanding of gender roles that will run through the text as a whole and contribute to the formulation of Vyry's final position. The black women introduced on the first few pages draw from their personal experiences in order to evaluate the present situation, but the focus of their thoughts and actions is clearly on Hetta, not on themselves. On the whole, this shows a typical role distribution along gender lines: the women engage in relational activities; they are care-givers and nurturers, trying to make a difficult situation more bearable to the best of their abilities. In contrast, both male characters are observers of the scene rather than active participants. Although they are both—albeit in very different ways—affected by the situation, there are no attempts on their parts to help alleviate Hetta's suffering.

This particular gender/race configuration is positioned within the location of the slave quarters; consequently, we also get information about various aspects of the slaves' everyday lives, as well as their personal assessments of the situation on the Dutton plantation. More than any other part of *Jubilee*, the first chapter effectively uses black religious beliefs to create a somber, subdued atmosphere, for which the squinch owl and the black pot become symbolic shorthands:

> Midnight came and thirteen people waited for death. . . . It was not a night for people to sleep easy. Every now and then the squinch owl hollered and the crackling fire would flare and the black pot boil. Aunt Sally kept wondering what would happen to the little girl, Vyry. (J 13)

Creating this initial scenery in which the community of slaves and their clearly black cultural practices play a central role, Walker sets out with the potential to challenge the privileging of the white man's thoughts and actions that I have outlined above.

However, the author's choice of an omniscient, but partial narrator renders this initial set-up problematic. Walker's empathy toward the slaves' difficult and painful situation risks being compromised by the narrator's perspective that seems to take white and/or male dominance for granted. This is apparent on the level of description, when the narrator appropriates white labels and calls Grandpa Tom "stable boy" and May Liza "house girl" (J 3). Additionally, it finds expression in a textual strategy that more or less subtly makes the slaves complicitous in their own subordination: Granny Ticey's positive characterization of John Dutton is the first of several instances in which a black person presents a defense of either an individual white person or of slavery in general. Accepting infantilizing descriptions of blacks instead of challenging them right from the start as inadequate, putting arguments in the slaves' mouths that make slavery appear justified and whites benevolent, and granting a surprising amount of space to pro-slavery defenses, the narrative voice jeopardizes some of the critical potential that is inherent in the novel's initially very explicit focus on the black slave community.

The granting of privileged narrative space to John Dutton that we see in chapter 1 is reaffirmed in chapter 14, when the pregnant Vyry gathers up her courage to ask her master/father to give her permission to marry. Although Vyry is the one who takes the initiative here, she is effectively silenced the very moment she walks into Dutton's study. He is clearly "master of the situation" (J 120), and the narrative voice leaves no doubt about the dynamics of the encounter: "*He* was watching her as *he* talked" (J 121, emphasis added)—she is not only literally his property, but also completely at the mercy of both his gaze and his definition. It could not be clearer that he is the subject in control, whereas she is the objectified intruder. Vyry is almost completely represented through Dutton's eyes or from the narrator's perspective. Only once do we get her own thoughts, and this occurs precisely at a moment when she is censoring her answers in the light of Dutton's expectations:

> She knew he expected her to say she didn't know. She started to speak the sober thought in her mind—that her husband would do these things for her—but she knew he would consider her impudent so she thought better of it and held her peace. (J 120-121)

While he runs the gamut of emotions from feeling ill at ease, patronizing, angry and furious, she largely appears silent and motionless, fearfully bearing his vehement reactions to her request until she is "dismissed, . . . [and goes] out without saying another word" (J 122).

These different ways of behavior clearly correspond to Dutton's and Vyry's respective roles as master and slave—there is no doubt that the situation reflects an extremely hierarchical relationship. What is disturbing is not so much that the scene describes a situation in which the black woman literally did not have much to say, but that the way this description is presented does not challenge the legitimacy of this power inequity. The narrative situation does not provide a counter-perspective, which would allow for a more critical evaluation of the difficult meeting between master and slave, or father and daughter. Instead, the narrator discursively supports the thematically inscribed hierarchies. If the purpose of this scene had been to show that slaves had to hide their emotions from their masters, the narrator could have focused on Vyry's thoughts, not Dutton's. This, however, would have required a different narrative attitude toward Vyry, but as it stands, the privileging of the white/male dominant view is maintained rather than challenged. We are implicitly asked to have sympathy for Dutton, who is said to be *made* ill at ease, and who experiences the encounter with his slave/daughter as "painful." How painful the whole argument must be for Vyry—whose whole future, after all, depends on Dutton's decision—remains unsaid.

This particular scene introduces the question whether moral conduct can be a convincing way of achieving reader empathy and establishing an authority that is based neither on social nor on discursive control—a question that will become increasingly significant toward the end of the novel. The assertion of Dutton's privileged position clashes with the equally clear moral assumption that Vyry is the one being wronged. In order to raise this issue, Walker has Dutton recognize "scorn" in Vyry's expression at the very end of the argument—a sentiment that fits into Dutton's initial feeling of unease, but is largely unprepared for by Vyry's behavior. It appears to be a rather contrived device that is needed to remind Dutton of his repressed guilt about denying his own daughter her freedom.

In his discussion of Harriet Jacobs's *Incidents in the Life of a Slave Girl*, William Andrews shows how "Linda Brent," faced with a situation similar to Vyry's, is nevertheless able to maintain a sense of agency for herself despite her powerless social status as slave:

> Nothing that Jacobs can say in these interviews can free her of her master, but her repeated dialogic struggles with Flint testify to the

power she could and did exercise against his attempts to manipulate and dominate her. (*To Tell a Free Story* 278)

What is most striking about Jacobs's description of the confrontation with Dr. Flint—especially in comparison with Vyry's encounter with Dutton—is the possibility inherent in the first person narrative perspective to add her own thoughts as critical comments to the argument that is represented in direct speech. What we get to know about Dr. Flint is what Jacobs chooses to tell us; within this narrative configuration, there is never any doubt who has the privileged perspective. So although Jacobs, too, is not given permission to marry the man she has chosen, the effect of the confrontation with her owner is totally different from the one achieved by Walker. After being told to leave, Jacobs even addresses her readers and asks them for empathy, which reinforces the impression that she is indeed controlling her own text: "Reader, did you ever hate? I hope not. I never did but once; and I trust I never shall again" (40) Vyry, in contrast, is left "[s]itting alone in her cabin door with her own bitter thoughts," because "[h]er beautiful dream of freedom again seemed forever lost" (*J* 122). At this point, it no longer comes as a surprise that we are not privy to these thoughts. In keeping with Walker's general focus on events rather than introspection, the chapter is here brought to a rather abrupt end.

Walker's strategy to demonstrate Vyry's unbearable situation is to show her exposed to emotional and physical violence in a quick succession of events. Again, Vyry's silence reaches disconcerting proportions, especially when she is put up for sale in chapter 16:

As each female slave was put on the block she was either stripped to the waist or wholly naked while the auctioneer recited her worth. Nobody seemed interested until Vyry was offered for sale. Her children cried when she was put up alone. The bidding picked up until it was clear that an old white man lounging in a corner . . . continued to bid higher for her than anybody else.

Then the bidding abruptly stopped. Vyry was told to dress again. Nobody was sold but the dumb boy, Willie. . . . Vyry saw that he would be taken away again and she was filled with distress (*J* 135).

Even though Vyry had a letter written to Randall Ware to send somebody to buy her, she could not at all be sure that her plan would work out. In this precarious situation, to be set up for sale is likely to have been extremely stressful and anxiety-ridden. The description of the auction, however, does not show any of Vyry's probable inner turmoil—with its brevity and restrained matter-of-factness, it stands in strong contrast to the emotional weight it carries. In anticipation of Vyry's later characterization as care-giver who is always concerned about the well-being of others, her only feelings that are explicitly mentioned are the ones directed toward somebody else: Vyry "forgot her own situation in pity for [Willie]" (J 135). It seems striking that not even a concern for her own children—which is so prominent in the flight scene—is brought in here. What did she feel when "her children cried" (J 135)?

In the next chapter, the plot moves rapidly to the planning of Vyry's escape—the auction is only mentioned in passing as the cause for Randall's decision to leave the area. The significance of Vyry's unsuccessful attempt to flee because she cannot conceive of leaving her children behind has repeatedly been commented on.[11] Again, however, the emotional ramifications of this scene are granted little representational space. And although the flogging Vyry gets immediately after being returned to the plantation is described in detail, there is no explicit remembering or mentioning of it later in the text. Only in the final discussion with Randall Ware and Innis Brown does Vyry bare her back. Significantly, however, neither of the men gets to see her chest—the scar on her breast remains totally "private." If the black men—both intimately connected with Vyry—learn their lesson by seeing only her bare back, the laconic remark that ends part I is addressed solely to the readers, whose gaze at this moment borders on the voyeuristic: "When she was able to examine herself she saw where one of the lashes had left a loose flap of flesh over her breast like a tuck in a dress. It healed that way" (J 145).

Walker is sublimating the physical and emotional pain that is inherent in that situation not only by comparing the wound to a "tuck in a dress," but by treating it as such. There is detachment rather than emotional investment on part of the narrator, which leaves readers to their own devices to "make sense" of the scene. This simile plays down and "normalizes" the injury—after all, a tuck in a dress is placed there deliberately, purposefully; it is also hardly noticeable, not really noteworthy. Bröck-Sallah's comments on the function of Vyry's scars reflect the disturbing implications of this scene:

> Never do we hear Vyry speak her minds and feelings about his wound to anybody, never does the text go back to this experience, not even in Vyry's final monologue that is, fulfilling the plot structure, the all revealing account of her martyrdom. Walker, even though she writes partially, as a witness to this slave women's suffering does not succeed

in wrenching Vyry's body from its status as a metaphorical site. ("Women Writing" 231)

The wound in Vyry's breast evokes shock in the reader at the very moment it is described. Had the whipping only scarred her back, it probably wouldn't arouse as much pity; to violate her "female parts," however, demonstrates how her being a woman and a slave cannot be separated. I read this as a preliminary stage of rape, which would be the ultimate expression of white/male power and which Vyry is—according to the novel—spared.

The first part of *Jubilee*—"Sis' Hetta's Child: The Antebellum Years"—functions particularly as evidence for Vyry's precarious condition as an enslaved woman; she is largely at the mercy of external forces with very limited spaces for self-directed agency. Her lack of control is exacerbated, as I have just shown, by the way in which she is discursively positioned in relation to other characters and the narrative voice. In order to actually make her the central, respect- and authority-demanding figure as whom she is finally presented in part III, Walker has to emphasize another way of gaining authority that is neither dependent on political nor on discursive power.

The focus on Vyry's bitter experiences during slavery, in combination with repeated manifestations of her natural "goodness" despite the evil that surrounds her, can hardly fail to rouse empathy and pity in readers—empathy that will later supposedly turn to admiration when it becomes clear that the victimized young woman unquestioningly assumes responsibility for herself and her family and makes a point of not expressing anger or hatred toward her former captors. The vivid descriptions of the various assaults on her spiritual and physical integrity can thus be considered central components of an authorial strategy to create an image of Vyry that draws its strength from its inherent moral force—a moral force based more on an "inner," i.e. "natural," strength in the face of unbearable hardship than on deliberate reflection.

Collective Silences

The slave community as a whole is exposed to a similar tension between material presence and a lack of narrative spaces that would allow an encompassing representation of the slaves' own perspectives. A situation that is in some ways comparable to the conversation between Vyry and Dutton is described in chapter 3, when the slaves meet with northern abolitionists in the swamp and discuss possibilities of escape. The scene itself ties in with other information about Ezekiel's and Randall's activities on the underground railroad, as well as Randall's northern connections. The overall impression, however, is one of suspicion and caution on part of the Dutton slaves. Although the narrator mentions both pros and the cons, the men who do not believe that it is possible to escape get the space to express their uneasiness about flight and/or rebellion. In a lengthy passage, Uncle Joe, one of the oldest men on the plantation, legitimizes slavery, using biblical references to make his point:

> "Does you know how many hundreds and hundreds of years we's been slaves? . . . You know how come? Well, you know what God told Ham, don't you? You know what we is, don't you? Just hewers of wood and drawers of water, that's what we is. That's our punishment for being black." (J 42)

Although the desire for freedom and the willingness to fight for it are also mentioned, the legitimizing argument is the one that is explicitly elaborated and thus given privileged narrative status.

This is one of several scenes in which textual space is granted to black characters expressing the very arguments that are then used against them. Internalizations of inferiority are granted much space; similarly, status attitudes that are not surprising in themselves, but disturbing because of the way in which they are portrayed, are given more than their share of attention—for example when Caline is airing her misgivings about "yard niggers" (J 72). These passages lack the kind of tolerance and open-mindedness that the novel as a whole purports to represent.

In contrast, the representation of white characters is often highly idealized; there is, for example, no indication in the text that the following description of John Dutton is not meant seriously:

> It was as if he stood on top of the world astride his beautiful horse, riding the crest of the sky like a young sun god, Phaeton, with the rays of sunlight highlighting his brown hair, and the earth spread before him in the low valleys like a golden brown and clay-red bordered carpet. (J 180)

Later in the Civil War section, the idealization of whites becomes even more poignant because it is immediately contrasted with a less-than-sympathetic portrayal of black characters. On less than a page, Lillian's nine-year-old son Bobby is described as being "old enough to understand what the war meant. He knew that now . . . he was the man of the house." Only fifteen lines below, Vyry's nine-year-old Jim is characterized by "Big Missy" as "a simple little nigger who just grins and says 'yas'm' and then won't do a thing" (*J* 220).

Portrayals like these clearly direct reader sympathies and provide spaces for positive identification where critical self-reflexivity might have been more appropriate. The dynamics behind *Jubilee* thus seem to have a particular stake in winning white sympathy and approval. Radical steps are always softened by some remark that supports the view of slaves as dependent and content, or as divided among themselves. Whites—often in contrast to blacks—are presented as emotionally complex characters whose racism is more the result of 19th-century southern socialization than a matter of personal responsibility.

The complete lack of explicit communication between house and field slaves that characterizes part I finally finds its counterpart in Vyry's condescending comments toward other blacks in part III. With the narrative focus diverted from the plantation community and instead directed almost exclusively toward Vyry's small family during the Reconstruction years, "Forty Years in the Wilderness: Reconstruction and Reaction" effectively silences the "hundreds of thousands of emancipated Negroes" (*J* 263) who are—just like Vyry and Innis—on the move after the end of the war. In part I, there is a wealth of detail in the description of black life on the plantation, intended to show the existence of a functional culture and thus to enhance the status of the slave community as a whole. All this provides a balance to the narrator's ambiguous discursive attitude toward individual black characters. However, nothing that would come even close to group identification, or a portrayal thereof, seems to survive the war.

The omission of a communal context in the novel's later chapters is partly due to the more explicit focus on Vyry and her family in part III, in which Vyry's concern for status, already apparent in part I, becomes even more pronounced. Although it is explicable in the light of Vyry's personal biases—her initially ambivalent attitude toward Innis is one case in point—it is still disturbing in not having anything to balance it or to explain it as one possible strategy for survival in difficult times. Vyry doesn't want to associate at all with the black people around her—who are, it can be assumed, mostly women and men in similar circumstances, trying to make a living out of little more than nothing. Although she extends her care to the black woman who gets tarred and feathered, being well aware that the woman is the victim of sexual exploitation, not the perpetrator, this does not have any effect on Vyry's basically detached attitude; she keeps herself and her family apart from the black community, "low-class folks . . . what doesn't do nothing but drink and give they money to them bad womens" (*J* 306), as she puts it. She only gets in touch with the preacher—obviously a man of learning and therefore of higher status. It is this very community, however, which scrapes clothes and money together to help the Browns out when their house is burned. This would certainly warrant at least a passing comment, but no further analysis of the incident occurs (cf. *J* 324).

Again, Vyry is set apart from other characters and presented as different on the basis of her high moral standards. I have outlined above that the opposition between Dutton's social and Vyry's moral authority is created in the text through complex negotiatons of voice, in which Vyry's personal integrity comes to be associated with silent suffering. In regard to her deliberate dissociation from other freedmen and freedwomen, however, her higher status is explained with her belief in proper "moral conduct," and her attitudes are presented as fundamentally different from those of "common negroes" in similar circumstances. In this context, the sheer possibility of Vyry's integrity is presented against the background of a black community that does not seem to be able to reach these standards. Vyry's becoming a black heroine who is convincing to a mainstream audience thus happens at the expense of the black community at large. This adds another problematic aspect to her fictional identity and to the way she functions within Walker's revisionary project.

Silences Broken, Voices Heard

Rather than placing the postbellum events literally in a black communal context, the novel creates a vision of a black folk culture with which the characters identify, and which gives shape and direction to their strivings. In keeping with the pattern already established through the paratexts (especially the chapter epigraphs), singing and storytelling are presented as predominantly black forms of expression that provide an alternative cultural framework to the western one implied in the genre of the historical novel. However, the shared knowledge of songs and stories evokes an atmosphere of communality that is—as the events especially of part III show—no longer supported by literal group identification. Nevertheless, the concept of a distinctly black cultural frame adds yet another perspective to the novel's chorus of voices.

In addition to the split between the novel's fictional and factual information and the split between the narrative representations of white and black characters, the text thus introduces the distinction between different modes of expression as another important factor to be taken into account. Spoken words are associated with concrete, rational acts of communication; they can also be cunning, deceiving—in fact they often have to be in the relationship between slaves and masters. To recognize and express honest emotional involvement, however, the novel uses culturally specific forms of expression like folk songs and spiriuals. As Eleanor Traylor puts it, "the world of the slave quarters 20 years before the Civil War . . ., visible only through memory, is a matter of historical document, yet its meaning is a matter of song, of lore, of myth, and of great story" (514). Within the context of subtle resistance, the symbolic potential of song is especially important. On the one hand, singing can be an expression of suppressed feelings that would otherwise find no outlet, and therefore help to make difficult situations bearable and to function as a kind of stress relief. On the other hand, to participate in song—to use a more mediated, less individual, more symbolic code than spoken language—is to speak in a culturally legitimized voice that inherently offers a sense of communality. Song thus functions both as communal activity—as during Brother Zeke's meetings—and as "mood pieces" for individual people. For Vyry, song later becomes her most tangible link to her past; her favorite hymn, "Flee as a bird to the mountain," accompanies her all her life.

In various instances, Vyry starts singing when she feels that it facilitates the expression of her thoughts and emotions. After the frustrating encounter with Dutton, for example, Walker decides not to work through Vyry's disappointment and likely feelings of anger, but uses the situation to shift from personal to communal ways of dealing with the experience of powerlessness. Vyry's frustration finds expression, but not consolation, in a song she recalls:

> My old marster clared to me
> That when he died, he'd set me free
> He lived so long and got so bald
> He give out the notion of dying at all. (J 122)

Embedded in the context of this song, Vyry's painful experience with her master/father loses its uniqueness and becomes one representative example of the ways in which white slave owners exercized their power. Similarly, the symbolism of hymns and spirituals provides a cultural contextualization that allows Vyry to back up her personal point of view when she is challenged by Randall Ware:

> I may not understand much. I'm just a poor colored woman traveling
> through this sinful world, like Brother Zeke useta sing,
>> I am a poor way-faring stranger,
>> I'm tossed in this wide world alone.

> No hope have I for tomorrow,
> I'm trying to make heaven my home.
>
> I wants you to bear me witness and God knows I tells the truth, I
> couldn't tell you the name of the man what whipped me, and if I could
> it wouldn't make no difference. (*J* 406)

This is one of the few instances in which singing is used as a means of communication for characters in the text. In most other cases, it rather replaces communication by creating a sense of belonging with little verbal exchange. In this function, it is carried into part III of the novel in which—in contrast to part I—lack of community is one of the defining features. To evoke life on the plantation through musical references in a situation in which Vyry deliberately avoids contact with other freedwomen and freedmen makes the ambivalent authorial attitude toward the black community in the Reconstruction section appear even more pronounced. Additionally, to identify singing as the personal expression invested with the most genuine emotion does not result in a privileging of song as structural model for the text. Again, there is a wide gap between story and discourse that underlines the ambivalent polyphony of the novel.

In contrast to the obvious significance of song, storytelling seems to be only of minor importance. The few instances in which it is integral part of a scene occur in part I when Vyry is still a small girl: Aunt Sally tells stories about their family histories, and Brother Zeke entertains the children with his tales. The two most important adults in Vyry's young life create and hold together a community by means of storytelling. Vyry obviously enjoys these community gatherings—after all they become some of her most treasured memories—but she does not actively engage in similar activities. Instead, she is presented as a predominantly solitary, quiet, uncommunicative person, who repeatedly refuses to talk to others. In part I, she apparently avoids contact with Lucy, her half-sister who is also working in the house (Cf. *J* 92), and she ignores the woman who is supposed to take Aunt Sally's place as cook, joining the house-servants who "swore all-out war with the woman and would not help her do anything" (*J* 71/72).

Later we learn that Vyry tries to forget the violence and hardship of her youth, but neither her memories nor the process of dealing with them are in any way focused on, not even in the education of her children—we hardly receive any information about her actively passing on to them what she knows. Her educational practices seem to be more concerned with the teaching of virtuous behavior and industriousness—things Vyry knows to be useful and absolutely necessary for their new, more self-determined life. For her son Jim, however, her admonitions seem unreasonable, and Vyry has a hard time dealing with his unwillingness to obey. Several possible reasons for this clash between mother and son are hinted at in the text: first, Jim is on the brink of puberty and needs to establish a sense of separate identity; secondly, it is his "nature" to be independent like his father; and finally, he symbolizes the difficult shift from forced labor to more self-directed work. However, only one possible solution is given: although Vyry can partially understand Jim's conflicting emotions, she still demands his submitting to his stepfather's rules. There is little effort to really make him understand, i.e. talk to him about why he is supposed to behave in a certain way (Cf. *J* 371-85).

The description of Vyry's temporarily difficult relationship with her son confirms Innis Brown's status as a father figure who is given the authority to decide on family matters. In the final chapters of her novel, Walker presents a concept of a black family that corresponds closely to traditional notions of how a functional nuclear family should work. This description explicitly counters the portrayals of dysfunctional, female-headed, black families that are, according to mid-20th-century sociological studies, the direct result of slavery and the reason for the continuing failure of African Americans to assimilate into mainstream American society (Morton 87-97). Despite their limited plantation experience, Vyry and Innis are shown as very capable of adapting to changing circumstances; in fact, their earlier experiences provide them with almost all the necessary skills to make a living after the abolition of slavery.

A break with the past occurs nevertheless: at this point in the novel, the old stories—born out of the experiences of enslavement—no longer seem adequate. Vyry's childhood experience was marked on the one hand by the absence of both parents; on the other hand she was cared and provided for by black "othermothers" who educated the girl by sharing their experiences. In contrast, Vyry's own children grow up in fairly protected circumstances, under the loving as well as demanding attention of both (step)father and mother. In this family constellation, however, communication is limited; the children are expected to comply to orders given by their parents, who in turn do not need to justify or explain them. There is hardly any verbal exchange between mother and son: Jim can only talk to Minna, while Vyry talks to Innis, trying—more or less successfully—to mediate:

> Vyry hushed because she was sure there was no way for Innis Brown to
> see Jim's side, but she also understood how anxious Innis was to make a
> crop, and she didn't want to encourage laziness in Jim. She knew he did

not like to work, but he was growing up and he needed to know how to work. (*J* 373)

Only once, after just losing some of their newly acquired land in a flood, the text mentions Innis and Vyry's engaging in storytelling. Significantly, they connect their immediate personal experience with the biblical story of Noah's ark and the Flood (Cf. *J* 281), which Vyry sings because she can "sing it bettern [she] can tell it" (*J* 281). This scene is part of an extended network of biblical allusions that replicates one of the basic notions of the spirituals by linking the destiny of African Americans with the Old Testament.

Vyry's singing of the spiritual on Noah functions both in retrospection and in anticipation of things to come: on the one hand, it presents a hopeful outlook in stating that the water will disappear; it also skips the encounter between the naked/drunken Noah and his sons that has been one of the justifications for slavery. On the other hand, the finishing lines of the spiritual—"God told Noah by the rainbow sign/No more water, but the fire next time" (*J* 281)—anticipate the later attack of the Klan who burn the Brown's new house to the ground. These coincidental parallels between Vyry's story and the biblical tale are one concrete manifestation of the widely held belief that the experiences of slaves paralleled those of children of Israel; again, concrete events are placed in—and explained by—a larger historical and cultural context, and thus given symbolic potential.

In regard to the black community as both social and cultural context for Vyry's life story, the initial focus on actual black people in the opening chapters shifts toward a literally disembodied, metaphorical notion of a black folk context in part III.[12] Whereas in part I, African American life on the plantation is presented as being rooted in and supported by a distinctly black culture, this harmonious whole of social circumstance and cultural self-definition is severed later on: while cultural context is maintained, and even elevated to symbolic significance, the living conditions of freedwomen and freedmen recede more and more into the background. Although the text maintains a connection between Vyry's family and other black people, this connection is no longer based on identification and support, but on the opposite impulse: Vyry is explicitly set apart from other African Americans. Her final authority as the novel's moral center is thus presented at the expense of possible group identification, because it is based on a gradual devaluation of a black communal structure.

Final Speaking Up: Vyry's Moral Voice

It is only in the course of part III, and particularly in Vyry's confrontations first with Innis Brown, then with both Innis and Randall Ware, that Vyry's voice is finally heard. At last, Vyry's central moral position that she has gradually achieved is connected with a discursive space in which she herself comments on her attitudes and beliefs. As the following analysis of chapter 57—"What will happen to poor colored folks now?"—will show, however, this space has clearly delineated boundaries: Vyry's authority is ultimately contained in a conceptual frame that limits her to a "private," female sphere. Confronted with the unexpected return of her first husband, Vyry needs to sort out relationships so that in the end, her dream of an intact and relatively stable family can prevail. The ending of the novel, with its climax in Vyry's claiming of authority vis-à-vis both Randall and Innis, requires an examination of how this authority is defined and what it entails for the critical consideration of the text as a whole.

The collapse of the old political order, which concludes the middle section of the novel, is symbolically represented by the disintegration of the Dutton household and Lillian's madness, and juxtaposed by Vyry's literal "growing up." Her coming of age as well as the major shifts in external circumstances contribute fundamentally to her growing sense of responsibility. The events described in part III—"Forty Years in the Wilderness"—continue this difficult process of self-definition in the face of adversity and function as a gradual preparation for the final climactic scene. More closely adhering to the immediate circumstances of Vyry's life than ever before, the plot in part III narrows in on her small family as the center of attention. In contrast to the Civil War section, in which the narrative focus is so often completely outside of Vyry's sphere, whatever we get to know about the period of Reconstruction is—except for the occasional shift to Randall Ware's situation—dependent on whom Vyry and Innis meet during their search for a safe home.

Narrative closure is possible only after the establishment of good neighborly relations with the white community and Vyry's final reconciliation with her slave past: Randall Ware has to come back, and the two men have to learn about the extent of Vyry's suffering on the Dutton plantation to bring the novel full circle. Only at this point is the past actively remembered: Vyry picks up the pieces of her former life and integrates them into her vision of the future, at the same time as these memories become tools to make the two men understand her position.

Challenged by Randall who accuses her of still being "divided between black and white" (*J* 402), Vyry responds:

> You done called me a white folks' nigger and throwed up my color in my face cause my daddy was a white man. He wasn't no father to me, he was just my Marster. I got my color cause this here is the way God made me. I ain't had nothing to do with my looking white no more'n you had nothing to do with your looking black. . . . They stripped me naked and put me on the auction block for sale. And worsetest of all they kept me ignorant so's I can't read and write my name, but I closed . . . [Big Missy's] eyes in death, and God is my witness, I bears her no ill will. (*J* 405)

Although Vyry's passionate speech clarifies her own personal point of view, it also clearly conveys her defensive position—even in a situation that appears comparatively safe because it is placed in a "private" context—in the dual sense of the word as both familial and textual.

In addition, it places her in a mediating role typically associated with women. As so often before, Vyry is more concerned about the well-being of others than about her own needs; in this instance, she tries to create an atmosphere of tolerance despite divergent opinions by bridging the gap between Randall's and Innis's positions. Even the primary purpose of very personal memories seems to be to cater to somebody else's needs and to make others understand her point of view; only as a side-effect does it wrap things up for Vyry herself.

Despite the apparent confidence and forcefulness of Vyry's words, however, they still do not carry enough authority to stand on their own. To bring her argument to a conclusion, Vyry finally lets the two men see her whip scars for the first time. Significantly, it is her back she exposes, not the scars on her breast:

> Snatching at her clothes, she tore them loose and bared her back. . . . [T]he two men stood horrified before the sight of her terribly scarred back. The scars were webbed and had ridges like a washboard. . . . Vyry was still weeping, but just as quickly as she had torn off her clothes she recovered herself and threw her apron around her shoulders to cover her back again. (*J* 405/406)

These scars, carefully kept from everybody including herself and the readers, speak a more powerful language than words. To show her mutilated body is a means to create compassion and pity—this time not in an extratextual audience, as in chapter 18, but in her immediate family. Bodily pain is thus functionalized to be visual evidence for the brutal treatment Vyry had to suffer. Her passionate speech alone does not suffice—the material inscriptions of slavery on her body speak a more authoritative language.

A Gendered Morality of Quiet Compassion

As described above, Vyry's encounter with John Dutton in chapter 14 is the scene in which his social and discursive control is contrasted with her alternative authority that is based specifically on moral grounds. It is initially the situation as such—inherently oppressive because of the larger context of slavery—more than Vyry's particular behavior that places her in an ethically advantageous position. Dutton's conduct may be legally permissible, but is otherwise considered unacceptable. Part of Vyry's alternative authority derives from the perverted father/daughter relationship, in which Dutton refuses any acknowledgement of parenthood; another part results from Vyry's condition as expecting mother who wants freedom not primarily for herself, but especially for her child. In clear contrast to her master/father, she thus tries to establish a framework of maternal responsibility in a situation in which Dutton himself leaves no doubt about how impudent he considers any such claim: "I own you and I own your unborn child" (*J* 120).

To present Vyry as being understandably concerned about the future well-being of her children, and therefore trying hard to have them born in freedom, brings up the complex issue of motherhood in slavery, as well as its textual representation and its function for the development of the narrative. Within the economy of the slave system, in which Vyry's manumission would also entail the freedom of her baby, she has to be prevented from having any influence over her children's fate. On the other hand, the fact that the request for her own freedom comes at a time when not only she, but also a child is affected, places her in a "maternal mode" that anticipates her later attitudes toward her children—particularly the decision not to flee without them, explicitly against Randall's advice. Vyry's moral integrity is thus closely linked to her being (or becoming) a mother in a situation in which she is denied even minimal influence over her children's lives. This is additionally supported by her willingness to extend her caring to anybody—black or white—who is in need of help.[13]

With her attitude of caring and her very pragmatic abilities to make ends meet, Vyry thus en"genders" a dedicated moral authority that is based on qualities traditionally associated with women—particularly forgiveness and unselfish behavior. The way in which Walker defines Vyry's character traits as unequivocally positive raises questions about gender roles and their function within specific social contexts. Again, the issue is more complex than it may at first seem: although Vyry disrupts some of the dominant myths about black women—she does not fit any of the common stereotypes—she also only approximates stereotypical notions of "adequate" white female behavior. Although she is the caring, nurturing mediator, she refuses submissiveness and insists on being taken seriously by the men in her life. She also stands her ground when she is (paradoxically) accused of selfishness after putting her family's needs before her white employer's. Shown as the direct result of her experiences in slavery and war, Vyry's personal integrity and strength gradually becomes a prominent motif in the novel.

Especially the capacity to nurture—like all her other qualities apparently "natural" to Vyry—is described as her most typical trait. Always pragmatically responding to the changing circumstances, Vyry habitually sees herself in relation to others, and defines her well-being as dependent on the well-being of those around her. However, this pronounced focus on incessant caring eclipses other aspects of Vyry's identity: there is, for example, hardly any mention of her sexual relationships. This fits well into a context in which female sexuality in general is shrouded in silence and denial. Hetta had to succumb against her will, and Vyry's babies spring from a few embraces and tender words. The birth of a child is graphically described only when it occurs in a white household, which gives Vyry the chance to prove her abilities as a midwife. In this framework, it is impossible to uphold stereotypical notions about black women's sexuality: neither Hetta nor Vyry can—by any stretch of the imagination—be considered "loose" or "promiscuous." Vyry herself does not at all refer to her body, not even to come to terms with the injuries that the whipping caused on her back and chest. Bröck-Sallah comments:

> The very individual story Vyry's body would have to tell is effectively silenced by Walker's survival plot that establishes the character as symbol of and within Black history. As readers we are permitted but a glimpse at that story which I think means that Walker did put the issue of female slaves' mutilation on the agenda of literary history—trying to counter the Black female's inscription into the patriarchal text as whore and slut. On the other hand she could not or did not want to make it a center moment of privileged response. ("Women Writing" 230)

Within the literary and historical parameters Walker chose for the novel and the additional difficulties inherent in writing family history, she probably carried this aspect as far as it would go. Within the narrative economy of the text, a different approach to Vyry's womanhood would also have necessitated a different concept of Vyry's character—one based considerably more on personal reflection and the textual spaces to represent it.

In contrast, it seems that Walker rather tried to reinforce the quality of Vyry's integrity by presenting it as largely unconscious, and not as the result of deliberate reflection.[14] Whereas Harriet Jacobs's narrative shows that "power ... is negotiated through speech acts, through dialogue in which the woman constantly matches wits with the man to define a margin of option for herself" (Andrews, *To Tell a Free Story* 278), Vyry largely acts on her "natural qualities" of patience and faith in changes for the better. The specific combination of innate virtuousness and motherliness, lack of bitterness, and limited exposure to historical and political information which seems to result in a lack of reflective capacity leads to an overemphasis of unexplained responses. This creates a constant sense of wonder in the reader that such dismal conditions could nevertheless bring forth such a person of integrity.

Vyry's incessant attempts to create dialogue and to make understanding possible correspond closely to Walker's definition of black humanism and to her beliefs about the necessary conditions for peaceful co-existence. They also, however, show a commitment to a conservative ideal of femininity. The closest we come to an authorial comment on Vyry in the text is in the guise of Innis's thoughts, after hearing her defend her position in response to Randall Ware's accusation that she "is divided between black and white" (*J* 402). This choice of perspective is noteworthy: within the discursive hierarchies of the text, the final praise is presented as being thought—not spoken—by Innis, arguably one of the characters otherwise bestowed with very little authority.[15] The passage warrants full quotation:

> This woman, who had stood so much outrage, had a wisdom and a touching humility that he could never cease to admire. It was more than her practical intelligence, or her moral fortitude; more than the fundamental decency and innate dignity that marked her character as an unusual one in the face of both these men that night. . . . Innis Brown knew that she was touched with a spiritual fire and permeated with a spiritual wholeness that had been forged in a crucible of suffering. She was, in that night, a spark of light that was neither of the earth or

September air, but eternal fire. Yet it was not that she stood there in pride for them to worship her or be in awe of her deep integrity. She was only a living sign and mark of all the best that any human being could hope to become. In her obvious capacity for love, redemptive and forgiving love, she was alive and standing on the highest peaks of her time and human personality. Peasant and slave, unlettered and untutored, she was nevertheless the best true example of the motherhood of her race, an ever present assurance that nothing could destroy a people whose sons had come from her loins. (*J* 406-7)

This highly idealized description has conflicting implications for the text as a whole: first, with Innis Brown as focalizing consciousness, this final authoritative characterization of Vyry is one rare instance in the text in which the narrative voice seems to merge completely with Walker's authorial attitude, and thus carries a strong impression of authorial approval. In this context, the quoted passage is the epitome of a development in which Vyry turns more and more into a positive symbol of black survival. Secondly, however, it is exactly Vyry's elevation to a symbolic figure that also functions as yet another instance of objectification. It takes away some of the authority that Vyry has just claimed for herself as an individual—with personal ideas, needs, and desires. Again, she is both represented and defined by others.

Spillers suggests *Jubilee's* strong religious subtext as one possible explanation for this kind of characterization—an explanation that can account for Vyry's lack of bitterness as well as for her lack of introspection (or representation thereof).[16] Describing the novel as "Historical" rather than "historical," Spillers places it, with reference to Paul Tillich, in a context of "theonomous" thinking: "Human history is shot through with Divine Presence so that its being and time are consistent with a plan that elaborates and completes the will of God" ("Hateful Passion" 186). If we accept this assumption, Spillers continues, Walker's narrative choices appear consistent and understandable:

From this angle of advocacy and preservation, the writer does not penetrate the core of experience, but encircles it. The heroic intention has no interest in fluctuations or transformations of palpitations of conscience—these will pass away—but monumentality, or fixedness, becomes its striving. Destiny is disclosed to the hero or the heroine as an already-fixed and named event, and this steady reference point is the secret of permanence. (187)

Although this argument is convincing in regard to Vyry, it cannot, however, be applied equally to all major characters. There are obvious differences in the narrator's decisions to either "encircle" or enter a character's mind, to describe somebody's actions or represent her or his own thoughts.

A privileging of the "unconscious" character on moral grounds contradicts the conventionally assumed hierarchy of textual voices in which the degree of access to a character's consciousness is linked with her or his textual authority. As Lanser explains,

> [c]onventionally, those characters are highlighted who are presented in some detail, whose presentation includes some subjective information, who are shown from an internal perspective (if the text shows *any* of its characters from that perspective), and who are presented with enough depth of vision that we know more than their outward act. (*Narrative Act* 214)

Whether characters remain objectified—always seen through the eyes of and spoken about by others—or are given the chance to present themselves as subjects in their own right thus impacts on any evaluation of the novel's overall distribution of authority. Within the power dynamics that the text describes, the differential treatment of characters becomes more significant than it might initially seem; it complicates any one claim to a privileged perspective that the spatial and temporal structure of the plot might otherwise suggest. In this context, Vyry's central position at the end cannot be seen as wholly unambiguous, because throughout the text, her thoughts, wishes, and fears are not given as much space as other characters'. This not only leaves her self-confident outspokenness during the final argument with Randall Ware and Innis Brown strangely unprepared for, but additionally raises the question of how these differently applied styles of characterization function for the text as a whole.

The passage representing Innis's thoughts about Vyry is significant in (deliberately) creating a "positive" image of 19th-century black womanhood that contradicts the dominant white cultural mythology of the 1940s and 50s. This image is substantially based on Vyry's "natural" goodness—a black female essence that is the result of both innate characteristics and their shaping through socialization in the context of slavery. It is placed in deliberate juxtaposition to white and/or male reflection. One could argue that Walker, after all, followed as closely as possible the known facts of her great-grandmother's life, and that it is exactly its transcendence of the individual life-story that makes *Jubilee* an important literary document.[17] The idealizing countermyth that the novel presents, however, runs the risk of creating new stereotypes that also deny choice and self-determined agency to black women. And it is the novel's inherent irony that this "positive" image of black women was no longer up-to-date even at the time when *Jubilee* was first published. Novels by younger African American women writers show that Vyry might have been a necessary step in the engagement with the history of slavery, but eventually had to give way to more complex analyses.

TEXT IN CONTEXT: *JUBILEE'S* PROBLEMATIC POLYPHONY

Walker's optimism that she would be successful in her attempt to challenge the dominant culture's perceptions of enslaved and recently emancipated African Americans was supported by her own definition of her authorial status. She deduced her claim to a public, authoritative voice less from the potentially problematic relationship to her intended audience than from her specific personal connection to the subject matter. First, she had privileged access to relevant factual information through her family's orally transmitted history. This authentic background to her fictional(ized) characters could always be refered to as indisputable evidence for the veracity of her narrative. Although she could no longer cite her own experience as legitimation—which, in the original slave narratives, was one of the most important authorizing mechanisms—the family connection still provided her with a close, albeit mediated, link with her protagonist's life. Together with the factual evidence mentioned in the "Acknowledgments," this configuration authorizes the novel's plot as a truthful depiction of historical events. Secondly, Walker used the intimate knowledge of her great-grandmother's story to position herself favorably in a historiographical context. Not only was her information different from that of other historians; after her own extended historical research, she also had more material and could, convinced that a big part of the problem had to do with a general lack of knowledge, offer her version of 19th-century black history as more comprehensive than others'.

Her choice of genre consolidates this claim to an authoritative position: with Walker's understanding that "the writer's responsibility is the same as that of the social scientist or philosopher: to be like God and show the way" (Graham 1993, 281), there doesn't seem to be any doubt on her part that the position of "author" inherently carries a certain degree of authority, regardless of the social identity of the person who fills it. Walker thus borrows the authority that the genre of the historical novel carries within an American mainstream cultural context, in order to be able to introduce a hitherto "marginal" topic into public consciousness.

The novel itself shows, however, that this issue is a lot more complicated. Although Walker does not state anywhere that her textual choices were influenced by her (conscious or unconscious) anticipation of reader expectations, the tensions and ruptures I have identified in the text suggest that the relationship between author and intended audience did create conceptual problems. My reading of *Jubilee* corroborates my thesis that the attempt to reach and convince a mainstream audience, whose willingness to accept the knowledge claims of a black woman writer was likely to be limited, resulted in the conflicting subtexts described above. How significant the manuscript's temporary status as a dissertation project was for the writing process is difficult to establish; I want to suggest, however, that the dissertation committee at the University of Iowa, consisting exclusively of white male professors, serves as a metonymic embodiment of an assumed mainstream audience, its attitudes and expectations.

Despite the authorizing function of the narrative's rootedness in family history, the (auto-)biographical component introduces yet another complicating factor: it implicitly brings in Walker's family as a second, "private" intended audience. However, a narrative that attempts to render an initially private family account in an explicitly public literary mode has to attend on some level to family considerations of what can and should be said, and how this can be done. The question of how Walker could possibly present her black female protagonist so as not to disappoint either group of readers on some level must have informed her thematic and discursive choices. Coming back briefly to individual sections from the novel, I will add to my above analysis by suggesting possible influences of Walker's complex authorial position on her text.

Within the context of reading Vyry's final authority as inextricably linked with the different ways in which she has been silenced—first, by the voices of more powerful characters, secondly, by historical circumstances that temporarily direct textual attention away from her, and finally by her elevation to a symbolic, larger-than-life figure—her textual representation is in keeping with her symbolic function. Nevertheless, the tension between the novel's emphasis on Vyry as the moral center of the textual world and the subtle devaluation of the black and female voice on the discursive level remains an issue, especially in regard to genre. Although Walker was confident that the form of the traditional historical novel would best accommodate her subject matter, this generic context implies a privileging of those characters who show some degree of introspection and reflection. In *Jubilee*, two contradictory authorizing strategies thus stand side by side, creating an uneasy tension.

In regard to part I, where this ambivalence is most apparent, there are a number of possible reasons: although the initial scenes of the book were substantially revised before publication, some of the problems in regard to structure and the handling of point of view might be due to Walker's own young age when she wrote the first chapters. It could also be the result of part I dealing with Vyry's childhood and adolescence, in which her perspective was not yet seen as forceful enough by the author to claim authority in the text. Whatever the case—the silence surrounding the young Vyry is so complete that not even the omniscient narrative voice—which otherwise slips in and out of other characters' thoughts rather easily—grants access to Vyry's mind. It seems that the young writer Margaret Walker found it hard to envision a black woman—or a black girl—on center stage; one way to achieve this was by granting her protagonist physical presence, but at the same time denying her a strong voice.

This particular way of characterization is especially obvious in scenes in which Vyry is confronted with people who have actual power over her—most importantly John and Salina Dutton. Walker's description of Vyry as a mistreated child and young adult shows her as being enveloped in an enormous silence, completely at the mercy of her white master/father and mistress. Although this is certainly "truthful" in a merely descriptive sense, it turns problematic when placed in the context of Walker's intention to give an empathetic account of her great-grandmother's life. Instead of presenting social inequities in a way that would also make it possible to critique them, Walker stylistically replicates the structures of oppression that are inherent within the encounters she describes in the text. It would make a significant difference if the narrator at least gave a balanced account of the thoughts and feelings of everybody involved, instead of largely silencing Vyry and giving voice to the perspective of the other person(s). Despite Vyry's otherwise central position, the discursive center thus still appears to be largely male and/or white.

One could assume that this hierarchy of voices is linked particularly to the first part, and that Vyry's development from childhood to womanhood, from slavery to freedom, is then accompanied by a growing authority of voice. For most of the novel, however, the impression that Vyry is spoken about rather than speaking for herself remains. This reaches huge proportions during the description of the Civil War years: the shift from the relative privacy of the Dutton plantation to the public event of war results in our losing sight of Vyry altogether. Whatever happens between 1861 and 1865, it seems, is completely disconnected from her life. And out of sight, she can also no longer be heard. What we get instead are detailed insights into Johnny Dutton's war experiences, with Randall Ware's and Salina Dutton's perspectives coming a close second.

Additionally, the fact that one of the novel's three parts is dedicated entirely to Civil War history—primarily from a white male perspective, secondarily from a black male one—calls into question Walker's initial intent to give an account of a black slave woman's life. Especially in this second part, the focus is almost completely away from Vyry and the other slaves on the plantation; their immediate surrounding is not the site of action and of decisive events, and therefore it is temporarily suspended in favor of a supposedly broader view.[18] This does imply a privileging of national events over personal or family life, and thus at least partly contradicts the initial claim to write "history from the bottom up." In the guise of "general information," we get all the details about the progression of the war, and this decision implies that the necessarily restricted perspective of an illiterate enslaved woman is not enough to make us understand her decisions and motivations.

The particular emphasis on the public/political in the Civil War section corresponds to Walker's own research process. She seems to have assumed that it contributes to our understanding of Vyry if we know the "big" events, even if Vyry herself does not. Particularly in part II, Walker shifts into an explicitly historiographic mode by focusing more on the events of war than on plantation life. This process is partly reversed in part III, where Vyry's concrete situation regains central importance. The novel ends with an exclusive focus on the private. The events during Reconstruction comprise the part of the story that Walker's grandmother actually remembered from her own childhood—in contrast to the antebellum and the war years that she herself must have been told about. This might be one explanation why the final part of the novel concentrates almost exclusively on events that happen to the family. In contrast to her treatment of the Civil War section, Walker here refrains from giving detailed accounts of the political developments that would lead us away from the small circle of people. Whatever we get to know are only those things that Vyry and Innis Brown—and later also Randall Ware—are confronted with. In this final part of the novel, Vyry gives voice to a symbolic image of herself. She is not speaking on her own behalf, but rather supports an idealized, positive image of black womanhood with her engaged speech in which she defends her caring, compassionate attitude that does not stop at racial boundaries.

The novel ends on a note of harmony: conflicts are sorted out and a model nuclear family, with roles and responsibilities clearly distributed, is awaiting a better future. Even if this ending accurately reflects the historical course of events for Walker's family, it describes a rather untypical situation in a larger political context. With the reinstitution of Jim Crow as a legal means of segregation, the late 19th century was very likely to harbor further hardships for Vyry's small family. The idyllic scene at the very end is therefore ambiguous; it might well be only an illusion of security, strengthened by Walker's choice to use it as the closing statement of the novel. Significantly, this was—according to Walker—not her initial plan. She wanted to carry the story on into Vyry's old age and have it finish with her death, but was discouraged from doing so:

> I didn't know the limits. I had carried it to Vyry's death at age eighty in the first version. And I remember a man telling me in 1948, "Well, you know that story really ends when Randall Ware comes back." He said, "that's the end of the story." And that was when I realized what the limits were. (Giovanni and Walker 56)

What are these "limits" that Walker so readily accepts? They seem to be limits set by conventions of closure, of a "female plot" that is considered over as soon as family affairs are finally sorted out. Having come full circle with Randall Ware's return—so that Vyry has a chance to settle her open accounts with the past—Walker decides to let go of more than half of Vyry's life.

What would have happened had she continued her account beyond its novelistic ending? It would certainly have implied a different approach toward the historical material, if only for reasons of space. More important than considerations of length, however, would have been the decentering of the Civil War part, in regard to both structure and content. As a result, Vyry would have been more obviously the center of attention, especially if the final focus on her family could have been maintained.

In being able to take recourse to the authenticity of her story, however, Walker is "safe" in both directions: against black criticism that she is not radical enough, and against white complaints that she is going too far. From her public statements, it can be assumed that she was more concerned with the latter—and the circumstances of the book's creation support that impression. Apparently, there is more at work here than to give a truthful, or plausible account of what (might have) happened. With a constant eye on reader knowledge and reader expectations, Walker shaped the different parts of her novel to correspond to what she perceived to be the informational needs of her audience, as well as her own needs that resulted from the intense personal connection she had with the material.

Conflicting Goals: Family Biography vs. Historical Novel

If *Jubilee's* biographical background helps to position and authorize Walker as the person most qualified to write this particular story, it might also have contributed to the novel's unevenness—especially in regard to the representation of fictional characters. I have argued that especially on the level of the third-person omniscient narrator, the text approximates a white/male point of view. One of Walker's most significant authorial choices in this regard is her portrayal of John Dutton, the most important white character in the novel. Vyry's owner/father is on the whole presented as a figure who demands reader attention. The focus is repeatedly directed toward the complexity of the situation he lives in—it reads at times as if he, too, is largely a victim of circumstances, tossed around by his wife's interests, his father's expectations, and the demands of his plantation as well as southern slave society at large. Torn between lust, greed, and guilt, John Dutton is presented as a highly complex character who demands attention, sympathy, and understanding in a way that is not encouraged as strongly in other characters.

With an exclusive focus on the dynamics of plot and textual discourse, Dutton's powerful presence is indeed disturbing. If we take Walker's authorial situation into consideration, however, this allows us to bring in an argument that might explain, though it should not excuse, the white master's privileged position. I see Dutton's and Vyry's characterizations—diametrically opposed though they might seem—as two facets of the same issue: Walker's need to find plausible ways of representating her ancestors. With Vyry, she obviously had a lot of very positive information, replete with the tacit understanding that this image of her great-grandmother had to be preserved. The refusal to enter Vyry's mind and to trace her behavior back to identifiable sources as well as the decision to show her possessing unexpected strength and integrity can be seen as a deliberate and enabling fiction to counter negative stereotypes about black women. There might also have been a sense of caution so as not to alter—and thereby implicitly criticize—the family myth of the heroic female ancestor.

With John Dutton, however, the interests involved were probably very different. Unlikely to have been treated extensively within the family narrative, he probably needed to be imaginatively recreated in a much more fundamental way.

The complexity with which the fictional character John Dutton is endowed, then, might in part be motivated by Walker's own interest in making sense of his thoughts and actions. After all, Dutton—like Vyry—is Walker's ancestor, so she might have tried—deliberately or undeliberately—to allow herself to accept him, by giving him positive as well as negative traits. As understandable as such an approach might be in a psychological sense, however, it also replicates the distribution of voice and silence of the dominant historical and literary discourses.

If the political subtext of *Jubilee* reveals some of the tensions and contradictions inherent in Walker's historical project, it might be possible to characterize her reticence about depicting Vyry's inner life as her own unconscious at work: trying not to destroy the impression of wholeness and personal integrity, which a more explicit unraveling of Vyry's fears, doubts, and desires might have done. In turn, however, this kind of characterization risks coming across to post-Freudian readers not primarily as a positive expression of moral strength, but as a simplification or flattening out of a person's complexity.

The Degree of Possible Revision

The hidden polyphonic structure of the novel is responsible for the impression that the text is not—in fact cannot be—an unambiguous, coherent historical narrative. On the other hand, however, this polyphony is also a chance for the text in that it provides moments of identification for diverse actual readers, and begins to open up conventional literary-historical discourse to marginal voices.

The question remains, however, if Walker's hints concerning the psychological, emotional and social significance of black expressive forms eventually carry enough "subversive" potential to balance the biases inherent in the conventions of 19th-century literary realism, as well as in her own remarkably favorable descriptions of southern whites. With the intention to reach a broad audience with various backgrounds, expectations, levels of knowledge and degrees of openness, the text might give necessary clues to readers who know the black cultural context and probably understand the implications of even brief references, whereas other readers are more likely to overlook them. Such an interpretation would make Walker's project look like a complex act of signifying on the dominant culture's historical ignorance, similar to Vyry's treatment of the poor white sharecropping family.

"If you thinks your chilluns would like some you is welcome to share what we got, sich as it is."

"Is you got enough?"

"Ma'am, I got plenty."

... [W]hen Vyry dished up the steaming hot stew she fed every one of the white family as well as her own and made *the poor white woman and her husband feel they were doing her a favor.* (*J* 291, emphasis added)

The significance of this scene lies in Vyry's clearly being in control, but pretending not to be in order to make communication possible. Similarly, in order to make the difficult topic of slavery from a black and female perspective less threatening for white readers, Walker uses narrative strategies that do not fundamentally challenge traditional structures of white/male dominance. She is putting all of her energy into a formidable educational effort, by giving readers as much information as possible, wrapped in a narrative form they are familiar with, and leading them through a process of developing sympathy with and respect for a 19th-century black woman and her difficult situation. What is missing, however, is an explicit awareness of the dangers of being too accommodating. If I take the text's double-voiced discourse as a deliberate authorial strategy, I am also still looking for some indication for this intention, e.g. an ironic undertone in descriptive passages that idealize white southerners. There is no evidence, however, that *Jubilee* is intended as a text deliberately "coded" in this way.

Nevertheless, the tensions and ambivalences inherent in Walker's novel implicitly lead our attention to the questions of black and female self-definition and agency within a traditionally defined historical and literary context. Despite Walker's own statement that a writer has to "be like God and show the way" (Graham, "Fusion of Ideas" 281)—a defiant claiming of authority as it is conventionally associated with authorship—her novel shows that this authority is not as easily claimed as it might seem. Lanser's contention that "whatever the reader knows of the author is brought to the reading of a text, the writer's and the text's authority are dynamically intertwined; either is capable of enhancing or diminishing the other" (*Narrative Act* 84) helps to highlight the dynamics at work here: Walker invests her narrative voice with an ideologically acceptable identity that does not, however, coincide with her own contested status in the center-margin constellation that she herself accepts as conceptual frame for her own writing.

In order to authorize the black female authorial voice, the narrator has to approximate white and/or male attitudes toward race relations, and consequently—within the "traditional" conceptual parameters in which the identity of the white and/or male subject relies heavily on "othering" black and/or female persons—has to deny discursive authority to the black female protagonist. To maintain the centrality that Vyry had at the beginning of Walker's conceptualizing a book about her great-grandmother, the author has to locate Vyry's fictional authority on a moral, ethical plane, because the prominent, authoritative place that she probably had in Walker's family history cannot uncontestedly be translated into the discourse of an inherently eurocentric and androcentric genre like historical realism.

CHAPTER 3

"Onliest mind I be knowing is mine"—
Sherley Anne Williams's *Dessa Rose*

> We, the black women of today, must accept the full
> weight of a legacy wrought in blood by our
> mothers in chains. Our fight, while identical in
> spirit, reflects different conditions and thus implies
> different paths of struggle. But as heirs to a
> tradition of supreme perseverance and heroic
> resistance, we must hasten to take our place
> wherever our people are forging on toward
> freedom.
>
> —Angela Davis, "Reflections"

> This novel, then, is fiction; all the characters, even
> the country they travel through, while based on
> fact, are inventions. And what is here is as true as if
> I myself had lived it.
>
> —Sherley Anne Williams, "Author's Note"

Questions of representation, privileged narrative perspective, and the contested
authority of an African American female voice—issues that shaped the above
discussion and critique of *Jubilee*—are the explicit concern and central thematic
focus of Sherley Anne Williams's *Dessa Rose*. From the very beginning, Williams's
novel directs readers toward an attitude that makes it necessary to challenge
conventional approaches to the transmission of historical knowledge. The first
part of the novel, a revised version of Williams's earlier short story "Meditations
on History,"[1] asks how the historical subject—in this case the black fugitive Dessa
Rose—is constituted in the privileged discourse of a white male scholar; how
standard procedures of "data collecting," paired with racist and sexist attitudes,
create not a credible, historically "truthful" image, but rather a distorted vision in
which the subject of inquiry is objectified, silenced, and made invisible through the
filters of an ideology that is based on the oppression of racial and sexual "others."
In part II of the novel, the effects of racism on black and white women's

perceptions of themselves and each other are explored. The main focus here is on Dessa's and the white woman Ruth's struggles to redefine their identities and to free themselves from the psychological constraints of the oppressive ideologies with which they grew up and which strongly affected both of them, albeit in crucially different ways. Part III finally presents Dessa's narrative in her own voice—a significant shift in narrative perspective that concludes the continuous development away from the white male point of view with which the novel opens.

Williams's critique of historical representation starts at the most fundamental level: rather than examining the risks and pitfalls of 20th-century engagement with historical material, *Dessa Rose* at first scrutinizes the construction of what is considered to be, and gets transmitted as, historical "fact." The novel thus not only critiques realist literary conventions of representation, but exposes claims to historical truthfulness as ideological fictions. What gets passed on as "fact" is often only assigned the status of "truth" by those who have privileged access to public discourse. In addition, the text extends its critique of the political construction of black identity by working through a white antebellum woman's psychological and emotional fictions about herself and the black people around her. They reveal the connections between the political system of a slaveholding society and one person's seemingly private self-definition, as well as the complex interdependencies of white and black women's lives—aspects that are also missing from the white man's "factual" account.

Secondly, the novel's formal and thematic emphases on the constructedness of knowledge make it necessary to reconsider the position of the 20th-century author, whose interest in finding/creating a "usable past" conflicts with her insights into the fundamental instability of historical knowledge and meaning. By making historical representation both a structural and a thematic issue, Williams self-reflexively negotiates any writer's investment in the stories s/he tells, as well as the impact of various narrative perspectives on how the text influences the process of meaning-making. This self-reflexive and self-critical approach includes both a critique of traditional historiography and of historical fiction. On the one hand, it creates conceptual complications for a writer who not only wants to criticize what is there, but also to change and/or replace it. On the other hand, the assertion that what we think of as reality is never a given, but always constructed opens spaces for re-visions of knowledge—spaces that Williams defiantly claims when she states that "[h]istory is often no more than who holds the pen at a given point in time. I hold the pen now, and that is what authenticates me and my children" ("Lion's History" 258).

Even a cursory glance at *Dessa Rose* reveals, however, that the point cannot be to simply replace one ideologically invested interpretation with another; neither do insights into the instability of knowledge result in a relativist dictum that "anything goes." The alternative conceptual context that Williams proposes demands that the writer's positionality and its impact on the processes of imaginatively engaging in historical "certainties" always need to be taken into consideration. As the work of many contemporary women writers of color suggests, the critical and revisionary potential of these recent challenges to mainstream representations lies in the insistence on the validity of political and moral responsibilities, and on the writers' own adherence to this alternative framework. Nancy Peterson summarizes that "[t]he focus on the textuality of history is liberatory, for it recognizes the validity of various emplotments of events and thus creates a space for new emplotments" (129)—new emplotments that not only expose the failures of the old ones, but also make a strong point of not replicating them.

Dessa Rose clearly shows Williams's authorial intentions to challenge the legitimacy of white power—social and discursive—over black slaves and fugitives, and of setting up a new model for non-oppressive interaction. In contrast to *Jubilee*, the scenes depicted in *Dessa Rose* in which narrative authority and discursive power are contested lead to a destabilization of hierarchical structures. Those who are initially empowered because of their race and/or sex invariably lose their privileged positions—not only thematically because of the course of historical events, but through active deconstruction of this privilege in the textual structures. How these shifts are intertwined with Dessa's gradual claiming of voice, which culminates in the confident first-person narrative of part III, has frequently been commented on by reviewers and critics. Drawing from the insightful critiques by Mae Henderson, Elizabeth Meese, Nicole King, Ashraf Rushdy and others, I am going to argue here that Williams negotiates possibilities of historical engagement that allow us to recognize the discursive nature of historical and personal knowledge(s), but still make it possible to claim a politically interested positionality that takes sides with the traditionally silenced and disenfranchised.

Critical Attention

Although not too plentiful, critical articles on *Dessa Rose* show an impressive scope and detailed overall analysis of the text. Unless the novel is used as one specific example in a thematically oriented study,[2] critics generally emphasize the theoretical complexities involved in any project of "historical representation," and analyze how Williams in particular challenges a-political and de-contextualized notions of "historical reality."[3] In "Everybody Knows Her Name," Mary Kemp Davis explores the multiple meanings inherent in the characters' names, and the importance of names and self-naming in the development of identity. Nicole King asks how "*discourse* is implicated in the literary interpretation of our histor*ies*" (353; original emphasis). She presents *Dessa Rose* as a challenge of stereotypical notions of slavery and a medi(t)ation of new definitions. Mae Henderson argues that Williams's project out of necessity "gestures toward intertextuality" ("(W)Riting *The Work*" 636), because she signifies on a number of (often identifiable) other texts. Focusing specifically on "Meditations on History," Henderson introduces the term "contratextuality" to strengthen the aspect of re-writing as "a corrective gesture" (657 n.2). She also describes how Williams, as part of her primary concern with the "critical relationship between discourse, power, and resistance," gradually dismantles the white man's knowledge claims. Anne Goldman significantly extends the discussion by emphasizing the connections between reproduction and literary production—how both body and word become commodified within the system of slavery, and how questions of "identity" must deal with both physical and linguistic appropriations of the enslaved woman. This dimension not only provides a very poignant link to *Beloved*, but also specifies the discussion of discourse and power by making gender a main concern. In "(Trans)forming the Grammar of Racism," Elizabeth Meese claims that through "structural intervention, Williams creates a break, a potential for relationship beyond the monolithic (white) master/(black) slave dialectic of oppression" (135). Meese's concept of a "free zone" or "borderland" in which false binaries are challenged and differences newly negotiated is also used by Jane Harrison in her description of Sutton's Glen as a liminal, utopian space outside of the white patriarchal order (121). And Ashraf Rushdy extends earlier analyses by examining how Ruth's attitude toward Dorcas/Mammy is as much an expression of control as Nehemiah's "reading" of Dessa: "What she [Ruth] needs to do is to develop a dialogical attitude towards the languages of others"—she needs to learn "to listen to fugitive slaves as a way of understanding her deceased one" ("'Reading Mammy'" 376/383). In general terms, the direction that the *Dessa Rose* criticism is taking suggests that increasing attention is given to the intersections of black feminist and narratological concerns in Williams's vision of more humane interactions beyond the strictures of racism and sexism.

Especially in early responses to "Meditations on History" and *Dessa Rose*, Williams's signifying relationship to William Styron's *Confessions of Nat Turner* is also frequently commented on (D. McDowell, "Negotiating between Tenses" 145). Although there is obviously a crucial connection between these texts, any analysis that reduces the "Dessa Rose"-material to being merely a response to Styron runs the risk of unduly limiting its potential. In this respect, an analysis of *Dessa Rose* in relation to *Jubilee* provides additional insights, as my questions about Walker's novel have already been shaped to some degree by the thematic and formal issues that Williams raises in her text(s). The generational gap between Williams and Walker, intensified through the events of the Civil Rights Movement, is important here, and the younger writer respectfully characterizes *Jubilee* as "presag[ing] the modern era in the written history of [African Americans] ("Lion's History" 248). Although it is not clear whether Williams implicitly refers to *Jubilee* when she comments in an interview that she "was influenced to some extent . . . by other novels I had read about slavery and slave women" (Ross 494), she nevertheless alludes to a conceptual shift—maybe a generational shift—in the literary representation of enslaved women.[4]

As this brief overview of the critical material on *Dessa Rose* shows, the issue of (self-)representation and its link with discursive authority is generally agreed upon as one of the novel's central concerns. In the opening section of the following analysis, I will outline the development of the "Dessa Rose"-material from its initial conceptualization as a short story to its final form as a novel. Taking Deborah McDowell's concluding statement that "Dessa Rose is the final authority on her story, controlling her own text" ("Negotiating between Tenses" 160) and Meese's focus on how *Dessa Rose* breaks the "grammar of slavery" (129), I want to support and strengthen these arguments by examining in greater detail how Williams validates this redistribution of authority by deliberately taking advantage of formal possibilities to direct reader attention and sympathy. In a short comparative analysis between "Meditations on History" and the first part of *Dessa Rose*—with an emphasis on the interrelationship between story and discourse—I will explicate Williams's intricate strategies of authorization. This will be the basis for a further examination of the explicit shifts in structure and narrative perspective from one part of the novel to the next, and their connections with the thematic issue of the characters' developments toward mutual acceptance and peaceful co-existence. It will be followed by a close look at the narrative strategies that Williams employs especially in parts II and III of the novel to create textual spaces in which the black woman can speak authoritatively, and the white woman can unlearn her racism.

The final section of this chapter will then deal with the possible implications of this textual analysis for considerations of the novel's context. The delegitimation of the white male voice makes it necessary to re-position *Dessa Rose* in the complex cultural text of black women's narrative representations. In addition to the obvious impact of Styron's *The Confessions of Nat Turner*, the novel shows intertextual relations to other texts that have not been focused on as much. Williams herself deliberately situates the "Dessa Rose"-material in alternative historical, literary and critical traditions, and thus creates dialogic relationships between and among conflicting discourses. If Styron prompted the shape and content of "Meditations on History," the polyphonic structure of *Dessa Rose* also engages intertextually in black artistic conventions, critiquing and re-visioning them in the process. On the surface level of the novel, black female oral discourse displaces white male and changes white female ways of thinking. And Williams charts Dessa's gradual reclamation of voice through a deliberate placing of her protagonist in a blues context that not only validates oral modes of communication, but is also significantly rooted in a different conception of gender relations. The blues becomes a structural and thematic model for the literary text, in which aspects of oral and written cultural traditions meet. *Dessa Rose* thus contains an implicit critique of how an African American literary tradition is being defined, and how authors situate themselves within the complex cultural situation of the contemporary United States.

AUTHORIAL POSITIONING:
THE NOVELIST AS RESISTING WRITER

In contrast to the wealth of public remarks by both Walker and Morrison, there are relatively few statements by Williams in which she comments on her work in general, and on *Dessa Rose* in particular. Nevertheless, some concerns stand out prominently in the interviews and articles on hand (esp. Jordan; Ross; Williams, "Lion's History"). One common theme is Williams's own longstanding engagement with matters of black public voice—of self-definition and self-representation in a still discriminatory society. What is at stake in any act of public representation? How does the identity of the speaker impact on what is said and how this is heard and understood? What are speakers' political and ideological investments and interests? Her own role as a writer, Williams's remarks imply, is to engage critically in these questions and, as *Dessa Rose* in particular shows, to lay open and clarify some of the mechanisms that are responsible for a continuing devaluation of African American perspectives from public discourses and public consciousness.

In this regard, the incidents that initially sparked Williams's engagement with the "Dessa Rose"-material are significant in epitomizing—albeit in different ways—the politics of public representation. William Styron's publication of *The Confessions of Nat Turner* in 1967 and the widely differing responses to the novel provided a first important touchstone: highly acclaimed in a mainstream cultural context—complete with the awarding of the Pulitzer Prize—the novel was severely criticized from within the African American community. This critique centered on what was perceived of as the text's racist politics of represention, hidden underneath a surface of authorial disinterestedness. Despite the publication of John Henrik Clarke's *William Styron's Nat Turner: Ten Black Writers Respond*, which I consider a public offer to engage in constructive dialogue, the objections brought forth against Styron's *Nat Turner* were not only offhandedly dismissed, but discredited as completely unjustifed and unreasonable by Styron himself (Styron, "Nat Turner Revisited" 71).

In comparison, the article that led Williams to the historical material that was then to become the basis for her literary project provided—through the person of Angela Davis—a tangible link between historical and contemporary black female resistance. "Reflections on the Black Woman's Role in the Community of Slaves," written during Davis's own imprisonment 1970/71 on what turned out to be false murder charges, made it possible for Williams to situate herself in a political context of radical social critique. It connected her historical interest in the 19th-century imprisoned woman's fate with an engagement in late 20th-century discursive practices in which black and/or female dissenting voices still met with derision and harassment from the dominant culture.

Considerations of Genre

In contrast to Walker, Williams explicitly approached her material under the aspect of revision, setting out to "signify on," and fundamentally challenge, the mechanisms of silencing inherent in the appropriation of an other('s) voice. On a metatextual level, this necessarily includes a critical attitude toward considerations of genre, especially as they hinge on issues of discursive control: not only the characters' relationships among each other and with the narrator, but also the author's attitude toward the complexities of both historical and literary representations are submitted to Williams's critical scrutiny.

Dessa Rose pays tribute to this approach in refusing to be subsumed under one clearly identifiable, conventional format. With its shifting narrative perspectives, it draws attention to the implications of different points of view for the meaning(s) of specific thematic aspects. It does so, however, in a gentle way that, as Williams asserts, strives to take into account and accommodate the reading abilities of a broad audience. Her rhetorical and formal strategies thus remain within an overall framework of recognizable narrative conventions: "[B]ecause I'm a writer who began by wanting to talk . . . to people who ordinarily might not pick up a book, it is obvious that I can't talk about it in a way that destroys traditional story and traditional narrative" (Jordan 290).

Within the bounds of acceptability set by this intended audience, Williams nevertheless re-directs readers' attitudes by clearly privileging some forms of literary representation over others. The audience's notion of what a "good story" consists of is linked with the author's revaluation of (unmediated) oral narrative and its positioning as the novel's privileged narrative mode. In the context of this commitment to the needs and expectations of readers, Williams's explicit statement about not wanting to destroy the traditional story can be read as a critique of postmodern assumptions about narrative. Instead of privileging formal experimentation in unconventional, "writerly" texts, she attends to the "readerly" qualities of her narrative. In addition, the very subject matter and her focus on speech and silence place her in an African American tradition of what Henry Louis Gates calls "speakerly" texts—texts that are concerned with "the possibilities of representation of the speaking black voice in writing" (*Signifying Monkey* xxv):

> The speakerly text is that text in which all other structural elements seem to be devalued, as important as they remain to the telling of the tale. . . . [Its] rhetorical strategy is designed to represent an oral literary tradition, designed to "emulate the phonetic, grammatical, and lexical patterns of actual speech and produce the 'illusion of oral narrativion.'"(181)

In this context, Williams's self-positioning in a tradition of realism does not mean that she does not simultaneously challenge many aspects of narration usually associated with realism. On the one hand, she states: "One of the things that was guiding me was realism. I wanted people to believe that this could actually have happened because I felt what I had to say . . . had some very real applications for today" (Jordan 287). This implies that plausibility—in the sense of giving readers a recognizable context—played an important role; it leads back to an initial didactic impulse. On the other hand and in marked contrast to Walker, Williams explicitly changes those aspects of conventional writing that are most likely to transport oppressive ideologies: the dynamics of narrative perspective—including especially the traditionally assumed hierarchies between narrator and characters, as well as between author and narrator—possibly being the most obvious. Again, what is important is the basic acknowledgment of every writer's positionality and personal investments in the stories s/he tells, and every writer's moral and political responsibilities.

Williams's intense engagement with the "Dessa Rose"-material is also obvious in the several different places within her work in which it appears: in her poetry, as the short story "Meditations on History," and finally as a novel. In this context, *Dessa Rose* can be described as the most recent result of a steadily evolving idea—an idea that spans the fifteen-year period between Angela Davis's article "Reflections on the Black Woman's Role in the Community of Slaves" in 1971 and the novel's publication in 1986. With Davis's reference to a young pregnant slave woman who took part in a coffle uprising as a starting point, Williams re-visions the original account that the woman got hanged after the birth of her child. Imagining a positive ending, she allows the woman she calls Dessa to survive, grow old and claim subject status and agency for herself in letting her tell her own story. The 20th-century writer thus remedies some of the cultural "forgettings" of female slaves' experiences by providing a fictional space in which contemporary readers can begin to imagine what these women's lives might have been like.

The "Dessa Rose"-Material: Gradual Development of an Idea

One segment of the "Dessa Rose"-material appeared in print for the first time in 1975 as the poem "I Sing This Song for Our Mothers." The poem shows that from the very beginning of her work with the material, Williams intended the fictional Dessa to be a survivor—unlike her historical counterpart. "I Sing This Song for Our Mothers" gives voice to "Odessa's" son and has him, as the first of several lyrical voices, praise his mother:

> I tell you now what my ma say, jes
>
> the way she tell it to me.
>
> I want you to tell it to yo woman, to yo sons: to yo daughters most
> especial
>
> cause this where our line come from. (79)

The son's proud self-definition is dependent on his mother's heroic acts: he does not even refer to himself by his own name, but simply as "Odessa's son." He thus links his self-image inextricably with his mother's, intending to pass family history on mainly along the female line. Although he is male, the strength of the mother also becomes his source of confidence and identity. The second part of the poem then is Odessa's voice—merging with the son's—telling him the story of his birth and the reason for his growing up free rather than a slave:

> . . . I had
>
> you in the wilderness unda
>
> neath a tree. Nathan and Cully
>
> hold my ha nd while Harker birth you.

In Odessa's poetic tale, the roles of the three black men involved in her escape are only slightly different from their respective roles in the novel. What seems extraordinary is how this early poem already anticipates events that are to come much later in terms of published material.[5]

Although Williams had also already completed the short story "Meditations on History" in the early 1970s, she could not publish it until 1980, when it was eventually included in Mary Helen Washington's anthology of short fiction by African American women writers, *Midnight Birds* (cf. "Lion's History" 253). It later became, with more formal than thematic modifications, the first of the novel's three main parts. The short time span between *Midnight Birds* and the publication of *Dessa Rose* in 1986 thus belies Williams's much longer engagement with the material. Additionally, the publishing history of "Meditations" and editorial objections Williams faced in regard to the "Author's Note" in *Dessa* Rose show that even today, black women's historical representation is still a contested space ("Lion's History" 257-58).

In several articles and printed interviews, Williams outlines the process of first conceptualizing the story and then reworking and extending it into the novel. She talks about her struggle to resolve the conflict between anticipated reader/editor expectations and her wish to tell a different story, and comments on the thematic and structural decisions that emerged from this conflict. In the initial phase of conceptualizing "Meditations," she states, it was the scarcity of available historical information that created a first difficulty:

> When I first did the short story, . . . there had not been a great deal of research on black women in history, and particularly of black women in slavery. To a large extent I was going off into virgin territory by even imagining a heroic slave woman, or a slave woman in heroic circumstances. (Ross, 494)

Secondly, Williams had to deal with the question of plausibility. What would 1970s readers be willing to believe, given the fact that so little was generally known about the lives of enslaved black women? She explains the white male scholar's presence as a necessity to be able to account for the very existence of Dessa's story, and the possibility of our knowing about it today:

> How had the tale of an illiterate slave girl survived? What possible interest could it have for the white people who, almost inevitably, would have to preserve it? . . . [T]he convention of presenting Dessa's narrative through Nehemiah's records of his conversations with her came to me only after her voice spoke its first piece. And that sequence of events was important to me, for the white man was created out of Dessa's need, to serve Dessa's purpose. ("Lion's History" 253)

These remarks explicitly draw attention to a conflict that is in some ways similar to what Walker was confronted with in the conceptualization of *Jubilee*. What was at stake again was the difficulty of inserting certain aspects of black women's lives into the public discourses on race and gender that contradicted the dominant culture's stereotypical assumptions. In contrast to Walker, however, Williams accepted the challenge head-on by making the struggle over "adequate" representation the central focus of her text(s). Williams's comments show that the intricate web of influences on the "Dessa Rose"-material led almost logically to a heightened awareness of the tensions between dominant and minority definitions of historical events, of the ideological implications of historical representation, and of the political investment of every writer in what s/he is claiming to do.

In "Meditations" (and later in part I of *Dessa Rose*) the main focus is initially on the notebook entries of the white male scholar. These entries consist of his transcriptions of Dessa's voice, his immediate commentary, and his evening comments after transcribing the day's notes. This multi-layered white-authored narrative is preceded by a (day-)dream, in which Dessa is imagining herself back on the plantation amidst the family and friends she lost when she got sold to a slave trader. This reverie stands in strong contrast to what is to come, and provides a first destabilizing challenge to the white man's interpretation. The immediately noticeable juxtaposition of these two very differently structured sections characterizes both story and novel as starting from oppositions: the oral text of Dessa's memory is contrasted with the interviewer's written "transcriptions," complete with date and location—the marginalia commonly associated with diary or letter writing. There is thus no mistaking Nehemiah's journal for an oral narrative, despite the first-person point of view in which it is written.

In contrast to the novel version, however, "Meditations" retains this initial focus on Nehemiah's journal until the very end.[6] This perspective, as well as Williams's repeated references to William Styron in interviews and articles, mark the story as a deliberate act of signifying on *The Confessions of Nat Turner*. Williams creates a scenario similar to the encounter between Nat Turner and Thomas Gray depicted by Styron, but makes it clear from the outset that what we are being presented with is not the black voice but a white rendition of it. She explicitly works through the dynamics of a forced relationship between black prisoner and white recorder, and she leaves no doubt about the stakes that Nehemiah has in the interviewing process. For him, Dessa's information is only a means to an end; his interest is not at all in the person in front of him, but merely in her potential usefulness for his book. He clearly expresses this attitude before he meets her for the first time, when he reflects on the possible reasons for the uprising in which Dessa was involved: "[I]f I do not discover the answer with this one negress, I have every confidence that I shall find an answer in the other investigations I shall make" ("Meditations" 211). Dessa's being pregnant is a case in point here: Nehemiah recognizes how instrumental her condition is for his opportunity to question her; he knows that he will have to remain on a good footing with her for the limited period of time in which Dessa is thus "protected."

What he is unable to recognize, therefore, are the meaningful connections between Dessa's memories of Kaine, her desire to gain freedom for herself and her unborn child, and the coffle uprising in which she was caught. Seriously doubting her capacities to reason, Nehemiah cannot even imagine that a black woman is capable of meaningful, self-directed behavior. This, in turn, leads to his complete disregard for Dessa's own self-definition as a person whose identity is shaped by and dependent on its communal context of family and friends. His search for "causes" for the uprising is thus reduced to an investigation of material clues. Dessa's genuine despair over her situation as a slave, as well as her final resolution to resist, remain incomprehensible within his frame of reference. Consequently, the transcriptions of Dessa's tale and Nehemiah's interpretations of it are full of oversights, clichés, and racist stereotypes. "The journal," Henderson explains, "is not a reliable text because its author is not a competent reader" ("(W)Riting *The Work*" 654).

Ironically, it is his striving for scientific accuracy that makes it possible for Dessa's countertext to become perceivable at all. Faithfully transcribing her words, the white man unwittingly creates a text that undermines his very goals, as his notes reveal Dessa's perception as well as his own. They show, for example, how important her relationship with Kaine, and especially the bitter experience of seeing him killed by the master, was for her resolution to claim agency for herself and take an active part in the coffle uprising: "'I kill that white man,' she said, [. . .] 'I kill that white man cause the same reason Mas kill Kaine. Cause I can.' And she turned her head to the dark and would not speak with me anymore" ("Meditations" 225). This act of resistance, of breaking the boundaries of submissiveness and passivity imposed on the slaves was, despite its harsh consequences, decisive for Dessa's self-image. "I bes" are, significantly, the first words the white man hears her utter:

> "I bes. I bes." Just those two words on a loud, yes, I would say, even exultant note. Her arms were now at her side and she stood thus a moment in the light. Her face seemed to seek it and her voice was like nothing I had ever heard before. "I bes. I . And he in air on my tongue the sun on my face. The heat in my blood. I bes he; he me. And it can't end in this place, not this time. Not this time. But if it do, if it do, it was and I bes. I bes." (216)

Nehemiah is thus immediately confronted with Dessa asserting her subject position. As he rightly understands, he "did not exist for her" (216); Dessa's identity is not dependent on his particular presence, although it soon becomes obvious that white people have been influential for her self-image as an immensely negative force. It is implied that in a system that is based on non- or mis-communication between white and black, the only way to "answer" to the degrading and violent conditions is physical action, although it is also clear that such a response leads to more violence and severe punishment. On first sight, Dessa's attack seems futile; in terms of her self-image, however, it is extremely important. Its significance does not lie in outward success; it lies in the sense of agency that it creates, and in Dessa's claiming her humanity by defining herself as subject.

Obviously, this subject position is continuously contested in the context of slavery. Not only does Nehemiah compare Dessa's appearance with that of an animal; the paradoxical situation of the interview in which he—despite his doubts about her mental capacities—wants information from her, but unfortunately not the kind of information she is willing to give, continuously attempts to reinscribe her as the object of his discourse. This attempt is thwarted to some extent by his own obvious inability to interpret Dessa's words and actions adequately. As Mary Helen Washington points out in her short introduction to "Meditations," the white interviewer, considered an expert on the "slave question," emerges as truly ignorant. Not only does he initially dismiss Dessa's self-constituting narrative as unimportant for his purposes; his view of the slave community is so biased that he is not capable of grasping the deeper meaning of anything Dessa has to say. Faithfully transcribing her words, however, he unwittingly writes down a text that undermines his very intentions. Therefore meaning is here more a matter of reading than of writing, and the interviewer reveals more to us about himself than he does to himself about Dessa; I agree with Washington that "[m]uch of the story's meaning is conveyed—unwittingly—through the writer-interviewer, . . . ultimately betrayed by his own presumptions of superiority to the slave woman" ("Sherley Anne Williams" 199).

It is this self-reflexive metalevel about the problems of representation that makes "Meditations" such a powerful piece of writing. Directing the readers' attention to the inadequacy of the alleged "expert" and refusing to accept the authority of his voice, Williams probes into the complex issue of "speaking for others"—an issue that has proved to be a delicate one indeed, especially in the context of an oppressive social system. It opens up reconsiderations of the way in which African Americans have been described, defined and represented not only during slavery, but ever since. It urges readers to reconsider not only the accounts of slaves, written down by whites, but by implication also the narratives of illiterate ex-slaves who entrusted their life-stories to northern abolitionists before emancipation, or to writers working in the WPA-projects in the 1930s (cf. M. Young). It urges us to reconsider stereotypes as they are perpetuated in historical and literary writing.

On the level of meaning, the juxtaposition of Dessa's (day-)dream—that most private of narratives—and the publicly privileged written discourse of a white male scholar, as well as Nehemiah's self-defeating blindness, certainly work to challenge the validity of his statements for the readers. As far as Dessa's concrete situation is concerned, the only way she has to exert some influence is to extricate herself not only figuratively, but literally from the white man's text/influence. In the long run, however, that still leaves us with Nehemiah's distorted perception as the one that stands as written "document." The socially and discursively privileged space that he occupies is not fundamentally destabilized. "Meditations on History" is a powerful story with its focus on misrepresentation, but—in contrast to *Dessa Rose*—it does not yet explicitly offer an alternative.

Williams's comments on the process of extending the story show how the decade between the writing of "Meditations" and the final publication of *Dessa Rose* opened new conceptual possibilities for her work. Research on black women's history expanded, and she

> . . . no longer had the excuse of ignorance. In the decade and more between the story's conception and the novel's inception, the history of black people in this country had become an accepted field of study on American college campuses. ("Lion's History" 255)

In addition to these external changes, Williams describes that she personally had not completed the work that the material required: the fictional characters continued to occupy her thoughts, and thus literally refused her the authority to let go of it:

> I knew that the test of Dessa's authenticity was going to rest not only on my willingness to allow the woman to tell her own story finally, but also on what she had to say and the authority with which she said it. . . . I would have been willing to let it go sooner, but she really wasn't. She wanted it told in a certain way; it was her story. (Ross, 495)[7]

What the novel has to achieve, then, is to back up Dessa's personal determination not to be dehumanized with the concrete presentation of her claim to be a "subject" within the discourses through which we get to know her. As a continuation of the revisionary process begun in "Meditations," *Dessa Rose* therefore has to go beyond Dessa's physical escape from Nehemiah's influence. The novel explicitly removes the black woman's *story* from the "mercy of literature and writing" and reclaims the "high art" of "surviv[ing] by word of mouth" (*DR* ix) in allowing Dessa to control her/story and in making its telling the only possible closing gesture of the novel. As Lanser points out, this includes having the space to choose the appropriate situation for speaking: "The transformation of [Dessa's] pseudopersonal voice must therefore entail the right not simply to speak but to speak freely, to choose a narrative situation and an audience that can be trusted not to appropriate her discourse for its own objectifying and annihilating purposes" (*Fictions of Authority* 199).

In the novel, the thematic representation of Dessa's gradual reclamation of voice—first turning the tables on Nehemiah and later claiming the right to speak in front of the white woman Ruth—is supported by a number of formal strategies, which include both textual organization at large and decisions about the distribution of discursive privileges in each section of the novel. Referring specifically to the first part of *Dessa Rose* and how it relates to "Meditations," Williams raises the issue of authority in direct relation to the text—in Nehemiah's case the sheer authority of his presence:

> The problem was to subsume Nehemiah's voice and presence under Dessa's. The short story is told solely through entries in Nehemiah's journal, so Dessa's voice is filtered not only through his consciousness but through his ability to hear and understand accurately what it is that she's saying. This puts him in control of the narrative to a great degree. . . . So I had to do the third-person narrative and subsume Nehemiah's voice and presence under that third person. (Ross, 494)

After thus stating the issue of misrepresentation in "Meditations," Williams attempts to give an answer in *Dessa Rose*: what emerges as the authoritative text finally is Dessa's own account of her life. She not only rejects being defined by others, but in appropriating the text for herself, she fundamentally undermines the value system inherent in Adam Nehemiah's narrative: instead of equating "white" with "human" and "black" with "animal-like," the novel as a whole refuses such naturalizing categories by showing the complexity of human relations, the emerging friendships between a black and a white woman, a white woman and a black man. And even white men are not exempt from this re-evaluation, as Dessa mentions in the novel's "Epilogue" how much help she and her black friends got from some whites during their journey west. Eventually, then, Dessa is not only able to tell a different story, but her countertext speaks of a different morality, supported by a situational, relational ethics, and the fundamental belief in social, not innate, reasons for human behavior.[8]

DESSA ROSE: SPACES FOR AN AUTHORITATIVE BLACK FEMALE VOICE

Williams's approach to her material becomes especially clear in the "Author's Note" that precedes the text proper (*DR* ix-x). She deliberately takes advantage of the option of inserting a paratext to clarify her own authorial position for the reader and to provide important information about the premises and goals of her project. In addition, the inclusion of such a separate preface in which readers are assured of the main text's truthfulness links *Dessa Rose* with the original slave narratives (Stepto, *From Behind the Veil* 7-12). It also refers to important extratextual sources, influences, and conflicts:

> I wrote the "Author's Statement" that opens *Dessa Rose* under protest;
> my editors seemed scared to death readers wouldn't know where fact
> ended and fiction began. Which in a way was precisely my point; white
> boys won prizes for doing just that and I didn't understand this sudden
> concern for "historical accuracy".... . It seems to me, still, that I
> wouldn't have been asked to write a disclaimer "separating fact from
> fiction," as my editorial guarantors put it, had I been white. I opened
> the novel with the Statement, rather than tucking it away in the back, so
> that Dessa would have the last word. (57-58)

From the point of view of the novel's editors, Williams's preface was thus supposed to function in a way diametrically opposed to Walker's: rather than affirming the verisimilitude of her narrative, she was asked to sever the obvious ties between her text and the historical events on which it is based.

Although it was not part of the "original plan" but rather an "afterthought to the novel" (Jordan 289), the "Author's Note" is more than a defiant response to the editors' expectations; it is also a valuable source of information for readers because it highlights the connections between the thematic issues raised in the text and the contemporary African American woman writer's situation. Williams provides historical documentation for her material, including exact references to her secondary sources, and thus takes a deliberate stand in the discussion about black women's specific situation(s) in slavery. She explicitly points out the significance of Herbert Aptheker's and Angela Davis's research and writings,[9] and covertly refers to *The Confessions of Nat Turner* as another important influence on her own work—an influence not because it was a source of information, but rather a reason for anger: "I admit also to being outraged by a certain, critically acclaimed novel of the early seventies that travestied the as-told-to memoir of slave revolt leader Nat Turner" (*DR* ix). Her choice to mention Aptheker and Davis explicitly but to withhold Styron's name challenges the prominent status and the high public visibility that his novel achieved, especially after winning the Pulitzer Prize in 1968.

Davis's "Reflections on the Black Woman's Role in the Community of Slaves" not only provided the specific starting point for Williams's literary project in mentioning the historical woman on whom the fictional Dessa is based; it also proved to be a powerful challenge to the almost complete silence of the historical record on enslaved women's active resistance. In addition, charged with murder and threatened with death, Davis herself was in a situation that in many ways resembled the historical Dessa's: each woman had stood up against an oppressive system, and as a consequence had to suffer unreasonable punishment. These parallels were certainly not lost on Williams, who in both "Meditations on History" and *Dessa Rose* responded to Davis's appeal to "resurrect [. . .] the black woman in her true historical contours" (Davis 15). With specific reference to "Meditations," Henderson explains:

> Davis concludes that the black woman has been central in the black community from slavery to the present as the "custodian of resistance." Davis thus provides Williams with a connecting link to the historical event within a continuum of political insurgency, establishing a community of purpose among Davis, Williams, and Dessa. ("(W)Riting *The Work*" 640)

And Williams acknowledges her debt to Davis both in the dedication to "Meditations" and in the "Author's Note": "I now know that slavery eliminated neither heroism nor love; it provided occasions for their expressions. The Davis article marked a turning point in my efforts to apprehend that other history" (*DR* 6).[10]

Henderson notes that with these explicit references to Davis and Aptheker, Williams also draws from a fundamentally different historiographic tradition than Styron with his reliance on U. B. Philips and Stanley Elkins ("(W)Riting *The Work*" 633-34). Davis's re-evaluation of the historical significance of black enslaved women is both a rejection of 1950s and 60s white historical and sociological explanations of "Negro pathology" and a critique of the male-dominated Black Power and Black Aesthetics movements (cf. Morton 70-76). The problematic of historical "truth" is thus further confounded by a political controversy between left/Marxist and conservative interpretations of history.

Implicitly, however, this preface is also a first act of signifying on Styron, whose own short introduction is called "Author's Note" as well. In contrast to Styron, who insists on his "rarely depart[ing] from the *known* facts" (*Confessions* 11), Williams states that "this novel [*Dessa Rose*] . . . is fiction." Yet it is also "as true as if [she her]self had lived it" (*DR* x). Already at this early stage, she raises the complex issue of the relationship between fact, fiction, and the writer's imagination, and formulates for herself the conditions of her narrative's credibility. In an act of deliberate re-positioning, Williams creates a space for herself away from positivistic historiographical truth claims, and at the same time opens the discussion of how "truth" can be, or should be, defined. In narrativizing and individualizing the truth claims of her text, she makes them less open to attack. In describing "truth" not as a stable entity but as an ongoing process of negotiation between present and past, she treats historical understanding as part of a continuously shifting cultural matrix that inherently requires constant engagement.

The "Author's Note" thus functions in several ways: it asks readers to accept the possibility of resistance—even the possibility of both black and white women's resistance, who have traditionally not been presented as self-determinedly active or heroic. The references to the historical sources for the fictional characters Dessa and Ruth work to quell suspicion in readers who might otherwise reject even the possibility of such characters and/or incidents. Williams uses the persuasiveness of historical "facts" to provide a context of potential plausibility; the novel then focuses not on a supposedly mimetic representation of "real" events, but on the conceptualization and articulation of possible relationships within the social and cultural context of the antebellum plantation system.

After the "Author's Note," the fictional text proper is framed with "Prologue" and "Epilogue," two short chapters that occupy literally marginal spaces—partly inside and partly outside of the central narrative. Representing Dessa's point of view, they rewrite, as Andrée-Anne Kekeh remarks, slave narrative conventions:

> The prologue and the epilogue surrounding the novel are told from Dessa Rose's perspective.... Graphically, then, Dessa Rose encircles the narrative, showing her full control over her tale. Setting Dessa Rose as the main narrator of the prologue and the epilogue shows not only her narrative authority in the novel, it is also Williams's strategy to undermine the conventions ruling traditional slave autobiographies. ... By framing her polyphonic novel with Dessa Rose's voice only, Williams goes against such official "voices" that were entitled to legitimize slave narratives. (225)

Taken together, these three sections thus provide different textual spaces for alternative means of authorization for both author and main character. The "Author's Note" is outer-directed, establishing a sense of historical plausibility and explaining the writer's imaginary project; "Prologue" and "Epilogue" direct reader attention into the text.

Like the dream section that stands at the beginning of "Meditations," the "Prologue" sets up a strong contrast between Dessa's memories of her past and her present situation. Especially the memory of her husband Kaine is associated with images of hope, power and agency—"[he looked] as if he could halt the setting sun (*DR* 1)"—that are directly opposed to the physical reality of her imprisonment, in which "chains rasped, rubbed hatefully" (*DR* 4). "Dessa's reveries, expressed in the language of private reflection, establish her as a speaking (rather than *spoken*) subject and provide the reader with a subjective and participatory point of reference for understanding the revelation of events which follow," Henderson explains.

> By opening the text with Dessa's reflections, Williams establishes the reader's narrative expectations, promotes identification with her protagonist, and provides clues about how to *read*, or decode, the real meaning of the narrator's ostensibly reportorial journal entries. . . . The effect of Dessa's prologue in "Meditations" is to subvert the authority and authenticity of the main narration. ("(W)Riting *The Work*" 641)

In "Meditations," Dessa's dream functions as an introduction for and an anticipated critique of the story's main part. It is not followed, however, by a similar concluding section—the white male scholar literally has the last word. In contrast, *Dessa Rose* closes with an "Epilogue," in which an aging Dessa is placed amidst a group of sympathetic black listeners. This final communal context is presented as an important basis for the possibility of black cultural expression and historical identity. In addition, Williams creates a storytelling situation within her novel that (supposedly) corresponds to her own authorial location. Placing herself in a "continuum of political insurgency" (Henderson, "(W)Riting *The Work*" 640) as it was outlined by Davis, she shares a (cultural rather than individual) memory with the generation of readers and listeners coming after her.

This intricate appropriation and redefinition of conventional(ized) fictional forms is also apparent in the novel's formal structure. At first sight, *Dessa Rose* shows what seems to be a straightfoward three-part format: it is divided into six chapters, two to each of the novel's three main parts. These parts are not numbered but entitled "The Darky," "The Wench" and "The Negress"; they are framed by "Prologue" and "Epilogue." However, the initial impression of a strict formal separation between sections, indicated through the chapter headings and a "Contents"-page, is not confirmed by the internal organization of individual chapters. Although there is, as I have pointed out above, the strong contrast between the "Prologue" and the beginning of chapter 1, the insertion of a dream-like passage similar to the "Prologue" later in chapter 1 links the two and creates a sense of simultaneity. Similarly, the transition between parts I and II of the novel is achieved through an extended reverie, in which Dessa's memories and present perceptions blend and initially create a sense of dislocation. Stylistically, then, the individual parts of the novel are intricately interwoven. Shifts in narrative perspective occur gradually and would not drastically disrupt the thematic coherence of the plot, if it were not for the strong structural separations, complete with a new title and motto for each part. The strongest sense of rupture is created when Dessa seizes the word—when the third-person narrative voices of parts I and II turn to first-person telling in part III. The "Epilogue" then shifts the temporal setting of the narrative as a whole, and serves as a corrective in retrospectively defining Dessa's audience as a private, textual one.

Part I: Escaping the White Man's Prison

Dessa's own narrative—comprised of memories, private reflections, and direct telling—stays largely focused on the past and maps out her specific situation as a pregnant young slave woman, deeply in love with the father of her child, and deeply concerned about the fate of her baby. She sees herself as stronger than the white women on the plantation—"was I white, I might woulda fainted" (*DR* 9)—and explains her especially charged relationship with the white family in terms of the sexual politics on the plantation: "I too light for Mist's and not light enough for Masa" (*DR* 10). One of the most significant events of her teenage years was that she could, at least temporarily, defy white orders by falling in love with Kaine. His assertion of agency—"he chosed me" (*DR* 10)—both enhances Dessa's feeling of self-worth and assumes a quality of resistance. Dessa's pregnancy, however, forcefully brings their desperate situation home to them. They know that in the eyes of their master, their relationship is "for nothin but to breed," without giving them any means to protect their children: "they [can] be sold off" (*DR* 10). Dessa mentions that one possible way of retaining some control is contraception, "the roots [that] stop his mouth and his seed" (*DR* 10), another is abortion, but she refuses to even think about forcefully ending her pregnancy. Rather than turning against her unborn child, she is willing to risk her own life trying to escape, because "even if she saved their baby from Lefonia, she would never be able to save it [from Master]" (*DR* 45). Dessa's comments situate her in a web of complex relationships and show her struggle to develop and maintain a sense of dignity and agency, both together with Kaine and within the larger community of slaves. The tension between desperation and hope that the two young people have to deal with confronts them with existential questions that are almost impossible to answer. Nevertheless, they do make decisions, even though that means risking—and in Kaine's case, losing—their lives.

Compared to Dessa's own very thoughtful examination of the forces that have shaped her life, Nehemiah's first impression of her comes across as sheer contempt: he describes her as a "female far along in breeding" with "a ghostly gleam [in] her eyes," whose "scars bespoke a history of misconduct" (*DR* 13). Clearly he does not "see" her at all; his perceptions are distorted by a racist image of blacks as subhuman. Dessa's femaleness is described in terms usually reserved for animals, and her blackness is referred to only through its negation—the white in her eyes stands out because it is implicitly contrasted with the darkness of her skin. And the scars—which Nehemiah cannot see but knows about—complete her status as "outlaw": not only is she a woman and black, but she has "visibly" broken the rules of behavior imposed on her.

During the period in which Dessa is questioned by Nehemiah, the spatial arrangement of the "interview" as well as repeated references to light and darkness metaphorically underline the white man's psychological distance from her and from the things she tells him: Dessa, who seemed to him "like a wild and timorous animal" (*DR* 15) is initially confined to the dark root cellar in which she is held captive; Nehemiah on the other hand is sitting in the sunlight at the door, several steps up from her. However, both the spatial setting and the color imagery change gradually, parallel to the dismantling of Nehemiah's privileged position and Dessa's claiming of narrative authority. First, Dessa is allowed to come out of the cellar: "[Nehemiah] sat now on a crude chair in the shade of the big elm. . . . The darky sat near him on the ground, . . . A chain attached to her ankle-bead was wound around the trunk of the elm" (*DR* 30). Accompanying the narrative shift toward Dessa's point of view, the descriptions of space eventually come to reflect her perceptions of Nehemiah, rather than vice versa: "He stooped awkwardly at the window, his face almost touching his knees. It was a ridiculous posture and she turned her face to hide her grin" (*DR* 65).

In the course of time, Dessa tries to make the best of her dismal situation and turns the involuntary interview into an opportunity to talk about what matters most to herself. Doing this, she relieves some of the tensions of her imprisonment, partly because it allows her to determine the direction of the interview and thus assume some power over Nehemiah: "Dessa had come to look forward to the talks . . . Talking with the white man kept her, for those brief periods, from counting and recounting the cost" (*DR* 51-52). As for his questions, however, "having no answers, she gave none. Maybe this white man would *tell her* something she didn't know" (*DR* 54; emphasis added). "Talking with the white man was a game" (*DR* 59).

"She saw the past as she talked, not as she had lived it, but as she had come to understand it" (*DR* 54): still assuming that she would be hanged after the birth of her child, Dessa lets her own voice transport her back into a part of her past in which she "knew herself to be enveloped in caring" (*DR* 58). But talking also has an exorcising function: "The dreams or haunts that had crowded about her . . . now allowed her peace at night" (*DR* 56). For self-protection, however, "memory stop[s]" outside the part that "was nightmare" (*DR* 56). This passage is one of the manifestations of Williams's intricate use of narrative voice: because there is no other way for us to learn about what happened "after memory stopped," the narrator keeps going to explain Dessa's attack on the white mistress. This subtle shift from Dessa's thoughts to the narrator's explanation is only noticeable because of the explicit comment on how much Dessa can bear to remember.[11] Despite this slight narrative inconsistency, the scene adds substantially to our later understanding of Dessa's first impression and description of Ruth. After the description of her former mistress as "hair screaming, red-faced, red-mouthed" (*DR* 57), Dessa's terror when she wakes up and finds herself alone in a room with a strange white woman whose "hair was the color of fire . . . [and whose] mouth was a bloody gash" (*DR* 88) becomes more comprehensible.

The function of Nehemiah's text as a stabilizing force within the political system of slavery is another important issue that part I of novel discusses. As part of his goal to find more effective measures of control over slaves, the purpose of his writing is the exact opposite of the original slave narratives': the slave's words are used in support of, rather than as a weapon against, the institution of slavery. Nehemiah's failure to recognize Dessa's humanity while exploiting her in order to enhance his own social status is made especially explicit in the short exchange they have about his intentions. Significantly, this scene is initiated by the first question that Dessa addresses to him directly. This then leads—in the structural context of chapter 2—to a general shift in narrative perspective, away from Nehemiah's and toward Dessa's point of view:

> "What you going do with it?"
> "I will use what you have said in a book I am writing." . . .
> "Cause why? . . . for what you want do it?
> . . . I write what I do in the hope of helping others to be happy in the life that has been sent them to live." (*DR* 41)

. . .
"If that be true, . . . why I not be happy when I live it?" (*DR* 47)
Thinking that "[m]aybe this white man would tell her something she didn't know"
(*DR* 54), Dessa turns the tables on Nehemiah here; he becomes a source of
information for her. His raising the issue of happiness, however, also situates both
in the context of the United States' (mythically enlarged) origin with its emphasis
on "life, liberty, and the pursuit of happiness," from which Dessa is obviously
excluded. What is highlighted in her exchange with Nehemiah is her function as
racial and sexual "other," who is necessary for the definition of an "American
identity," but to whom the basic tenets of American citizenship do not apply.
"Why I not be happy when I live it?" (*DR* 47) is not only a self-determined
question—which in itself challenges her objectification—but demands a reconsid-
eration of the slave's status within the discourse of American liberty. Dessa's
question, with which she defines herself as a thinking and speaking subject,
expresses both her expectation that she should also profit in some way from her
work (and her words), and her refusal to be excluded from Nehemiah's definition
of "people." Additionally, Dessa's questions frame the passage in which she
describes Kaine's—and her own—concept of freedom, and the frustration of not
being able to achieve it:

> "I say 'Run' and he laugh." . . . "'Dessa, run where?' 'North' . . . North
> had been no more to her than a dim, shadowed land across a river, as
> mythic and mysterious as heaven: rest, when the body could bear no
> more. But . . . if there was rest for the body, there must be peace for the
> heart. "Dessa. . . . You know what is north? Huh? More whites. Just like
> here." (*DR* 43)

The textual organization thus reflects the larger social configuration: Dessa's
argument with Kaine about the risks of escaping from slavery is embedded in the
context of the dominant white society, which is here represented by Nehemiah's
definitions.

In this scene of the novel, then, Williams's deviation from the basic structure
of "Meditations" becomes most apparent: Dessa's claiming the right to talk back
is, in contrast to the short story, accompanied by a decisive narrative shift away
from the representation of Nehemiah's point of view. The remainder of the
chapter is predominantly told from Dessa's perspective, through an additional
third-person narrative voice. Nehemiah is reduced to his nightly diary entries;
except for the passages of direct speech, his "text" is thus removed both spatially

and temporally from his own privileged position during the interviewing process. Williams explains in "The Lion's History":

> I used Dessa's dream of home, in Chapter One of the novel, to counterpoint Nehemiah's narrative, and reined in his self-important haughtiness under third-person narration. And in Chapter Two, Dessa quite literally snatches even that partial control from the white man, yanking the narrative from his point of view, relegating his voice to the journal entries that have by then been thoroughly invalidated. (255-56)

However, the doubleness of this formally "third-person" perspective is important to note. Despite the narrator's ability to "read" the characters' minds, s/he is never presenting both Dessa's and Nehemiah's thoughts at the same time, but clearly distinguishes between the two points of view and uses only one in any given passage.

Nehemiah's impression that he is getting closer to whatever it is he wants to know is thus juxtaposed not only by his obvious misinterpretation of Dessa's words on the thematic level, but also by a process of formal distancing. The combination of both reaches its peak when Dessa literally escapes, while he is out searching for the maroon settlement: "We did not even know that she was gone, had, in fact, sat down to eat the supper left warmed on the fire-half against our return, to talk of the futile venture of the last few days. . . . Unsuspecting we were" (DR 69). That Dessa finally escapes on the fourth of July is a concluding ironic comment on Nehemiah's corrupted understanding of the concept of freedom (cf. Nielsen 272).

Part II: Dessa and Ruth—Unreconcilable Perspectives?

The introduction of a limited omniscient narrative perspective in part I, which represents either Dessa's or Nehemiah's perspective, then allows Williams in part II of the novel to present both Dessa's and Ruth's points of view without automatically creating a hierarchy of voices. If the frequent use of derogatory names is startling at first, because the third-person passages suggest a non-person-alized omniscient narrator, it is explicable when it becomes apparent that the narrator in fact assumes a partial stance and switches sides, depending on whose perspective is foregrounded at any given time. Accordingly, Dessa is often referred to as "the wench" in Ruth's passages, whereas this appellation logically never appears in Dessa's parts. This rhetorical strategy makes it hard to locate any strong sense of authorial control, despite the third-person perspective that implies a level of narration outside of the plot level.

It seems that Williams is trying to keep readers' awareness of authorial influence as subdued as possible. Any opinion or attitude that is expressed in the novel is attributable to one of the characters. She thus manages to largely withdraw from her text, first handing the authority over to a disembodied, but personalized narrative voice, and finally directly to Dessa. Within this framework of negotiating narrative positions, important processes of individual transformation take place. The following section will explore the overlapping, yet distinct developments that Dessa and Ruth go through until their final moment of mutual recognition and acceptance. Again, Dessa's identity is initially "made up," appropriated by someone else, although the circumstances are much less threatening than in part I. What is examined in part II is the fallaciousness of Dessa's earlier assumption that "where there is rest for the body, there must be peace for the heart" (DR 43).

The situation that Dessa finds herself in at the beginning of part II is at first more frightening than her imprisonment in the cellar, because for a while she is incapable of reading the clues of her environment:

> I didn't have no words to make sense of what my eyes was seeing, much less what I'd been doing. I was someone I knowed and didn't know, living in a world I hadn't even knowed was out there. So that bed was grave and birthing place to me. (DR 215)

In her state of physical and psychic exhaustion, her retreat into memories is even more pronounced than it was earlier. The present makes so little sense and is so frightening that the past offers welcome oblivion. Dessa emotionally removes herself from a situation that is too hard to bear, but she finally realizes that her memories are no longer "real": "[O]nly the Quarters had been a dream ... [and] she was the one who was missing" (DR 88). Even when she is fully conscious, however, Dessa tries to blank out what Ruth is saying: "She knew she could understand the white woman if she would let herself" (DR 119).

The spatial and discursive organization of this scene is the exact opposite of the initial set-up of part I: Ruth is in the shadow of the room, talking to herself about a past that appears so much more appealing than the present. "Unlike Nehemiah," Meese comments, "Ruth is not 'fearful of being drawn into the shadows'" (142). Dessa, in contrast, finds herself em"bed"ded in terrifying light and whiteness.[12] In juxtaposition to Nehemiah's claiming the right to ask the first direct question in part I—"And what has that to do with you and the other slaves rising up?" (*DR* 12)—it is now Dessa who interrupts Ruth's monologue, challenging what the white woman is saying: "Wasn't no 'mammy' to it" (*DR* 124). This first open response to Ruth is reminiscent of Dessa's earlier thought that there "wasn't no darky to it [the uprising]" (*DR* 58), when she was full of resentment about Nehemiah's "careless references" (*DR* 58). Significantly, she could then not openly express her indignation, although she reacted strongly against the imposition of the term "darky" on her and other blacks; the situation did not allow her to raise the issue of signification. In Ruth's presence, however, Dessa realizes that she is no longer immediately threatened, and can therefore respond more openly and spontaneously: "Maybe [the white woman] was crazy, Dessa thought, but not a killer. No, not a killer. Nathan and Cully would not have brought her here" (*DR* 121).

Figuratively, the scene in Ruth's bedroom initially replicates the conventional (mis)communication patterns between whites and blacks: the white monologic voice takes no notice of the racial other who shares the same space; it does not even consider the possibility of establishing genuine contact. In Sutton's Glen, however, "normal" mechanisms are suspended: physically, Dessa is no longer a slave, and Ruth no longer a slave mistress. These changed circumstances make it possible for Dessa, who is rendered invisible through Ruth's soliloquies, to seize the very moment in which her own story meets Ruth's—in the shared term "mammy"—and thus insist on being acknowledged as a presence.

Psychologically, however, the process of truly freeing herself from slavery is much more difficult; it makes a fundamental rethinking of her former strategies of self-definition necessary. King outlines:

> The abandonment of a familiar order carries with it the loss of
> previously available forms of agency. Dessa Rose has achieved her goal
> of freedom for herself and her son. And yet, in her flight, she too left
> behind much that was familiar in her world, most importantly, easily
> identifiable constructs of power. And although Dessa is experienced in
> confronting bastions of power, she is unaccustomed to their absence.
> . . . [B]y specifying how and where her mother, her sister Carrie, herself,
> and Dorcas fit into the white power structure, Dessa manages both to
> disrupt its power for Rufel and retain its ordering principle for herself.
> (363)

The process of rethinking her assumptions about white women in general already starts before the argument about "Mammy": Dessa sees Ruth nursing her baby, and that goes "against everything she had been taught to think about white women" (*DR* 123). It takes a long time, however, before Dessa is able to gather enough information about Ruth and develop enough trust for a closer relationship. Ruth's later involvement with Nathan for a while threatens to jeopardize Dessa's acceptance: "White woman was everything I feared and hated, and it hurt me that one of them would want to love with her" (*DR* 182). In retrospect, however, Dessa is able to see the dynamics behind her own earlier behavior: "Where white people look at black and see something ugly, she saw color. I knowed this, but I couldn't understand it" (*DR* 184). Her final recognition comes in part III when she realizes that even white women are subjected to violence— that the power Dessa had attributed to them because of their race is partly undermined by their sex: "The white woman was subject to the same ravishment as me" (*DR* 220).

Part II: Ruth—Approaching Connection

At the beginning of part II, Dessa and Ruth are confronted with each other in an abrupt way that is very unsettling and disorienting for both. In order to negotiate the difficult beginnings of a relationship that remains ambivalent and tense for some time, the narrative shifts back and forth between Dessa's and Ruth's perspectives, and thus presents us with two different but complementary angles of vision. Although the women occasionally talk to each other, the contact between them is, at this stage, not yet characterized by genuine dialogue. Both are still caught in conceptual frameworks that do not allow them to truly "hear" what the other is saying, and this leads to serious misunderstandings. In maintaining a clear-cut distinction between the two different perspectives, the personalized third-person narrative voice(s) reflect—on the discursive level—the lack of real communication that is occurring on the social plane. These two basically monologic and parallel voices also justify an interpretive focus that separates them for the sake of analysis; the following section will therefore concentrate particularly on Ruth and her development.

Reconstructing Dessa's life from various vantage points, Williams cannot but show the diversity of perspectives—a diversity brought about by race, gender and class influences. With Dessa and Nehemiah as the most diametrically opposed, the book breaks down more binaries by arranging the meetings between Dessa and Ruth, as well as Ruth and Nathan—incidents that unsettle both characters and readers because they go against simplifying notions of rigid social categories. In contrast to Styron, who presents Nat Turner as a black man driven by his sexual lust for a white woman, controlled by biological determinants, Williams shows her characters to be motivated by a complex web of experiences, expectations, and restrictions (cf. Styron, *Confessions* 289-92, 313-19; Poussaint 20).

When Dessa arrives at Sutton's Glen, Ruth is in the worst possible situation: she is stranded with her two small children in a half-finished house, without financial means, without contact to family or friends, even without her "personal maid" and confidante of many years, the black woman Dorcas. For the first time in her life, Ruth is required to show some initiative; this initially consists of her grudging acceptance that she is providing a place to live for the group of fugitive slaves who have temporarily settled on her land. Despite her spontaneous help when Dessa arrives half-dead with her newborn baby, however, Ruth's basic attitude is still one of suspicion and distrust, and she needs a long time to develop enough understanding to overcome her doubts that she is unfairly taken advantage of.

This process of (un)learning takes her through a number of stages in which she becomes more and more aware of her own situation. Brought up in the racist and sexist ideology of her time, she has never before been confronted with the need to question the circumstances of her life. Now she not only has to admit to herself her feeling of being betrayed by a patriarchal system that falsely promised happiness in marriage and motherhood; she also recognizes her own complicity in racist structures. This complex re-positioning makes Ruth "ambiguously (non)hegemonic" in the best sense of the term: she is victimized as a woman, but simultaneously takes part in the oppression of others because she is white.[13]

In this context, Ruth's taking care of Dessa's baby initially appears to be little more than a simple reversal of roles; it is, however, one key manifestation of her complex psychological and emotional state. First, her spontaneous reaction to such basic needs as a baby's hunger already shows a fissure in her self-definition as a slaveholding white woman—it does not matter at that moment that the baby is black. Only later, when reflection sets in, does Ruth recognize that her behavior must indeed seem strange within the framework of southern conventions:

> She shouldn't have done it; Rufel had been over that countless times also. If anybody ever found out. . . . But nothing of that had entered her head as she picked her way carefully up the steep back steps, the baby hugged close to her body. The girl's desolate face, the baby's thin crying—as though it had given up all hope—had grated at her. (*DR* 98)

Secondly, Ruth is also suffering from a lack of opportunity to assert herself as a person in her own right. Socialized from early childhood into expecting the leisurely life of a lady—as wife of a well-to-do planter—she is disappointed when things do not work out, and for a while gives in to her sense of loneliness and frustration.[14] The arrival of Dessa and her baby is the first chance Ruth has to act in a self-determined, independent way:

> [S]he could do something about this, about the baby who continued to cry while she waited in the dim area back of the stairs for the darkies to bring the girl in. . . . She—Rufel—could do something. That was as close as she came to explaining anything to herself. The baby was hungry and she fed him. (DR 98)

To be of use—which is what Ruth is longing for—can only happen when she "*chooses* to act, to interpret and to respond to the black baby's call" and thus breaks one of the fundamental rules of white accepted behavior (Meese 143; original emphasis). Her personal development toward genuine connection starts by means of establishing a bond with Dessa's baby that is—in the deepest sense—both physically and emotionally relational.[15]

As surprising and positive as this first spontaneous reaction might seem, it quickly becomes obvious that the intellectual processes of questioning her self-definitions and gradually moving toward a new, fundamentally revised sense of identity are much more difficult to work through. For quite some time, Ruth is hovering between the wish to avoid the emotional pain involved in confronting her own shortcomings and her need to change the situation. The initial confrontation with Dessa functions as an important catalyst here to set a process of development in motion. In contrast to the baby, who naturally accepts Ruth's care and thus implicitly affirms what she is doing, his mother clearly shows discomfort about seeing him nursed by a strange white woman. At first Dessa's state of fatigue allows for an uneasy truce, but conflict breaks out when she interrupts one of Ruth's soliloquies, and they start arguing about "Mammy's" identity.

This "nominative struggle" (Meese 146) touches a raw nerve in both women, although they are aware that they cannot possibly be talking about the same person. Their argument becomes a "probing of categories and labeling, through multiple referents attached to the single word 'mammy'" (King 361).[16] Although Ruth and Dessa cannot yet really "hear" each other, the important point is that Ruth's monologue—in which she seeks reassurance by creating a positive fiction of her past—is broken into. A seemingly unequivocal term is suddenly contested and confronted with the possibility of multiple meanings, and unavoidably changes in the process.

If Dessa reappropriates "mammy" to stand for the black (biological) mother—and thus insists on the significance of black family ties despite the continuous threat of disruption—she simultaneously exposes the hypocrisy of white family life. Not personal closeness and affection, but status considerations appear as motivating factors behind Ruth's upbringing. The need for companionship, for trust and acceptance, can only be expressed in a relationship in which it is also immediately compromised, and in which genuine, mutual closeness is in fact impossible: between the white girl and her black maid. The estrangement from her family obviously started a long time before Ruth was married to Bertie. As her thinking about Dorcas reveals, she felt disregarded and unloved even as a young girl, and consequently the black woman turned into a substitute "mother," alone able to provide the attention and sympathy Ruth craved for.[17] As a result, King explains,

> Rufel's entire being crumbles when she realizes that her construction of herself rested upon a construction of "Mammy" as incomplete and faulty as the stairway of her house which leads to nowhere, to the never built second floor. In effect, once her construction of "Mammy" is made problematic by Dessa, and Mammy's name, Dorcas, is revealed, Rufel is bereft of any assuredness about a single aspect of her life. With that foundation gone, the previously unshakable knowledge that Mammy loved her unconditionally evaporates. (363)

Ruth's identity was built on the pretense of dialogue and the simultaneous avoidance of it: "Rufel . . . want[ed] desperately to believe that Mammy had loved her not only fully, but freely as well" (DR 147). "What else had she refused to see? she wondered bitterly" (DR 166). This illusion of a close relationship collapses at the very moment when the conventions for communication between whites and blacks are suspended and the hitherto parallel, but disconnected discourses meet. As long as Ruth is left to her own devices, ignorant of what is going on around her and feeling more "at home" in her memories than in the present moment, there is nobody to check the adequacy of the fictions she creates of her past. Only when she can no longer avoid taking notice of the other people in her house, because their actions disrupt and challenge the world of her thoughts, is she forced to confront those aspects of her memories that she had tried to forget.

This confrontation is painful and results in new attempts to deny and repress; the circumstances, however, do not allow that to happen. Once the process of self-questioning is initiated, it develops a dynamic of its own and completes the process of Ruth's growing up. Her former state of prolonged childhood— characterized by a certain naïveté and dependence on others that was conventionally considered becoming in young ladies—is irretrievably over. Especially her lack of knowledge about Dorcas creates a strong sense of guilt:

> Mammy might have had children and it bothered Rufel that she did not know. Mammy had liked blackberries, Rufel knew. . . . That much and no more, Rufel thought, somehow shamed; eleven years and only then to know the feel of a loved one's hair under a loving hand. Truly, such ignorance was worse than grief. (*DR* 136-137).

Between these flashes of recognition and understanding, however, Ruth repeatedly shies away from her new insights and falls back into old patterns. If she is seeing herself as "Mammy's child" at one moment, she is soon afterwards revolted by the idea: "[H]ow absurd it was to think of herself as Mammy's child, a darky's child. And shuddered. A pickanninny" (*DR* 132). The specialness of one individual connection to a black person is not transferrable; to "know" Dorcas does not change Ruth's stereotypical perceptions of blacks as a group. Even while she is getting to know Nathan better, she hovers between genuine surprise and relief about his civility and a feeling of being offended.[18]

It is this relationship with Nathan, however, that ultimately pushes her to do the decisive step and really "see" the person in front of her, rather than some stereotypical distortion:

> She turned to the darky aghast, and caught her breath. Never had she seen such blackness. She blinked, expecting to see the bulbous lips and bulging eyes of a burnt-cork minstrel. Instead she looked into a pair of rather shadowy eyes and strongly defined features that were— handsome! she thought shocked, almost outraged. (*DR* 132)

With appreciation for being at last taken seriously, "[s]he sought Nathan's company more often—he at least treated her like a person" (*DR* 160). Unlike Dessa, whose feeling of personal loss and utter distrust of white women prompted her response to Ruth's musings about "Mammy," Nathan is able to react empathetically: "A dark hand obligingly offered her a ruffled cloth. . . . 'Dessa didn't even know Dorcas, and just met you. Why you so upset?'" (*DR* 132-133). He is the first person with whom she is able to break her monologic mold and have genuine conversations. Nathan becomes the necessary mediator who can explain things to Ruth, including the likely dynamics of her relationship with Dorcas, whom he never met personally:

> "Bertie was a gambler, wasn't he, Nathan?" ... "Yes'm," he said. Sighing heavily, he looked at her steadily. "Yes'm, he is." "Why didn't Mammy tell me?" Rufel wailed, feeling more betrayed by Mammy's silence than by Bertie's deception. Had they conspired against her, plotted together to keep her in the dark? "It wasn't her place." "She should have told me anyway," Rufel insisted. "I spect she tried," Nathan said dryly. (*DR* 164-165)

Because of his background—his literally intimate knowledge of white women as well as the fact that he didn't physically suffer as much under slavery as Dessa—he is the right person for Ruth to talk to. He has enough self-confidence to stand his ground, and he is not personally threatened by anything she can say or do.

When Ruth accidentally walks in on Dessa and actually sees the whip scars on the black woman's body, she is shocked: "Rufel leaned weakly against the door, regretting what she had seen. The wench had a right to hide her scars, her pain, Rufel thought, almost in tears herself" (*DR* 166-167). She finally gets visual proof for what Nathan told her but what she could only half believe, and this prompts her to offer Dessa a first gesture of reconciliation: "'That other day'—she stopped and cleared her throat—'that other day, we wasn't talking about the same person. Your mammy birthed you, and mines, mines just helped to raise me. . .'" (*DR* 167). In this context of Ruth's careful attempt to approach Dessa, Dessa's calling her "Miz Ruint" when she sees her and Nathan in bed together becomes a painful reminder that it needs two to change a situation, but that Dessa is not yet able to reach out to Ruth.

Interestingly, there is no description of Ruth's liaison with Nathan from Ruth's own point of view. Nevertheless, the fact that she can go that far after only a few months of separation from "society" is meaningful in itself. On the one hand, it shows the intensity of her development in the short time since Dessa's arrival; on the other it makes explicit how deep the emotional estrangement from her husband and her family must have been.

In a 1989 interview, Williams commented on the way she conceptualized Ruth's character and her personal development. With Aptheker's very brief reference about a white woman who helped fugitive slaves as historical back-up, she still had to imagine the exact circumstances that might have motivated someone to defy morality and law in such a way:

> I wanted her to come on as this stereotyped conception of the Southern belle, but now in dire straits as opposed to the very secure circumstances that we usually think of such a character in. Also, I felt that the

kind of alliance that I was proposing between a white woman and a slave would most logically come about out of necessity rather than some kind of liberal feeling. Where was a Southern woman going to be educated to that kind of liberal feeling in the South? I just happened to believe that people for the most part really try to rise to whatever the circumstances are, that given the need, they can in fact grow and develop. I felt that in establishing that initial image of Rufel as this kind of stereotype and then giving her circumstances in which she could grow, I would be able to create a very full and complex character. (Ross 495)

Ruth might be racist because of her upbringing as a southern belle and her growing into southern slavocracy without much personal choice. Her behavior certainly reflects that socialization, even long after the relationship with Dessa has begun to turn into a kind of friendship. Because she is geographically removed from southern society and deserted by her husband, however, Ruth is literally separated from the influences of those institutions that produce and perpetuate racist ideology. The only link that remains is her former education, but without an occasional affirmation, its effects gradually wear thin.

Without any racist influences around, she is challenged to take a second look at her previous assumptions about black people, and is forced to realize that her well-being depends on the fugitives' industriousness—a dependence that "normal" power relations would obscure. Sutton's Glen exemplifies the inter-dependence of black and white lives: the fugitives certainly do not need any white person to tell them what to do to make a living of the land. In the larger context of southern life, however, they need Ruth—if only to pretend she is their "lawful" mistress and not to arouse suspicion among neighbors. The white woman, who would not be able to provide for herself if left alone because her upbringing always included the service of others, and both black men and women are trapped in a system that denies all of them a public voice and political agency. Within the confines of the system, however, Ruth's class status allows her a certain amount of influence. This is on the one hand ridiculed by setting it up in contrast to her disempowerment as deserted wife and mother without any legal rights, but on the other hand is later used to fight the system so that she can finally leave her ruined backwater plantation.[19]

In this context, the "cult of true womanhood"—set up to ensure white women's ungrudging submission—ironically turns out to be a space for agency. Although we do not know what Ruth is doing exactly after leaving the South, the implications are that she not only leaves behind the slavocracy of the South, but that her experience of having chosen a certain course of action will have left its mark on her future decisions about her own and her children's lives. She is not likely to accept the role of submissive wife and mother again, despite the great odds awaiting her with such a frame of mind.

The major learning effect for Ruth is to become able to recognize the racist restrictions of her culture, and to acknowledge her own involvement. Meese explains that "[i]n the process of figuring (out) the stories of Dorcas and Dessa, and how those stories are bound up with her own, Ruth discovers her complicity" (142). She learns to see and acknowledge the humanity of the black fugitives around her, and eventually to relate to them in an atmosphere of mutual trust— despite some instances of conflict brought about by her liaison with Nathan. This is a process paralleled by the one that Dessa is going through, who also has to learn to recognize Ruth's humanity, after painful experiences in which whiteness has come to stand for irrationality and brutality.

In the course of part II of the novel, Ruth thus moves from a monologic to a dialogic, relational attitude. Harboring the fugitives, nursing Dessa's baby, arguing with Dessa, and meeting Nathan are all important steps within this development. Particularly the encounters with Nathan illustrate the difficulties inherent in this process of (un)learning, as well as the ultimate impossibility to avoid it. The white woman's conversations with the black man are the first instances of real dialogue, and stand in marked contrast to her talking *at*, not *with*, Dorcas. In comparison, Dessa's development—her coming to terms with her experiences and integrating them into a new, freer, definition of self—has not yet reached a similar level at the end of part II. The emotional injuries she suffered because of her former mistress's brutality make it a lot more difficult for her to revise her attitudes toward white women in general, and to develop a basic trust that would make it possible to associate with Ruth after such a short time. The learning effect that Ruth achieves for herself through her talks with Nathan cannot substitute for a direct engagement with Dessa. This, however, is focused on in part III from Dessa's point of view.

Part III: Dessa's Own Voice and Story

In part III, the initial reading impression is one of great spontaneity. Dessa directly responds to the love-making scene she has accidentally walked in upon. What is not immediately obvious is a shift in regard to the time frame—the narrating consciousness is no longer part of the plot, but looks at events retrospectively— and the implied audience. Dessa neither tells her story at Sutton's Glen, nor to one of the people living there. Who this changed addressee is, however, is only made explicit in the "Epilogue": it is not, we come to understand, an extratextual reader, but instead a group of family and friends, adults as well as children. When Dessa finally emerges as the maternal storyteller who reconstructs her past for her children and grandchildren, it becomes clear that the narrative is shaped by the presence of this particular black (female) audience, and thus by-passes the actual readers of the novel in its process of self-authorization. Clearly, the "outside audience" is not the primary one. In a retrospective move, we thus have to modify our earlier impression—of being the privileged audience to whom Dessa is recounting significant events of her early life—toward a recognition that we might, in fact, be inconsequential for her tale. Lanser explains that "[t]hrough its own complex narrative structure, *Dessa Rose* illustrates the misuses of a black woman's voice and makes clear why private rather than public voice seems to be for black narrators a necessary first location of power" (*Fictions of Authority* 198). Part III is the only section of the novel in which an extratextual, public audience seems to be addressed directly. This impression is invalidated, however, when the "Epilogue" clearly specifies an alternative private audience. By making us eavesdroppers in a narrative not altogether meant for us, Williams ingeniously deals with a predica- ment every writer has to confront: that s/he cannot control who is actually going to read the text. Defining an internal audience for whom (oral) storytelling is a privileged means of learning, the writer effectively decenters the expectations of readers who might want to deny the validity of a private, oral narrative.

The privileging of Dessa's perspective is additionally supported by her being granted the advantage of hindsight through temporal distance. Instead of showing her spontaneous reactions while or shortly after events take place, the retro- spective narrative allows Dessa to engage in a process of revaluation and revision of her own. She deliberately contrasts first impressions with the knowledge that comes with experience, and thus presents her growing older as a continuous process of growth. Her later insights into the processes of her own development are probably one direct result of her talking about her earlier life; storytelling thus functions to organize and evaluate her experiences in order to make sense of them, as well as transmitting her hard-won wisdom to her audience of children and grandchildren. In the final storytelling scene it becomes obvious how much the act of telling is a central aspect of family life: "I told that West part so often, these childrens about know it by heart. [And] Mony tell it to his babies like the memories was his . . ."(DR 236). To connect generations through the ritual of storytelling is one of the few things that the turbulent events which robbed her of her family and friends could not take away; to replicate the patterns of communication that Dessa learned from her mother thus ensures generational coherence and a stable sense of belonging. At the same time, orally transmitted stories of the past have the potential openness to allow for re-evaluations and modifications as they become necessary over time.[20]

Part III's final scene in the city prison also concludes the process of "seeing" and accepting each other for both Dessa and Ruth. It also completes the dismantling of whatever was left of Nehemiah's authority by making him look utterly ridiculous—not only for Dessa and Ruth, but also for the sheriff. And because at this point it is Dessa's own rendering of what happened, she can directly oppose Nehemiah's claim to the validity of "Science. Research" (DR 255) by modestly stating the subjectivity of her narrative. In contrast to Nehemiah, Dessa is not interested in an illusion of objective mimesis: "This not exactly what he say, you understand; what none of them said. I can't put my words together like they did. But I understood right on—I was something so terrible I wasn't even human" (DR 250). As part of Williams's underlying critique of oppositional thinking, Nehemiah ends as "slave" to his epistemological framework that requires the (racial and/or sexual) "other" for its own self-definition: "Nemi without Dessa, without the other, cannot function as a speaking subject; he has no language without her to under/write his symbolization" (Meese 151).

In addition to showing the total rejection of Nehemiah and the value system he represents, the last scene in the prison simultaneously completes the process of recognition for Dessa and Ruth. Their final joining of forces is made explicit in the ritual of naming and figurative embracing after Ruth has managed to free Dessa:

> "My name Ruth," she say, "Ruth. I ain't your mistress." Like I'd been the one putting that on her. "Well, if it come to that," I told her, "my name Dessa, Dessa Rose. Ain't no O to it." . . . "That's fine with me." We was both testy. Clara started petting me in the face and I hugged her to me. I wanted to hug Ruth. . . . [T]hat night we walked the boardwalk together and we didn't hide our grins. (DR 256)

Not only have they literally and figuratively freed themselves from Nehemiah's definitions; Ruth's newly-won integrity, which was comparatively easy to uphold in the secluded space of Sutton's Glen, is put to the test when it is confronted with the forces of education and law—the schoolteacher Nehemiah and the sheriff. Her decision to take sides with Dessa even under this kind of pressure completes both her own and Dessa's process of (un)learning. "The dismantling of Dessa's slave identity," King states, "both necessitates and is implied by the dismantling of Rufel's identity as slave mistress. Thus, Dessa's identity as slave is dependent upon Rufel's identity as slave owner" (364). This intersection of identities makes it clear that Ruth's presence in the text is a necessary condition of Dessa's becoming "free" in a psychological sense. Identity in this context is a constant negotiation between other voices and oneself/one's self. As Shoshana Felman explains, "[d]ialogue is thus the radical condition . . . through which ignorance becomes structurally informative; knowledge [including self-knowledge] is essentially, irreducibly dialogic" (83).

TEXT IN CONTEXT: *DESSA ROSE*'S SIGNIFYING ACTS

Williams's approach to narrative conventions is, as outlined above, informed by her intention to reach an audience of "common readers." In this context of creating an amenable, responsive text-audience relationship while scrutinizing the implications of traditional genre conventions, she nevertheless engages in a highly complex act of deconstructing the southern ideology of racial and sexual control with which slavery was rationalized. She exposes hegemonic claims to superior knowledge as fictions, necessary to maintain and stabilize the status quo of white/male supremacy. For the vicious cycle of physical and psychological violence to be broken, Williams suggests, the monologic imposition of one group's definitions on another must make room for genuine dialogue. This is a difficult, arduous process that shatters the very basis of white southern identities; nevertheless, it is imaginable—as Williams shows with the character of Ruth. Her use of a variety of narrative perspectives reflects and supports the novel's thematic development toward responsible, empathetic interaction based on genuine dialogue. And as a logical consequence of the textual development that finally allows the main character to continue the telling, Williams destabilizes conventional expectations of her authorial role as final authority over the text. This implicit relativization of her own position and status as author is an integral part of her cautious attitude toward mainstream writers' claims to empathy and "fair treatment" when writing or speaking about African Americans.

Because of deliberate shifts in narrative perspective that are clearly intended to catch the reader's eye as they disrupt any expectation of coherence, Williams draws explicit attention to the discursive aspects of her narrative. The influence of point of view on any evaluation of what is said is thus presented as a central textual concern. So despite Williams's statements about her general adherence to realist conventions of storytelling, the objective to focus on discourse as well as plot places *Dessa Rose* in a revisionary mode: the narrative voice gradually hands over its authority to the protagonist and thus destablizes the traditional hierarchy of textual voices. Although this shifting of responsibilities is obviously in the long run always an authorial decision, the very dynamics of the process call into question any unreflected claim to privileged knowledge—whether of the narrator or the writer. In this regard, *Dessa Rose* can be considered an "interrogative text," which Catherine Belsey defines as follows:

> [An] interrogative text refuses a single point of view, but brings points of view into unresolved collision or contradiction. It therefore refuses the hierarchy of discourses of classic realism, and no authorial or authoritative discourse points to a single position which is the place of the coherence of meaning. (92)

Such a self-reflexive engagement in the intersections of point of view, content, and ideological implications sets Williams's novel apart from earlier texts which present their stories of the past as supposedly transparent representations of historical events in which the perspective of the 20th-century teller is rendered invisible.

(En)slave(d) Narrative: The Confessions of Nat Turner

With "Meditations on History" and the first part of *Dessa Rose*, Williams clearly signifies on Styron's *The Confessions of Nat Turner*. The intertextual nature of her literary project is already obvious in the choice of the short story's title, which is lifted from Styron's preface, as well as from her own "Author's Note" that explicitly states her revisionary ambitions. As Henderson describes it, Williams "repeats in structure and subverts in meaning" the premises of *The Confessions of Nat Turner* ("(W)Riting *The Work*" 639). In contrast to Styron, she reveals the ideological implications of historical representation through both structure and content of her texts:

> Styron's work . . . is meant to be a meditation, or reflection, on history itself, whereas Williams's can perhaps be more aptly understood as a meditation on historiography—in the sense that it provides the reader a guide to the contemplation of historical and literary-historical works such as Styron's and Gray's. (636)

As a "meditation on historiography," the main questions surrounding *Dessa Rose* are questions of legitimacy, of authoritative voice, and of the political and ethical responsibilities of authority. If Styron—whether consciously or not—runs the risk of solidifying the racist myth about the Nat Turner rebellion by silencing him through the appropriation of his voice, Williams, on the other hand, is engaged in a complex process of signifying, relating to both the historical material about slave uprisings and Styron's interpretation of a particular one. She critically examines the conditions under which historical "data" are being generated and recorded, and uses this awareness of the procedural nature of knowledge production as one main focus of her own novel.

Additionally, Williams addresses in more general terms the practice common in the 19th century to have imprisoned fugitives or former slaves who fled successfully tell their stories to white amanuenses. Drawing explicit attention to the ideological underpinnings of "speaking for" in her own narrative, Williams critiques Styron for disregarding the impact of his own historical and cultural positionality as a white southern writer on the process of taking on the voice of an African American slave. That Styron's novel is based on a 19th-century white man's record of Nat Turner's "voice" additionally reveals the 20th-century writer to be part of a longstanding tradition of white-controlled representations of supposedly "authentic" black voices. As Andrews explains,

> [r]eaders of black autobiography then and now have too readily accepted the presumption of [white] . . . 18th and 19th century editors: namely, that the experiential facts recounted orally by a black person could be recorded and sorted by an amanuensis-editor, placed in various institutional contexts (aesthetic, philosophical, or moral, for instance), and then published with editorial prefaces, footnotes, and appended commentary—all without qualifying the validity of the narrative as a product of Afro-American consciousness. (*To Tell a Free Story* 20)

By treating the content of the narrative as separable both from the form in which it is presented and the context in which it is produced, this approach hides the white presence in the text. It is one of the achievements of *Dessa Rose* that the novel exposes this very claim to disinterested representation as an ideological fiction.

Even a brief comparative glance at the issues raised by Williams and Styron reveals the political implications of any project of historical re-creation. Deborah McDowell's question of "[w]ho has been publicly authorized . . . to tell the story?" ("Negotiating between Tenses" 146) becomes especially relevant in a context that is characterized by a history of racism and sexism, in which any authorial position is necessarily invested. The question is simultaneously leading in two different directions. First, it asks whose perspective meets with broad cultural agreement, and who is thus more likely to be regarded as an authoritative voice. Secondly, it examines who has—for whatever reasons—privileged insights and a "better" understanding of the historical material at hand. These two issues can only appear mutually dependent, if there is a larger consensus that the presentation of "good" (i.e. well-researched, well-documented) arguments has enough persuasive power to automatically bestow authority on the researcher—the position that Margaret Walker embraced in *Jubilee*.

This attitude, however, does not take into consideration that the question of cultural authority is always also contingent on the writer's identity—whether real or assumed (Lanser, *Narrative Act* 84). The discussion about and critique of white southern William Styron's ability to "recreate a [black] man and his era" (Styron, *Confessions* 11) challenges a wide-spread assumption: that traditionally accepted "mainstream" versions of history—whether in historiographical or literary texts— are also the most adequate ones. In contrast, they might in fact be so ideologically charged that their implicit or explicit truth claims can no longer hold.

In this context, the question of privileged perspective cannot be avoided. It has occasionally been remarked that Williams and Styron are basically trying to do the same thing, namely to recreate a historical situation in fictional form (cf. Inscoe). This assumption contains the slight reproach that Williams claims for herself an epistemic privilege because of race and gender congruences to her protagonist Dessa, while she is simultaneously denying the possibility that Styron is able to perform that "miracle of empathy," that "imaginative leap not only into history, but across cultures" (Thelwell 80). In contrast, I consider Williams's epistemological premises to correspond to Spillers's evaluation of African American women's attitude toward other black women:

> Whatever the portrayal of female [and/or black] characters yields, it will
> be rendered from the point of view of one whose eyes are not alien to
> the humanity in front of them. What we can safely assume, then, is that

black women write as partisans to a particular historical order—their own, the black and female one, with its hideous strictures against literacy and its subtle activities of censorship even now against words and deeds that would deny or defy the black woman myth. What we can assume with less confidence is that their partisanship . . . will yield a synonymity of conclusions. ("Hateful Passion" 185)

For Williams, it is a clearly political and moral choice to side with the hitherto silenced, and speak for them in a way that does not negate their essential humanity.

Especially within black feminist criticism, there have been several attempts to counter the authority historically bestowed on the white male point of view with the assertion that black women, because of their specific place within the North American social matrix as the "other of the other," have a privileged understanding of both the "hegemonic" and the "ambiguously (non)hegemonic"—i.e. white male, as well as black male and white female—points of view.[21] Rather than declaring this ability to be the new "truth," however—and thereby simply reversing the old binary of white and/or male privileged knowledge versus black and/or female lack of insight without challenging the system as such—Henderson deliberately calls this standpoint "an enabling critical fiction—that it is black women writers who are . . . empowered by experience to speak as poets and prophets in many tongues" ("Speaking in Tongues" 24).

The point of the argument is not that black women naturally have a greater propensity for understanding others; it is rather that they might be—because of their particular socio-political situation—more likely to see through unjustified claims to disinterestedness and objectivity, especially as it affects their own experiences and living situations. It is through "Meditations" and *Dessa Rose* that Williams affirms this assumption. She argues that any kind of writing that aspires to some degree of accurate historical representation in a racist and sexist society is—out of necessity—politically invested, especially if it deals with representation across race and gender lines. Styron's re-creation of "a man and his era" is not possible without paying dues to the context of this project, especially if the teller is in the position of the traditionally privileged, and the person whose life is told in the historically silenced position. Meese comments:

In a sense, Williams too, with her "happy ending," presents a distortion of history (all that writing ever is or can be, or that history as text also is), but unlike Styron's text, Williams's (re)figures the lessons of the slave narratives, as the black story of history which the white story has un/written and denied in the process of writing itself. The issue . . . is again one of respect, or its obverse—the willful blindness this (white) writing cultivates in order to produce its insights—since Styron, who reviewed Aptheker's book on slave revolts, should know better than to represent compulsively and unquestioningly the southern white male story of slavery. . . . In this sense, the outrage of enslavement is recuperated and perpetuated in *The Confessions of Nat Turner* through a writing of racism in the "place" of race: the African-American is once again, in a discursive repetition compulsion, (re)presented as the victim of representation. Nat Turner's story is held captive by Styron's, and the revolution against both the oppressor and his discourse are (un)written. (152-53)

This sharp evaluation of the hidden dynamics of Styron's text succinctly describes the opposing orientations of the two novels, by once more drawing attention to Williams's goal to reveal and invalidate these dynamics.

Finally, despite the well-founded critiques of *The Confessions of Nat Turner*, it cannot be the issue whether Styron should have written his novel or not. Rather, the implications of his insistence on the fiction writer's "creative freedom" are at stake, which in his case includes the disavowal of any political accountability. Although Styron has repeatedly stated that the initial motivation for his interest in the persona of Nat Turner was very personal, he still refuses to acknowledge any influence that his own positionality might have had in the process of conceptualizing and writing the novel. Within this self-established, supposedly value-free context, he then feels entitled to reject any kind of critique—after all, he wrote the book with the best of intentions. This abnegation of responsibility is exactly what he is held accountable for. One of Williams's accusations is that Styron did not approach the historical data about the Nat Turner rebellion critically enough but simply took them at face value; instead, he should have been aware of the possible distortions and misrepresentations due to the specific context of the historical situation. Rather than an attempt to acknowledge the historical importance of the black rebel, *The Confessions of Nat Turner* is—according to Williams and the critical voices of *Ten Black Writers Respond*—little more than a re-run of stereotypical notions about black men, insidiously wrapped in the cloak of "authenticity."

Again, the issue of contemporary cultural authority comes in: part of the black critics' exasperation about *The Confessions of Nat Turner* is caused by the way historical fiction like Styron's is likely to be received and understood by a general reading public. If veracity is one major part of reader expectations—especially if the fictional narrative itself does not contain any obvious disclaimers but pretends to be a truthful account of historical events—Williams is right in arguing that Styron's novel is yet another attempt by a historically privileged white man to define African Americans in a way that underscores their alleged "inferiority." The fact that Nat Turner is one of the few better known black historical figures that have gained great importance within the African American community adds to many readers' taking offense at Styron's novel.[22]

"Liberation Narratives"

When Williams says in the "Author's Note" that she now "own[s] a summer in the 19th century" (*DR* x), she raises the question of what constitutes historical knowledge on a very fundamental level. This statement makes explicit how an imaginative act can in fact "become real"—not necessarily only by adding select data to the already available pool of information, but by clarifying connections, by sensing possible motivations behind actions, and by creating plausible coherence, and thus by entering a dialogic relationship between present and past. Like Morrison in *Beloved*, Williams uses historical references mainly as a jumping-off point. Considering the scarcity of information, this might not only be a decision on creative grounds, but a necessary procedure: the existing evidence about the historical "Dessa" is not extensive enough to create a coherent narrative that could claim "truthfulness" for itself.

Veracity, then, shifts from the historical material to the narrative itself. It becomes a matter of what JoAnne Cornwell-Giles calls "epistemic accuracy": the conceptual, aesthetic, argumentative cohesion of the text (97). Rather than pretending to mimetically represent a "reality" that consists of somebody's skewed representation of yet another person's state of mind—which is what Styron is charged with—Williams quickly moves away from mimetic truth claims to look at the processes of relationships that occur between and among various people, each person caught in the confines of her or his personal history and experiences. This focus on the text's inherent plausibility emphasizes its diegetic qualities and the power of storytelling to "make sense."

Williams's identification with the fictionalized past of her narrative also blurs the distinctions between the storyteller Dessa and the writer Sherley Anne Williams: she situates herself in the slave narrative tradition by "reveal[ing] that in writing the novel she found freedom in her history" (King 355). However, *Dessa*

Rose also signifies on the tradition of the slave narratives—called "liberation narratives" by Williams herself ("Lion's History" 246)—by redefining the primary audience for Dessa's story as black and private, rather than white and public, as I have outlined above. A comparative look at 19th-century writer Harriet Jacobs and the strategies she used to catch her white female audience's attention and turn them into sympathetic listeners reveals thematic emphases in the 19th-century text that are significantly different from Williams's. Much of Jacobs's narrative takes into consideration the conventions of "true womanhood," and she self-consciously positions herself in relation to societal norms that a black woman could not fulfill. As Andrews outlines,

> Jacobs wrote on a precarious margin as she composed her autobiography, hoping "to kindle a flame of compassion" in her female reader's heart without searing her sensibilities with a frank account of such inflammatory subjects as seduction, rape, and miscegenation. (*To Tell a Free Story* 240)

The necessity to attend to the sensibilities of white female readers thus had considerable impact on the writing of *Incidents in the Life of a Slave Girl*. For Williams, however, the narrative situation is notably different. Having Dessa finally talk to a group of people who are likely to share her perceptions, Williams can provide her protagonist with the textual space to use herself as the normative center against which she measures both the white woman's and the black men's ways of behavior, instead of having to prove her own humanity and adherence to the dominant culture's standards of femininity.

The Blues as Conceptual Model

Williams argues that it is in black music—particularly in the blues—rather than in literature that "we get some inkling, not only of the circumstances out of which . . . new male and female roles evolved, but also of the ethics which were their underpinning" ("Cultural and Interpersonal Aspects" 50). In contrast to the oral, conversational, communicative concept out of which the blues have emerged, recent African American literature presents "portraits rather than group scenes, monologues and soliloquies rather than dialogues or conversations" (51) and thus deprives its readers of a sense of community that is based on shared values and philosophies:

> Our oral culture is a source that is largely omitted from consideration, from real investigation in thinking about our lives in this country. But until we know the blues intimately and analytically, we will not know ourselves. (51)

Williams's explicit intention, then, is to find a connection between different available modes of communication, attempting an artistic synthesis between oral and written discourses, in which important issues of African American life can be adequately expressed. In regard to her poetry, critics have repeatedly commented on her use of blues conventions as an important source of and influence, and she herself has theorized the "Blues Roots of Contemporary Afro-American Poetry."

This theoretical argument can easily be extended to include Williams's prose fiction. Already in the "Prologue" of *Dessa Rose*, a blues framework is established for the whole text, with personal loss—which is extremely painful, yet at the same time strengthening—as one defining aspect. By beginning the plot after the husband's death, Williams rewrites the conventional 19th-century script for women's lives: Dessa's life is by no means over when she expects a child from Kaine. Rather, lasting relationships are jeopardized by the brutality of a system that fails to recognize personal commitments between black women and men. In addition, the novel signifies on the sentimental tradition through Dessa's mournful reveries, by showing the precariousness of "romantic love" in the context of slavery.[23] As Meese states, "the opening situates us in the tradition of the romance revised in the tradition of the blues" (137).[24]

The conversations among the runaways on Sutton's Glen then embed Dessa's past experiences within a second communal context. Again, the disruption of personal relationships is presented as one of the prevalent and most pain-inflicting manifestations of slavery, but in this new communal situation, Dessa's individual voice is validated (from) within the community of slaves. This setting is the fictional expression of Williams's attempt to envision a communal spirit in the individual voice: "The particularized, individual experience rooted in a common reality is the primary thematic characteristic of all blues songs no matter what their structure." ("Blues Roots" 126).

The novel's representation of gender relations is another integral part of this overarching attempt to imagine a communal structure that can accommodate both female and male perspectives. Accordingly, the granting of subject status to the women in *Dessa Rose* does not necessarily lead to tensions in their relationships with men. Thematically, Williams's treatment of gender can be seen as a comment on conventions of male slave narratives—with their often strong emphasis on individual achievement—as well as recent evaluations of today's relations between black women and black men as strained. In her contribution to a 1979 *Black Scholar* open forum on gender relations in the black community, Williams joins critics of Michele Wallace and Ntozake Shange by pointing to a history of mutual support and acceptance among black women and men. She explains that African Americans in the 20th century have lost an earlier understanding of gender relations that was not based on male supremacy to the same degree as white society's, because they have constantly been surrounded by European American norms as expressed in "mass culture, records, films, newspapers, and television":

> I don't think we even realized that we had made ourselves a new people ... for the sixties found us hungering after roles which we had already discarded in practice, though not in principle, some hundred years before. ("Cultural and Interpersonal Aspects" 50)

Again, Williams identifies a discrepancy within African American culture between concerns raised in the literature and those expressed in traditional musical forms; she sees the possibility to imagine relationships between "equal and opposing forces" (51) expressed most powerfully in the oral tradition of the blues, but does not find this sense of cross-gender commonality adequately represented in black literature. Instead, the images that emerge from the writing of contemporary black authors fail to acknowledge a core aspect of a distinct aspect of African American culture—different from both African and European-American cultures:

> The African patterns were syncretized, transformed, sublimated, forgotten as Afro-Americans accommodated and adapted to the European norms as these in turn were changed and shaped by life in the New World. (50)

Her own fictional exploration of positive female-male relationships was not, however, inspired by the *Black Scholar* debate, but was an issue that she had been concerned with before. Nevertheless, the discussion surrounding Wallace's *Black Macho and the Myth of the Superwoman*, Shange's *For Colored Girls Who Considered Suicide / When the Rainbow is Enuf*, and Alice Walker's *The Color Purple* might well have affirmed her perception that there is a need for a broader spectrum of representations of black female-male relationships.

Williams's male characters—first Kaine and later especially Harker and Nathan—confirm this notion of mutual respect despite occasional differences in opinion. With Nathan and Harker, she portrays two men whose attitudes toward Dessa show deep respect and understanding for her situation. In one of his conversations with Ruth, Nathan explains:

> You see so many people beat up by slavery, Mis'ess, . . . turned into
> snakes and animals, poor excuses even for they own selfs. And the
> coffle bring out the worst sometime, either that or kill you. And it didn't
> in Dessa. (*DR* 149)

And later, when Dessa is hurt and angry about Nathan's involvement with Ruth,
they find a way to accept each other's decisions without invalidating either one.
There is an underlying basis of trust that can accommodate some difference and
change, even though this isn't easy and demands constant negotiation. After an
argument with Nathan about Ruth, Dessa says:

> I guess this was always my pain, that things would never be the same. I
> had lost so much, so much, and this brother was a part of what I'd
> gained. . . . "Damn fool negro," I told him, yet and still leaning against
> him. His arm tightened around me. "Hankty negress like you need a
> damn fool negro like me." And I laughed. (*DR* 205)

Likewise, Dessa's relationship with Harker is characterized by great tenderness
and caring, which is most movingly expressed in Harker's reaction to Dessa's scars
during their first lovemaking:

> I sat up afterwards and kind of draped my dress across my hips and
> scooted so my back was against the tree. . . . "Dess?" Voice quiet as the
> night, "Dessa, you know I know how they whipped you." His head was
> right by my leg and he turned and lifted my dress, kissed my thigh.
> Where his lips touched was like fire on fire and I trembled. "It ain't
> impaired you none at all," he said and kissed my leg again. "It only
> increase your value." His face was wet; he buried his head in my lap.
> (*DR* 191)

Recognition of the other person's individuality—including her or his past
experiences and how they affect the present—is the basic quality of their evolving
relationship, and this sustains them even beyond the moment of storytelling, many
years later: "Harker . . . he still overcome my senses and never mock at me for my
weakness, say I'm his weakness, too" (*DR* 235). Williams thus creates black
female-male relationships that are inherently non-hierarchical and develop and
deepen outside of a white patriarchal script, apparently almost untouched by its
definitions of female inferiority. In the liberatory space of Sutton's Glen, the
rejection of hierarchical thinking is the first step toward a new community which
is not based on oppressive structures.

Because of its dialogic set-up, especially the final communal setting of the
novel also harks back to Williams's earlier definitions of heroic behavior. In

contrast to the solitary, explicitly individualistic notions of heroism in the western tradition,[25] Williams describes the heroic black woman as a strong agent without implying that this automatically results in a threat to black masculinity. That her early definition of heroism as culturally specific holds even if the concept is extended from black men to black women is demonstrated by the various interpretations of the term "devil woman" with which Dessa is described—with positive as well as negative connotations, depending on circumstance. Dessa rejects this label as long as it is used by whites to designate her supposed lack of humanity; she can finally accept the term when she realizes that it is meant by blacks as a name of honor: "After that last jail, I couldn't mind Cully and them keeping up that name" (DR 259).

Williams's explication of the concept of "heroism" in an African American context—associating it mainly with black male characters in Give Birth to Brightness—is one way of pointing out contrasting interpretations of black history: "A hero is one who is on the side of and supports his society's version of morality and/or order and/or history" (56; emphasis added). Consequently, black heroism contains "some measure of revolt against social structures, for those structures were the instruments of their [Black American's] oppression rather than their protection" (57):

> The rebels, such as the slave revolt leaders, Nat Turner, Gabriel Prosser and Denmark Vesey, [have], [d]espite William Styron's meditations on history, . . . come down to Black people in legends, in historical and fictional accounts of their deeds, as men of great nobility and physical prowess. . . . The point is that the term rebel, in the case of the Black revolt leaders, is a synonym for hero, for they established through their actions a heroic model and tradition based on Black necessity. (59)

Give Birth to Brightness has been criticized for focusing almost exclusively on male authors and their approaches to "writing the Black experience," and Williams herself has stated that she put on a disguise and "was a 'man'" when she wrote the study (Introduction to "Meditations" 198). By making an enslaved woman the center of her concerns as a creative writer, Williams significantly expands her own critical project, including her earlier definition of black heroism.

Commenting on the texts she read in preparation for her work with the "Dessa Rose"-material, Williams explicitly mentions "other novels about slavery and slave women." These novels might have given her some ideas for her own project; especially in regard to characterization, however, they could not provide a useful model, because Williams came away with the impression that "in many of them slave women perform their heroic actions in a kind of trance, as though they would not have been able consciously and rationally to come to decision to do what they had done" (Ross, 494-95). To reinstate rationality in slave women's actions means to hand over the responsibility for their decisions to the women themselves, rather than attributing it to some higher force that cannot be controlled. The focus is therefore not only on establishing spaces for agency, but for deliberate agency. This is an important step in actually imagining and presenting women as subjects, whose circumstances might have been extremely restricted, but who nevertheless refused to be totally objectified.

Dessa Rose thus becomes a cultural space where a positive identification with the African American past becomes possible—an experience that Williams felt she had been lacking:

> I had felt so strongly that young black women and young girls *now* not have to go through the same kind of experience I did [as a child], that they understand that whatever our historical circumstances that those circumstances had never barred us from heroic action. . . . I think it is very, very important that children—that black children—be able to imagine themselves in heroic roles in history without having to imagine themselves as white. (Jordan 289)

In the sense that "heroic" African Americans enjoy the respect of the community they have emerged from, they can be said to have earned the right to occupy a position of authority within that community. Williams's critical project of engaging in African American history and scrutinizing the ways in which it has been made and passed on in language has been committed to creating imaginative spaces in which black people—both female and male—have positions of authority that can no longer be invalidated by the dominant, white and male-oriented culture. This project now spans more than twenty years, and consists of texts in many different genres. They are linked by Williams's commitment to open, dialogic forms of communication that are characterized by moral and political responsibility—responsibility to show how language has been ideologically (ab)used to maintain a status quo of racist and sexist oppression, and how a different model of interaction might in fact make dialogue across differences of race and gender possible.

CHAPTER 4

"A ritual engagement with the past"—
Toni Morrison's *Beloved*

> There is no place you and I can go, to think about
> or not think about, to summon the presences of, or
> recollect the absences of, slaves; nothing that
> reminds us of the ones who made the journey and
> of those who did not make it. . . . And because
> such a place doesn't exist . . ., the book had to.
>
> Toni Morrison, "A Bench by the Road"

> Everybody knew what she was called, but nobody
> anywhere knew her name. Disremembered and
> unaccounted for, she cannot be lost because no
> one is looking for her, and even if they were, how
> can they call her if they don't know her name?
> Although she has claim, she is not claimed.
>
> *Beloved*, 274

> I will call . . . her beloved.
>
> *Beloved*, epigraph

Emphasizing the psychological and emotional effects of oppression and imagining possible strategies for recovery, Toni Morrison's *Beloved* leads away from a focus on historical events that have remained unspoken because of deliberate oversights and slanted perceptions in traditional historiography. The novel is also not so much concerned with providing a general reading public with knowledge held within the African American community. Instead, it directs our attention to those aspects of slave life that remained "unspoken" because they were—according to 19th-century slave narrators—"too terrible to relate" (Morrison, "Site of Memory" 110). Morrison thus enters the difficult terrain of traumatic experiences and their repression—the "unspeakable" that literally could not be spoken because it was too painful even to be even remembered, let alone put into words. To gain access to this unrecorded part of the black historical experience, Morrison returns the site of her narrative to the inner lives and private needs of her recently "unowned"[1] African and African American characters.

In contrast to both *Jubilee's* and *Dessa Rose's* initial spatial and temporal settings in the antebellum South, *Beloved* is set in a northern state eight years after the end of the Civil War. The novel takes us back to 1873, into the black community of Cincinnati, Ohio. Although the former slaves who fled to Cincinnati from slave-holding Kentucky are now officially "free," their lives are still overshadowed by the physical and psychological aftermaths of slavery. Sethe, Morrison's main character, is still struggling with the traumatic memory of having killed one of her children in 1855 to prevent the family from being taken back to the South. Although her former owner gave up his claim on her then, Sethe has not been able to break away from slavery. Eighteen years later, when the plot of *Beloved* starts, she is still in a state of intense emotional paralysis, and she has to spend most of her energy "beating back the past" (B 73).

Yet despite Sethe's desperate struggle to prevent the surfacing of tormenting memories, the incident of the killing remains a controlling presence in her life, and it quickly becomes clear that in order to break its hold on her, she has to meet the challenge to confront it. The different stages necessary for this process become one of the novel's organizing principles; they divide the twenty-eight (unnumbered) chapters into three clearly designated parts. Part I (chapters 1-18) outlines the first impulses for a renewed effort to lay the past at rest: with the appearances of Paul D (an old friend who was—like Sethe—enslaved on the plantation cynically called "Sweet Home") and of the strange young woman who calls herself Beloved, Sethe is prompted to rethink her situation, and cautiously toys with the idea of a future with Paul D. Toward the end of part I, it temporarily looks as if this hope were an actual possibility. At this particular stage in her life, however, it cannot yet happen, because Sethe's real work has not been done: she has not yet been able to confront the traumatic experiences that are primarily responsible for her state of emotional paralysis, and that the character Beloved comes to represent. This necessary confrontation takes place in part II (chapters 19-25): Sethe turns all her attention on the girl—whom she gradually "recognizes" as the dead daughter returned—and the two women slide into a deadlock of guilt and desire, of accusation and the desperate need to explain. In part III (chapters 26-28), finally, the conflict is brought to an end through the intervention of Denver, Sethe's living daughter, Stamp Paid, the old black man who helped Sethe cross the Ohio river in 1855, and the women of the community. This leads to Beloved's disappearance, Sethe's reintegration into the community through a rebirth ritual, and the tender beginnings of a new "family" that includes both Denver and Paul D.

Morrison has repeatedly commented on the function of black and/or female objectification and silencing within the dominant literary and historical discourses. In *Beloved*, too, the role of slaves as "other"—essential for the definition of white southern identity—is obvious. Sethe's thought that "[f]reeing yourself was one thing; claiming ownership of that freed self was another" (*B* 95) astutely raises the question of how it is possible to renounce white definitions that were imposed on one('s)self and how, ultimately, to define oneself as a "free" subject. Morrison sets out to find answers to these concerns, by making the main characters Sethe, Beloved, Denver and Paul D unambiguously central for the thematic and formal structuring of the text. What they cannot say or think is not represented; how they come to be able to think and/or speak about their experiences is respectfully traced, with careful attention given to the enormous psychological and emotional difficulties involved. As Morrison explains to A.S. Byatt in a videotaped interview:

> If I had put the Civil War there, or even the institution, it would have central place. It would disappoint me as a writer to have to deal with it, but also it would require that I dissipate the energy from the interior life of those people.

Consequently, nothing is explained primarily for readers; if something is unspeakable for the characters, neither the readers' interest in learning about it nor the author's conventional "privilege" to explain it from a position of authorial control is sufficient reason to say it. The "unspeakable" remains "unspoken" until the characters themselves are ready for it. Just as Ella, a member of *Beloved's* fictional black community, is "listening for the holes" in the fugitives' stories (*B* 92), and Morrison is trying to fill—with genuine concern, empathy and imagination—the gaps in the 19th-century slave narratives, readers are implicitly asked to listen attentively, to accept that the characters themselves have a claim to be finally listened to.

Although this narrative strategy is of course a deliberate authorial decision, it is an intentional gesture of handing some of the authority to define the extent and directions of their development over to the characters.[2] Especially Sethe's world view is posited as the text's conceptual center; any evaluation, any judgment of what happens has to be carefully measured in relation to it. Unlike Morrison's earlier novels, in which the community often occupies this central place by providing a relatively stable value system in and against which the characters have to act, *Beloved* describes the community as a group of people who are also, like

Sethe, still struggling with what it really means to be "free." They, too, are still trapped in "enslaved" notions of love and relationship, and are therefore—although involuntarily—complicitous in Sethe's desperate act of motherlove. Baby Suggs's teachings, convincing and necessary though they seemed, for a long time cannot really take root and displace the bitter experience of slavery that one has to "love[ ] small" (B 162) in order to survive. Before the community can represent a genuine ethics of self-respect, care and mutual responsibility—and thus become a supportive "holding space" for Sethe—they have to undergo their own processes of unlearning, eventually repudiating the internalized messages of slavery that initially made them judge Sethe and exclude her from community life. In addition to the community's long inability to accommodate Sethe's behavior, Paul D's lack of understanding when he accuses her of love that is "too thick" (B 164) for some time also threatens the promise of a bearable future.

For readers, the implications and risks of passing judgment over a person who has done something so unfathomable that it is literally "beyond saying" are thus repeatedly demonstrated in the textual world: they result in the failure of communication, in the lack of the ability to "hear" and respond sympathetically to that person's plight. This forfeiture of genuine dialogue locks everybody into preconceived, and thus necessarily decontextualized, notions of morality—notions that invariably fail to address adequately the complexity of any situation. Implicitly, Morrison therefore cautions her readers, too, not to objectify Sethe by imposing 20th-century attitudes onto her. We are asked instead to accept the process of Sethe's struggle with her past as key to the meaning that we can finally give to the killing of the little girl—the unspeakable center of the text.

The shift in thematic and structural organization toward a clear validation of psychological and emotional processes that Sethe and her extended family have to go through thus signals a concomitant shift in basic conceptual assumptions, especially in regard to issues of authority. Morrison asserts that as long as dominant literary and cultural expectations demand primary attention, the imaginary spaces in which the effects of slavery on those who suffered most under it can be explored are severely limited. In the following chapter, I argue that Morrison is carrying the project of constructing historical black (female) voices—of "represent[ing] captive persons as subjects rather than as objects of oppression" (Abel, "Race, Class and Psychoanalysis" 199)—a significant step further than both Walker and Williams. Morrison's historical project starts from a fundamental critique of the very epistemology that has provided the context for earlier explorations of the "meanings" of slavery. She asserts that as long as issues of race and gender are approached within a conceptual framework that automatically defines white men as central and black women as marginal, a black and female person cannot unambiguously occupy the position of a subject; she will always already be reduced to an objectified "other," as long as the categories of perception and representation implicitly assume whiteness and maleness to be the inherently normative center (cf. Moyers).

It is the framing assumption for this chapter that Morrison adopts a writerly position marked by a confident, non-defensive claim to a public voice, and thus redefines and claims for herself the position of "black female author" as an authoratitve space; this stance then allows her to clear a fictional "safe space" that does not constantly have to engage in legitimizing activities. Instead of trying to accommodate the dominant culture's expectations, Morrison displaces the concern with readers that is necessarily part of texts with a more explicitly didactic goal.[3] This, in turn, makes more respectful, "response-able"[4] attention to the fictional characters possible, recognizing them as the primary loci of (narrative) authority for the shape and development of the narrative. My thesis is that Morrison is doing this by significantly expanding her general critique of conventionalized processes of novel writing (and reading)—including the expected roles of author and readers. This does not mean that the needs and expectations of readers are disregarded; rather, Morrison creates what Holloway calls a "collaborative community of author, character and reader" (*Moorings* 35). She is able to achieve this delicate balance between all parties involved because she embraces the same "both/and" conceptual orientation that she develops within the text.[5]

Much of the novel's power and effectiveness lies, I will argue, in the tension between always implicating its readers in the epistemological processes that happen within the text, as well as also clearly privileging the textual needs of the characters over the extratextual individual and communal needs of the readers. To put it differently, Morrison implicates readers so much in the characters' processes of recovery that their respective needs can no longer be separated. As a result, the fictional characters' struggles to confront their pasts and find their own, bearable interpretations become ways to recognize our own needs to confront those aspects of the past that have been individually and socially repressed, and to envision the possibility of similar healing processes in a 20th-century context. *Beloved* thus becomes, as Linda Krumholz suggests, a cultural healing ritual, "in which the acquisition of knowledge is a subjective and spiritual experience" ("Ritual, Reader, and Narrative" 376).

After a brief survey of the relevant secondary material on *Beloved*, I will first describe Morrison's own definition of the concept of authorship in which "black female author" is not a contradiction in terms, but rather an authoritative position that stands for possibility and growth. I will then examine in detail how this authorial stance is inscribed within the text, and how it creates conceptual spaces in which new strategies for a coming to terms with a troubled past can be imagined. On the textual level, I will emphasize how Morrison displaces—and thus literally decenters—events that have traditionally been considered of "central" significance in the historical imagination. Within this thematic framework of a refigured historical scenery that is based on and defined by the knowledge(s) and experiences of the 19th-century African American characters, the second section will focus on the complex intersections of content and formal structure, with the dynamics of (re)membering as an organizing principle for both. The third issue to be discussed will be the implications of point of view for the distribution of narrative authority within the text, to specify how Morrison not only challenges the ideological investments of traditional literary genres, but even revisions language and its concrete usage in her attempt to tell a story of black history that was, until *Beloved*, largely assumed to be unspeakable. This will also include specifications of the novel's explicit and implicit signifying relationships with earlier written and oral "texts," to examine the extent of revision that is needed to "rip that veil drawn over 'proceedings too terrible to relate'" (Morrison, "Site of Memory" 110) in the original slave narratives, as well as to rectify some of the distortions and/or shortcomings of later historiographical and fictional texts. As a final step, I will then return to extratextual considerations and examine how the relational model of interaction that the text develops becomes a model for the extratextual community of writer and readers.

Critical Attention

Since 1990, critical material on *Beloved* has been rapidly proliferating, and critics have—generally with great sophistication—examined and analyzed the novel in its extraordinary complexity. Most of the critical attention to *Beloved* to date is presented in scholarly articles. In addition, several recent black and white feminist literary studies include *Beloved* as one textual example in overarching theoretical inquiries,[6] and a number of recent "author-studies" on Morrison's work as a whole also include either a separate chapter or longer sections within thematically arranged chapters on this fifth novel. Finally, even a metalevel of criticism dealing with *Beloved's* critical reception is already emerging.[7] In contrast to the approach that I could take with both *Jubilee* and *Dessa Rose*, it will therefore not be possible here to give a comprehensive survey of the critical material. I will rather group articles in terms of their specific points of interest, and refer in more detail to those that are immediately relevant for my own analysis at the appropriate moments in my analysis of the text.

Whereas early reviewers and commentators were often concerned with establishing Beloved's "true" identity (e.g. House), the urge to come to an unambiguous conclusion about who this enigmatic figure really is quickly shifted toward an agreement that part of her significance lies her symbolic openness, her "stubborn" refusal to be unambiguously explainable (cf. Phelan). In this line of thought, the intricate intersections of memory, language, and narrative form in *Beloved* have become one privileged critical focus (e.g. Rodrigues; Page; Rushdy, "Daughters Signifyin(g) History"). Several articles focus on how slavery has been inscribed both on Sethe's psyche and on her body, and how this imposed inscription is countered in the novel (e.g. Henderson, "Toni Morrison's *Beloved*"; Goldman). Others examine the difficulties of mother-child relationships under conditions of slavery and their significance for black female identity formation (e.g. Hirsch; Schapiro; Fultz). The need to scrutinize language itself and its ability to limit and expand knowledge is also the focus of a number of insightful critiques; they attend to Morrison's exploration of the workings of language and the need for self-determined language use and explore how Morrison both draws from and reconceptualizes western linguistic and philosophical traditions (e.g. Wyatt).

Most critics approach *Beloved* in a way that shows their basic willingness to engage in and struggle with the novel's complexity. Although the critical readings do not always show the kind of conceptual openness that Morrison asks for, the overall impression is one of respectful engagement. This critical behavior supports my presumption that Morrison's status as an acclaimed writer, which she had already established through her first four novels, made it very likely that the fifth one would also be met with positive public responses. Morrison therefore did not have to deal with the particular pressure that is part of publishing a first novel. Instead, her established status provided a more secure basis for making *Beloved* an imaginative "safe" space for substantial conceptual revision.

In accordance with the notion that Morrison's status as an important writer is by now largely acknowledged, there is not much critical attention on how she takes advantage of the authority that this status entails in creating the imaginative worlds of her novels. The one study that explicitly deals with issues of authorization in *Beloved* is, as I have mentioned above, Lanser's chapter on Morrison in *Fictions of Authority*. Despite Lanser's somewhat problematic theoretical framework and my disagreement with some of the conclusions she draws in her critical reading of *Beloved*, the description she offers of some of the novel's textual features can be a useful starting point for a discussion of Morrison's authorial stance. One advantage of Lanser's approach is that she surveys Morrison's work as a whole and places her interpretation of *Beloved* in the context of the earlier novels. This makes visible a conceptual development in which the fifth and—at the time when Lanser published her study—latest novel is shown as a (temporary) climax:

> Through shifts from the double narrative structure of *The Bluest Eye* to the complex "fluidity" of *Beloved*, authoriality remains a powerful presence in Morrison's novels, but . . . the use of Western culture as a source of authority virtually disappears. (*Fictions of Authority* 129)

Lanser's perceptive analysis of the stances that Morrison's narrators take from *The Bluest Eye* to *Beloved* confirms my reading of *Beloved* as a novel in which some of the basic parameters of novelistic conventions are rewritten.

In addition to the growing number of studies on Morrison's work, the publication of all of her novels has been accompanied by numerous interviews and articles in which Morrison herself elaborates her role as writer, her attitude toward readers and critics, and the thematic emphases and poetic characteristics of her writing. With these comments, Morrison not only creates a public image of herself as writer, but provides an important critical framework for the interpretation of her fictional texts.[8]

AUTHORIAL POSITIONING:
THE NOVELIST AS "RESPONSE-ABLE AUTHOR-ITY"

In *Beloved*, Morrison explores the contemporary possibilities to imagine a historical subject—a subject who is respected as such not only by other characters, but also by the narrative voice and the author—and examines how this destabilizes and redefines conventional assumptions about the writer-text-reader configuration. If the shift to the interior life of a black enslaved woman is to be more than a narrative appropriation of her thoughts and voice, Morrison asserts, it requires a simultaneous rethinking not only of this fictional character's relationship to other characters in the text and to the narrator, but also of the writer's attitude to the text and, as it is expressed through the writing, toward an anticipated or actual audience. This immediately touches on questions of positioning and authorization. Starting from the assumption that Morrison intends *Beloved* to be a "safe space" for her fictional characters, I will outline in the following section how she describes the conceptual premises on which her writing is based in her nonfictional public statements.

The discussion of Morrison's authority as a writer could follow two different tracks: the one pursued here starts from her own contention that the subject matter she is writing about and the forms she is using need no special justification because they "are already legitimatized by their own cultural sources and predecessors" ("Unspeakable Things" 33). The integrity and self-confidence that is so characteristic not only for Morrison's texts, but also for the way in which she presents herself and her writing in public is part and parcel of her understanding that to be a black woman is nothing to be defensive about. As she formulates it in the interview with Byatt:

> [Because of the existing categories] you have to say, no I'm not a black writer, I'm a writer, or, no I'm not a woman writer, I'm a writer; or, as I do, I say, yes I am, a black woman writer. And that makes my world larger than those who are neither.

The other possible track would focus on the question why Morrison has achieved such high critical acclaim in European American literary and academic circles, if white readers and their expectations are apparently of so little explicit concern to her writing. The relevance of this inquiry has been highlighted by Morrison's being awarded the Nobel Prize for Literature in 1993. Why is it necessary or desirable at this particular historical and cultural moment to have an African American woman become Nobel laureate? Whose needs are being met?[9] Because the focus of these questions is directed away from Morrison and what she is trying to achieve—back toward reader interests and the workings of a mainstream culture industry and literary market—they are outside the objectives for this study.

Morrison has repeatedly explained how she sees her role as a writer both within an African American cultural context and vis-à-vis the dominant society. What is most notable is her explicit identification with black traditions, and her insistence that both her authority as a writer and the legitimation that is necessary for her work comes out of this very particular cultural mooring place.[10] To stop insisting on "see[ing] things differently" because this alternative knowledge is contested by the dominant culture is out of the question for Morrison. In "Memory, Creation, and Writing" she asserts:

> If my work is to confront a reality unlike that received reality of the West, it must centralize and animate information discredited by the West—discredited not because it is not true or useful or even of some racial value, but because it is information held by discredited people, information dismissed as "lore" or "gossip" or "magic" or "sentiment." (388)

Leaving no doubt that she sees herself as belonging to and identifying with this "discredited" community, Morrison has often explained how this standpoint shapes her work. This is—besides being an expression of genuine identification—also clearly a political gesture of a writer who has repeatedly been asked to "move on to larger issues."[11] Obviously, this deliberate positioning of herself and her work vis-à-vis the "West" has important conceptual consequences, one of which is that the dominant European American society loses its privilege to be the primary legitimizing authority. Morrison is very clear about this, and consequently redefines the identity of the implied audience to whom she addresses her novels:

> If the critics felt that they could force me to "write positive images," then clearly they assumed that I was writing for white people. It was a demand that I create an image for the "other" as opposed to making an intimate and direct account to the people in the book and to black people. . . . It's humiliating to be asked to write propaganda. That's not literature. ("Bench by the Road" 38)

These thoughts about the implicit expectations that are brought to texts written by African American women can be placed in the larger context of the significance of "race" for U.S.-American self-definition. Morrison herself has done this very astutely in the lectures collected in *Playing in the Dark*, in which her textual discussion starts from the premise that "for both black and white American writers, in a wholly racialized society, there is no escape from racially inflected language" (12-13).

Morrison's own efforts to take the implications of this complex historical and social situation as seriously as possible and to break the American "habit" of belittling and silencing the lives and experiences of African Americans create conceptual and moral spaces to challenge readers and critics who continue to practice these devaluations. She explicitly does not want her work discussed in terms that have little or nothing to do with black traditions:

> Other kinds of structures are imposed on my works, and therefore they
> are either praised or dismissed on the basis of something that I have no
> interest in whatsoever, which is writing a novel according to some
> structure that comes out of a different culture. (McKay 425)[12]

Accordingly, the writer's relationship to both a critical and a general audience
needs careful consideration. By unhesitatingly setting up her black female
protagonist's worldview as the epistemologically central one in *Beloved*, Morrison
makes it clear that it cannot be the text's primary goal to explain anything specifically to an extratextual audience; the fictional character has too many things that
she first of all needs to explain to herself. It is by being privy to these psychological processes within the text that some of the issues at stake might become clearer
to the readers as well. In a conversation with Gloria Naylor, Morrison agrees with
Naylor's assertion that "if the readers want to extrapolate a message, then they can
do it on their own; I haven't put one in for them. That's not my responsibility as a
black or as a black woman" (Naylor 579). Naylor and Morrison both echo Audre
Lorde's insistent remarks that it cannot be the task of African American women to
teach others about their prejudiced behavior:

> Oppressed peoples are always being asked to stretch a little more, to
> bridge the gap between blindness and humanity. Black women are
> expected to use our anger only in the service of other people's salvation
> or learning. But that time is over. ("Uses of Anger" 132)

In a televised interview with Bill Moyers, Morrison also opposes expectations
that it should be her primary concern to educate readers. In this highly public
forum, she instead outlines an alternative approach to the conventional didactic
situation in which one authorized person passes on privileged information to a
group of uninitiated readers. She challenges this hierarchical set-up by suggesting a
model of literary communication in which author, readers, and text are positioned
in a larger matrix of shared work and learning. Responding to Moyers's question
why he, as a white man, felt so drawn to and impressed by the novel, she answers:

> You were ready for the information. You were available to the book. . . .
> The person inside you has to be accessible. There has to be a little crack
> in there already, some curiosity. Some willingness, you know, to know
> about it. Some moment when you really don't have the blinders on. We
> know people who just zip their eyes shut, who are totally enclosed in
> the neurotic and frequently psychotic prison of racism. But if ever any
> chink can be made from the inside or outside, then they become
> accessible to certain kinds of information. (Moyers 62)

What does it mean that readers need to be "accessible"? There needs to be at least a basic willingness to accept that a black and female writer has enough authority to speak publicly. Morrison is very clear about not seeing it as her primary obligation as a writer, though, to bring about that openness in reluctant or outrightly hostile readers. As it is obvious from numerous public statements, she is increasingly less willing to accept compromises for her texts in order to make them easier to approach for some readers.[13]

Despite these very clear statements about her own expectations, Morrison still wants readers to become "partners in struggle" and actively work with the text; this emphasis on what she calls a "participatory relationship between the artist or the speaker and the audience" ("Rootedness" 341) links *Beloved* with all of her other novels. Her authorial control over the text is manifested in the deliberate creation of spaces for the 20th-century audiences to read and interpret the textual events for themselves—the symbolic openness of Beloved's identity is probably the most obvious case in point, but there are numerous other—formal and thematic—"entry points."[14] The safety of (intellectual and emotional) distance is no longer possible, because the processes of reading and getting involved are what is important, not any supposedly privileged information that the author "possesses" and merely passes on. "The moral issues," says Trudier Harris, "lock us into participation in the novel" (171). And in the interview with Moyers, Morrison explains:

> I want the reader to feel, first of all, that he trusts me. I'm never going to do anything so bad that he can't handle it. But at the same time, I want him to see things he has never seen before. I want him to work with me in the book. (Moyers 62-63)

This shift from product- to process-orientation not only creates spaces for a dialogue between writer and readers, but even goes hand in hand with a partial authorial withdrawal: the mysterious young woman offers a variety of different but equally plausible interpretations and thus allows everybody—characters and readers alike—to invest her with highly personal meanings. Instead of fixing meaning in the attempt to pass it on to readers, which any supposedly mimetic representation would do, Morrison provides "reminders and spaces to throw knowledge [as well as the processes of knowing] into doubt"—a necessary condition, according to Jane Flax, to recognize the positionality of every individual (whether writer or reader) in the socio-cultural matrix (224). The novel thus becomes a dialogic cultural moment in which the plight of the historical black community is made recognizable, and can in turn initiate individual and communal processes of healing and revisionary self-definition for the 20th-century author and her readers. In this sense, as I have already suggested with the first epigraph to this chapter, *Beloved* also functions as a memorial—as a site of memory or a *lieu de memoire* (Nora)—particularly, but not exclusively, for African Americans.

Within this redefined framework of authorization and reader engagement, Morrison situates the key thematic and conceptual issues of her writing. In "The Site of Memory," she challenges the conventional assumption that "fiction, by definition, is distinct from fact." Out of her disagreement with this statement, she formulates the theoretical premise that instead of being a self-evident given, the distinction between "fact" and "fiction" is—like the definition of narrative authority—also based on public agreement: "[N]othing in [fiction] needs to be publicly verifiable, although much in it can be verified" (112). Fiction is thus a space that allows writers to deliberately "stretch boundaries" (Moyers 62) and to challenge accepted notions of behavior—to effect a willing suspension of disbelief in readers so that development and growth become possible. "Art can do what other things cannot do," Morrison says (Byatt). And because "fiction is not random, . . . the crucial distinction . . . is not the difference between fact and fiction, but the distinction between fact and truth. Because facts can exist without human intelligence, but truth cannot" ("Site of Memory" 113).[15]

Morrison thus not only creates her own implied audience, insisting on the integrity of the culture and the work that emerges out of it. As a response to the notion that "until recently, . . . the readers of virtually all of American fiction have been positioned as white" (*Playing in the Dark* xii), she also deliberately "change[s] the definitions" (Byatt) of who is addressed, who has the authority to speak, and what is sayable whenever she deems that necessary. Once the hegemony of the white male voice is thus broken, more and different things—"a reality unlike that received reality of the West" ("Memory, Creation, and Writing" 388)—can be imagined and described. In regard to *Beloved*, this has a plethora of results. Giving a "voice" and an inner life to Sethe, Morrison breaks the cultural silences that have surrounded enslaved black women; she contextualizes motherhood in a political and social matrix, and she presents "motherly" and "daughterly" needs as crucially interwoven. Maternal violence is not only addressed but also put into a context that precludes quick judgment. Additionally—as part of Morrison's general challenge to western culture as privileged legitimizing instance—she addresses the collective trauma of the Middle Passage as an issue that finally demands the attention that it has been denied—for different reasons—both in traditional historiography and in the literary imagination.

If these are some of the constitutive elements of Morrison's approach to narrative, they have the following implications for the reading process: first, there is quite explicitly a strong sense of authorial guidance. This guidance does not, however, express itself through an authoritarian attitude, in the sense of the writer imposing one particular reading on the audience. Although there is undoubtedly control over the narrative, to interpret this as an undue exertion of control over the reader and her or his perceptions is unwarranted.[16] Secondly, the author's attention to interaction and dialogue translates into process- rather than product-orientation for the characters as well as for the readers. What is important here is the active engagement of each reader with the text, not a preconceived, fixed notion of the text's deeper meaning. In this regard, Morrison's characterization of her own writing several years before the publication of *Beloved* still applies: "Something in . . . [the novel should suggest] what the conflicts are, what the problems are. But it need not solve these problems because it is not a case study, it is not a recipe" ("Rootedness" 341).

These comments clearly show the contours of the public space that Morrison is defining for her writing; as such they provide an important frame of reference for the following discussion of *Beloved*. If, and how, these extratextual claims are actually put into practice in the fictional text remains to be seen. What is remarkable in any case, however, is the self-confident matter-of-factness with which Morrison outlines the terms both for her work and for its critical treatment by others. The public image she thus creates is one of a challenging, authoritative writerly presence—a presence that anticipates the way in which the implied author in *Beloved* presents herself and defines her role vis-à-vis the novel's audience.

The "Beloved"-Material

Like *Jubilee* and *Dessa Rose*, Morrison's novel is based on historically verifiable information. The starting point for *Beloved* was an 1856 newspaper article that Morrison came across while co-editing *The Black Book*, a "scrap-book" of black history, in the early 1970s. In this article, a white minister tells of a fugitive slave mother who, after escaping from Kentucky to Ohio, tried to kill her children to prevent them from being taken back into slavery, and whom he was allowed to talk to in prison (Bassett 10). Although the article does not mention the woman's name, other sources identify her as "Margaret Garner" and also provide information about what happened to her after her imprisonment: because of several disparities in the federal laws and the state laws of Ohio, she was handed over to her former owner under the Fugitive Slave Law before she could be tried for murder. Together with her children, she was sold down the Mississippi (S. Campbell 144-47; Lerner 60-63).

These events must have been well known at the time.[17] What was obviously most surprising for Margaret Garner's contemporaries was the claim she made. To decide her children's fate, to take the responsibility for their death, was remarkable for a slave who had no legal rights whatsoever. Morrison comments: "This was a slave who, if she owned anything at all, it certainly wasn't her children. And she claimed them. It's an outrageous claim, not only of property, but rights, and sovereignty" (A. Smith 51). In "Rediscovering Black History," Morrison describes her own reactions when she first read the article in the *Black Book*-material: "I lived through a despair quite new to me but so deep it had no passion and elicited no tears" (16). The story stayed with her for more than a decade and eventually became the starting point for *Beloved*. However, she refrained from doing much further research on the Garner case to give herself and her characters more space to develop:

> I did research about a lot of things in this book in order to narrow it, to
> make it narrow and deep, but I did not do much research on Margaret
> Garner other than the obvious stuff, because I wanted to invent her life,
> which is a way of saying I wanted to be accessible to anything the char-
> acters had to say about it. (Darling, "In the Realm of Responsibility" 5)

Morrison's effort to "mak[e] an intimate and direct account to the people in the book" ("Bench by the Road" 38) is reflected in her treatment of the killing which, in the historical sources, always occupies central space. In the novel's 1873 narrative present, this historically sensational(ized) event is displaced and relegated into the past. Within the text's distribution of narrative responsibilities that I will outline below, it can only be approached through the minds of those who witnessed it.

This shift from the event itself to people's reaction to it draws attention to the relationship between language and "reality." Although the violent death of Sethe's child remains a constant presence in the characters' lives, the temporal setting prevents any supposedly transparent representation. Instead, the text negotiates the immense difficulties inherent in remembering and attempting to speak about it. In addition to thus focusing on the characters and their struggles to free themselves from the psychological and emotional shackles of slavery, Morrison simultaneously scrutinizes the role of language in the conceptualization of "free" African American subjects, and the precarious double-sidedness of historical representation. On the one hand, an old newspaper article is almost all that is known about the historical Margaret Garner; on the other hand, a white-authored report's perspective might make it impossible to comprehend the woman's desperate act.

Morrison's conceptual premises for her writing in general and *Beloved* in particular, which she has formulated and publicly presented in many articles and interviews, clearly place her in an intertextual, signifying relationship with the original slave narratives. Morrison argues that the 19th-century situation, which demanded of the African American writer disproportionate attention to the attitudes and expectations of a white audience, precluded any sustained and honest concentration on the needs and perspectives of the black people whose lives were being represented. To make this concentration finally possible, Morrison defines her own authorial position as authorized from within African American culture and thus in no need of legitimation vis-à-vis a white and male-identified dominant culture. With an outer-directed, authoritative attitude toward readers, and an innerdirected, "response-able" attitude toward her characters, she sets out to explore the possibilities inherent in such a textual "safe space." Textual choices—generic, structural, discursive and thematic—are inextricably connected with these extratextual conceptual emphases.

BELOVED: THE LANGUAGE OF CAREFUL REMEMBERING

Unlike Walker and Williams, Morrison does not include a preface or an introduction to alert readers to the circumstances of her text's genesis. She deliberately makes do without the orienting measures that both Walker and Williams employ to focus their readers' attention on the historically verifiable bases of their texts. Although *Beloved* is also based on historical persons and events, nothing in the presentation of the novel draws attention to this extratextual dimension. The implied author of *Beloved* establishes a first contact with her readers through the few short paratexts that precede the text proper: the readers' attention is directed from the novel's title to the dedication "Sixty Million and More"—a number not explained at this point—and then to the epigraph, which is clearly identified as a passage from the Bible:

> *I will call them my people,*
> *which were not my people;*

and her beloved,
which was not beloved.

ROMANS 9:25

This instantaneous combination of the novel's title—at this point still inter-pretable only as an adjective, expressing the attitude of an as yet unspecified speaker to an also still unidentified person—with the bible quote that starts with a prophetic "I" marks the extrafictional voice as a confident, authoritative presence whose agenda is already apparent before the text proper has even started.

Hence, Morrison establishes contact with her readers not on the basis of historical verification, but on the basis of the enigmatic character of her introduc-tory, extrafictional structures. Especially the dedication introduces a mythic dimension that describes the novel as of greater conceptual scope than those texts dedicated, for example, to an author's immediate family. In addition, instead of attending to outside demands and expectations that might challenge her project, Morrison uses the epigraph to create an atmosphere in which it is her prerogative to define the priorities of the text. She even assumes the authority to appropriate the "Word of the Father," both to set the terms for her narrative and to create a space for a redefinition of historical "truth." Choosing a quotation from the bible, Morrison already anticipates that she will later take the word of God literally and actually "call . . . her beloved which was not beloved."

The concept of creating something by naming it has, as Janheinz Jahn and other scholars of African cultures have shown, parallels in West African thought systems (*Muntu: Outline* 121-55). Unlike assumptions based on Christian mythology that attribute the creative power of naming to God alone, the appropriation of the word in an African context does not—according to Jahn—imply a preposterous or even blasphemous claiming of God-like abilities. Rather, within the African philosophical and epistemological framework that Jahn describes, every person—living or dead—has the ability to create reality by naming, by using words (128). Morrison's extrafictional self-positioning in black cultural traditions, her construc-tion of a revisionary historical community and the great respect and care with which she treats the "reality" she has thus created correspond in many ways to this non-western thought system.

Because of these conceptual affinities to African patterns, it is relevant to note that *Beloved* begins with an explicit reference to Christian traditions. This focus functions in different ways. First, it initially presents authorial presence in the text as powerful and authoritative, even if this very kind of authority later comes under critical revision, as the novel gradually moves away from a monologic toward a dialogic, relational concept of human connection. Secondly, Morrison's choice of this particular quotation shows the potential inherent in the bible to act differently toward "others" than white Christian American society has chosen to do toward African Americans.

Chapter 1: Setting the Stage

The very opening of the fictional text then establishes the theoretical frame on which the novel as a whole rests. There are two aspects in particular that are relevant for the discussion of Morrison's alternative approach to authority: first, the way in which she introduces the roles of narrator and characters and the relationships between them, and secondly, how she has Sethe introduce different ways of dealing with memory, and thus outlines a model of forgetting and remembering that will provide an important conceptual basis for the remainder of the narrative.

Only the very first paragraph of the first chapter is completely told from the perspective of a third-person narrator—a storyteller's voice who introduces listeners to the fictional world that is about to unravel (Rodrigues 153). The information she gives here is purely descriptive and extremely sparse: time, place, names and kinship relations, and the barest outline of how Sethe and Denver came to be on their own, living in what appears to be a haunted house. The overall sense is one of loss and family disintegration, but much of what is said is not, at this early point in the text, understandable for readers. There is, however, no effort to explain. The tone of this introductory passage is very matter-of-factly, and confidently assertive that however puzzling it may seem, what is said is enough for the time being. In its mixture of enigma and concreteness, the novel's opening is indicative of the narrator's general attitude toward the text's implied audience: it is a gesture that is both inviting and demanding, and it also makes clear that the characters have the advantage of an understanding that readers lack: "124 was spiteful. Full of a baby's venom. The women in the house knew it and so did the children" (*B* 3).

Morrison has commented on this beginning as being part of her overarching authorial attitude toward the extratextual audience:

> The reader is snatched, yanked, thrown into an environment completely foreign, and I want it as the first stroke of the shared experience that might be possible between the reader and the novel's population. . . . I

wanted the compelling confusion of being there as they (the characters) are; suddenly, without comfort or succor from the "author," with only imagination, intelligence, and necessity available for the journey. ("Unspeakable Things" 32-33)

This positioning of the audience destabilizes preconceived readerly notions of what might happen in the text; it opens up the novel to explore paths that do not adhere to the expectations evoked by the genre "historical novel." As Morrison explains,

[l]iterary references ... can also supply a comfort I don't want the reader to have because I want him to respond on the same plane as an illiterate or preliterate reader would. I want to subvert his traditional comfort so that he may experience an unorthodox one: that of being in the company of his own solitary imagination. ("Memory, Creation, and Writing" 287)

This deprives her audience of the comfort of being "in the known"—of being in a position of control because we know what "should" happen. What we have to do instead is to keep reading and trust that things will eventually become clearer.

From the second paragraph on, the narrative is then squarely situated in the fictional world. In the remainder of the chapter, the third person omniscient narrator gives way to a limited omniscient point of view, in which the narrative voice takes over the characters' perspectives and refrains more and more from outer-directed comments and explanations. While thus gradually moving us into the characters' world, the chapter also introduces a number of key thematic concerns that will prove significant in the course of the novel. Both the shift in point of view and the thematic emphases provide necessary clues for reading and understanding.

Although the introductory outline defines the narrative present as "1873," the chapter does not get to that date until three pages later. The first described action happens approximately ten years earlier, when Baby Suggs, the grandmother, is still alive. This time shift is not accompanied by a shift in tenses—an early indication that present and past are not clearly separable in the textual world. We enter the scene through Baby Suggs's perspective, and we are offered a key statement for a deeper understanding of the text when we learn that "she knew death was anything but forgetfulness" (B 4). Her significance as an important presence in the lives of Sethe and her daughter Denver is established here, because it is through Baby Suggs's perspective that the relationship between the living and the dead is presented as a central concern. The second character to be introduced in some detail is Sethe herself, through whose thoughts and memories the narrative is eventually brought to what will then largely remain the narrative present.

Without yet mentioning the event that forms the core conflict of the text, these first few pages circle around painful memories and various ways of dealing with them. Already at this early stage, the importance of memory both as a leitmotif for the characters' actions and as an organizing principle for the text is apparent, as these processes are clearly linked with the disturbing ghostly presence with which the chapter opens. It also becomes clear that Sethe and Denver consider this spirit, which has for years been interfering with their lives in 124 Bluestone Road, to be one of Sethe's children who "wasn't even two when she died" (B 4). The ghost's actions are seen as causally related to Sethe's: they are "no more powerful than the way [she] loved her" (B 4).

"The way I loved her"—a sentence uttered in response to a question from Denver—triggers Sethe's memory of trying to get a headstone for her dead daughter. In a symbolically very rich and complex scene that has ramifications beyond the textual world, we are given crucial insights into the dynamics of remembering, as well as into Sethe's self-image and self-definition as a mother who is willing to take even sexual abuse for her children's sake. By having her love writ large in stone, Sethe demonstrates her motherlove for everyone to see. Her "payment," however, remains hidden; it expresses a "see-how-much-I-endure-to-give-evidence-of-my-love-for-you." To accept and submit to the engraver's "offer" is Sethe's way to symbolically make up for her own violence—which is an important gesture for herself. It suggests that the maybe misdirected agency that Sethe showed in resisting schoolteacher's claims can be countered—undone—by an act of deliberate self-objectification. She endures becoming a victim of sexual abuse not with the intention to be called "beloved" herself, but to have her child called so.

Sethe's self-definition is thus shown to be crucially dependent on her being a mother. The encounter with the stonemason is an act of making herself invisible, because the locus of her identity lies not primarily within herself, but within her children. After turning against these children in desperation, she then turns against herself in agreeing to trade her body for the engraving.[18] This scene can be considered a middle piece that fits between the parallel scenes of schoolteacher's arrival in 1855 and Bodwin's coming to pick up Denver in 1874: if Sethe's reaction to schoolteacher was to try and kill her children, she is later able to turn her anger to the outside and attack the white man whom she can only consider a threat. In the graveyard scene depicted in chapter 1, Sethe figuratively kills herself/ "her self" to get the engraving on the tombstone. Although not a repetition in a strict sense, it is another marker of how Sethe has internalized the notion that "[w]hites might dirty *her* all right, but not her best thing, [her children]" (B 251).

The manifestation of Sethe's love as the one word chiselled into the gravestone is also meant as an explanation for the dead girl. This doesn't work, however, as the presence of the angry, spiteful ghost makes clear. In this case, simply to be called "beloved" does not mean that she—the dead child—can actually see or feel herself "beloved." To say it makes it so, and thus creates a reality for Sethe, but for Beloved, who cannot forget or forgive the violence, this is not the case. Sethe's words are not meant to instigate dialogue. And what the one word on the headstone also does not achieve is its implicit primary function: it does not provide Sethe with the necessary space in which she can mourn her dead child.

If the stone itself is meant to signify permanence, the letters on the stone raise questions in regard to writing/literacy as a means of control: only through obeisance to a white man can a poor black woman like Sethe pass on the written message that "She is/was my beloved." Sethe is also responding to what she perceives as community expectations: "That should certainly be enough. Enough to answer one more preacher, one more abolitionist, and a town full of disgust" (B 5). As it turns out shortly afterwards, however, it is not enough: the black community resents what they see as Sethe's pride—she does not talk to them. The inscription on the stone is an attempt at communication that fails because its addressees are not clear; it does not reach those who need to know. The gravestone—conventionally a symbol for mournful remembrance primarily for the family and friends of the deceased—is used by Sethe for a different purpose: she obeys a custom that is ultimately meaningless for her own attitude toward her dead child. And it does not bring about any support from the black community, because it does not "explain" anything to them.[19]

Additionally, the stone that testifies to Sethe's emotions could also be, like the newspaper article mentioned later on, one of the few pieces of historical evidence that would have had the chance to survive until today—another symbolic facet of this scene. If these two pieces of documentation—the gravestone and the article—are taken together, we have two conflicting versions of the same event, one of which is so stripped of context that it basically loses the story that goes with it. In order to "write" a story that would be intelligible to us today, Sethe would have had to go through unbearable humiliation—the ten minutes that she endured were already "longer than life" (B 5). Only the barest necessity—"the one word that mattered"—can be passed on. This part of *Beloved* states the public aspect of remembrance—the public display of emotion that in Sethe's case does not state the obvious but attempts to convince the community that the violence they saw had nothing to do with hatred, but was rather an act of love.

The private aspects of remembrance—of the need to mourn, the need to forget as well as to remember, and the inability to keep painful memories from surfacing at unexpected moments—are dealt with in the following scene, which also brings the story line into the novel's present. Sethe's memory of Sweet Home is triggered by some insubstantial, seemingly unimportant sensory impression in the present situation:

> Then something. The plash of water, the sight of her shoes and stocking awry on the path where she had flung them; or Here Boy lapping in the puddle near her feet, and suddenly there was Sweet Home rolling, rolling, rolling out before her . . . in shameless beauty.
> (B 6)

The important part of the Sweet Home memory is its doubleness: if Sethe only remembered the terrible things, she could deal with those more easily. It shames her, though, to remember beauty, although this is of course a way to show how repression works. Margarete Mischerlich describes this process as "derealization" (cf. 13-14): if something is too painful to be looked at directly, it needs to be covered with a layer of something else—if only with the leaves of a tree hiding the bodies of the lynched men hanging from its branches. The selectiveness of memory thus becomes a burden for Sethe; instead of being reminded of the "beautiful" aspects of "Sweet Home," she would rather not think of the plantation at all. This, however, is not a choice: she cannot reduce her perceptions of the present moment—those potential triggers for memories—to such a minimum that they would not lead to reminiscences.

The first few pages of chapter 1 do not give a detailed and extensive introduction to characters and thematic background for the plot that is about to unfold. Rather, the novel starts by taking us right into the textual world, with only the barest outline of characters and setting. Accordingly, the omniscient third-person narrative voice that opens the text quickly retreats behind the perspectives of the individual characters, who then introduce some of the novel's central thematic and structural concerns. In this textual set-up, the central position of the characters is obvious; readers are inherently situated in a marginal position, privy to the developments in the textual world, but not instrumental in shaping it.

With the workings of memory as an organizing principle, present and past are no longer clearly distinguishable; memories of past events intrude upon the present moment, sometimes welcome, often unwelcome and painful. The characters' present sense of self is still distinctly shaped by their past experiences as slaves, because political emancipation was not accompanied by psychological liberation. As Sethe thinks later, "[f]reeing yourself was one thing; claiming ownership of that freed self was another" (B 95). From chapter 1 on, the novel follows the course that this process of freeing oneself demands of the characters. It will be the focus of the following sections to show how this thematic and conceptual concern intersects with and is supported by *Beloved's* structural and discursive organization to form an integrated whole in which "the form becomes the exact interpretation of the idea the story is meant to express" ("Site of Memory" 388).

Textual Displacements of the "Master('s) Narrative"

Morrison's conceptualization of a fictional world that is as independent as possible of the dominant culture's definitions works on several levels: one major aspect is the expropriation of the "right to define" from those who traditionally held it by thematically exposing the inherent inhumanity of both the ideology and its underlying epistemology that made slavery possible. I will show in detail in a later section how Morrison invalidates the slaveowner's perspective by positioning it within an alternative ethical framework. In a more indirect way, she extends this critique of the slaveholders and their ideology of white supremacy—personified especially in schoolteacher—by structurally disregarding the traditionally positivistic, chronological ordering principles of historiography, which are by implication related to schoolteacher's social-darwinistic categorizations.

Not only does the formal abandonment of chronological narration make the narrative structure correspond much more closely to the psychological developments of the characters; it also allows the author to relegate the Civil War—a period of time that is conventionally given a privileged position in historical accounts of 19th-century America—to the very margins of her fictionalized world. To have the actual plot start several years after the end of the war is, in this respect, a significant act of displacement. In addition, Morrison challenges conventional assumptions that associate the 1860s with political turmoil and change, by describing this period primarily as a time of stasis: a time in which Sethe's emotional paralysis is most intense, and nothing at all seems to be changing. The novel's temporal structure brackets the war in having Sethe's thoughts move back and forth between 1873 and 1855 or earlier, and thus skipping the "no-time" in-between. This almost complete omission of the Civil War gains additional relevance because readers are likely to know that it took place between the two key dates of the novel. Part of its significance thus lies in its not being mentioned.[20]

In contrast to her treatment of the Civil War, Morrison's dedication of the novel to "Sixty million or more" very pointedly leads the readers' attention to the Middle Passage, and to the Africans who did not survive the transportation from Africa to the Americas. Sethe's individual struggle is therefore not embedded in a framework of liberation—as a privileging of the Civil War would have implied—but in a framework that still links even the freed African Americans' situation with the historical beginnings of their enslavement.[21] Political and material changes—the end of the war and the emancipation of the slaves—have not yet superceded the old order of slavery, and the term "Reconstruction" takes on a much more complex meaning. *Beloved* suggests that only through a renewed practice of selection and a radical restructuring of what are conventionally considered "logical" ordering principles of historical information does it become possible to approximate the silenced world view of the former slaves.

Another important displacement of the white man's script—an instance in which textual and extratextual concerns intersect—is Morrison's treatment of the one historically verifiable event on which *Beloved* is based. The killing of the child, the unfathomable event around which the novel circles, is only accessible to us in a mediated way; it is never directly described in the 1873-present of the text. In a sense Morrison is protecting her characters and the narrator from having to recreate the event in language; in an interview, she comments:

> It seemed important to me that the action in *Beloved*—the fact of infanticide—be immediately known, but deferred, unseen. . . . I thought that the act itself had to be not only buried but also understated, because if the language was going to compete with the violence itself it would be obscene or pornographic. (Schappell 110-11)

However, we are confronted with one textual representation of it, and significantly, Morrison gives us schoolteacher's 1855 version. Only the person who caused Sethe's violent reaction is at all capable of describing it. It is immediately obvious in this description, though, that the white man's fundamental failure to recognize Sethe's humanity has to result in an incredibly distorted account of her life and—by implication—black life in general.

Schoolteacher's description evokes other manifestations of white-authored "texts" that the novel mentions, but doesn't directly represent. These written or printed texts are nevertheless talked and thought about; they are relevant because they have consequences for people's lives. One that is directly connected with schoolteacher and the time when Sweet Home finally became unbearable for Sethe is a list of "slave characteristics" that he had his nephews assemble. The second is Baby Suggs's bill of sale, in which she is defined as property and identified as "Jenny Whitlow." Finally, a newspaper article about Sethe's act of resistance gains particular relevance when Paul D is confronted with it by Stamp Paid. What connects these three texts is their explicit intention to establish slave identities. These literal definitions of who African Americans are supposed to be in the ideological, political and economic system of slavery symbolically represent what the "free" black community has to renounce.

Paul D's reaction to the newspaper clipping pointedly expresses his well-founded suspicion about white interpretations of black behavior. Unable to read, he nevertheless understands its implied politics: "[W]hatever it was those black scratches said, . . . there was no way in hell a black face could appear in a newspaper if the story was about something anybody wanted to hear" (B 155). Paul D's evaluation appears especially astute because it immediately follows schoolteacher's blatantly racist account of the killing (cf. B 148-151). Although we never get to know the exact wording of the clipping, the textual organization suggests a connection between the two scenes. They are part of Morrison's critique of any belief in a simple referentiality of language, and a forceful reminder that written records, the staple of historical inquiry, are never objective accounts of "how it really was," but are always in some way mediated.

This critique of representation links Beloved with Dessa Rose and Nehemiah's miserable failure to interview the imprisoned Dessa. In Beloved, it is the schoolteacher who makes the slaves objects of study. In defining Sethe as partly human and partly animal, he places his racist conceptions of blacks within a scientific framework; this "proof" then lets him justify his inhumane treatment without any moral scruples. How little this "knowledge" has to do with the reality of Sethe's life, however, is revealed in his account of Sethe's capture. Both the "scholar" and the schoolteacher, then, are representatives of an oppressive system, whose claims to superiority and dominance are based on scientific racism. Kate Cummings explicitly stresses the intersection of ideology and education when she elaborates that

Schoolteacher's actions are undeniably repellent, but none have the impact of his obsessional studies which underwrite and thus legitimize the slave economy with the pseudo-science of race. . . . [He is] intent on codifying the alterity of Blackness. . . . [T]here's a perfect marriage here between the pedagogue's discourse on knowledge and the material requirements of slavery. By "raising" the black body into metaphor, that is, schoolteacher has made it signify, strategically, according to the needs of the slave regime. (563)

Nehemiah and schoolteacher are particularly dangerous because within their roles as "experts" and "educators," they are expected to pass their knowledge on to the generations to come and thus to contribute even more effectively to the stabilization and perpetuation of the system.

One significant difference between the textual treatment of white racist ideology in *Dessa Rose* and *Beloved* is that Morrison deliberately refrains from repeating the slaveholders' dehumanizing attitudes. Not even the intention to show their unacceptability is reason enough to grant them the discursive space to be presented and thus in some ways re-enacted. This deliberate act of displacement is one prominent example of Morrison's careful approach to language and its power to create realities.

Closely connected with this textual decentering of the master('s) narrative is a shift in emphasis and attitude toward a silenced part of the African American historical experience and possible—bearable—ways of representing it. Morrison has mentioned "awe" and "reverence" as two important components of her writing[22]—and this authorial modesty and reticence is most noticeable in how she approaches the Middle Passage. The 20th-century writer does not claim the ability to comprehend fully what happened, and instead cautiously approaches the enormity of the event.[23] The references we get are characterized by an intense sense of loss: Sethe can no longer remember her mother's African language, and Beloved speaks a fragmented language that only partially makes sense to those who hear her. Especially through Beloved's speaking about the Middle Passage in cryptic images, the task of "remaking" that experience—imagining and telling it— falls largely to the reader.

Part of this narrative decision is surely an authorial strategy to create a sense of displacement in the readers when Beloved finally starts recounting her experiences. Acording to Wyatt, "[their] confusion . . . imitates the disorientation of the Africans who where thrown into the slave ships without explanation" (480).[24] Morrison herself has used a similar formulation in her description of the novel's first pages; the sense of displacement that Wyatt identifies specifically for the Beloved-passages is thus deliberately evoked as part of an overarching authorial strategy ("Unspeakable Things Unspoken" 32-33). In addition, however, Morrison's reticence might also be an expression of authorial respect for the enormity of the task to put the atrocities of the Middle Passage into language.

In this light, it is an ingenious move to equate the experiences of death and the Middle Passage through the mind of a pre-verbal child—and then use language to express all three components, because language is ultimately the only means to re-create these experiences for us. Both death and the Middle Passage, Morrison implies, escape symbolic representation; and the 20th-century author deliberately refrains from assuming the authority to imaginatively recreate something that has literally been beyond expression—"unspeakable"—for so long. This is certainly an unusual posture for a creative writer, but it also underscores Morrison's understanding of the potential of language both to create a historical "reality" and to distort it.

Morrison's strategy of allusions and ambiguous references is a way of raising the Middle Passage as an important precondition of African identity in America without having to go all the way and "say it all." There are several African characters in the text: especially important are Sethe's mother and Sixo, who demonstrate an integrity of spirit that becomes a model for the American-born blacks and a source of support and strength for their own attempts to fight dehumanization. Thus, the image of Africa that pervades the text is one of resistance: Sixo, rejecting any form of "assimilation," dies fighting, defying his tormentors by laughing into their faces.[25] Sethe's mother, unable to care for her daughter, has important information passed on to Sethe through Nan before she gets hanged, probably also for some act of defiance. The African "brother" and mother thus become important figures of identification in both Paul D's and Sethe's developments. After surviving the ordeals of the Middle Passage, they continued to resist the conditions imposed on them. Looked at in conjunction, the Civil War and the Middle Passage stand for fundamentally different approaches to historical inquiry; as metaphorical shorthands, they come to represent different frames of reference for the development of the narrative. Morrison's deliberate displacement of the former and foregrounding of the latter emphasizes her concern with the explicit and implicit influences that the conceptual context of an inquiry has on the questions that can be asked and the answers that can be imagined.

Instead of directly describing the events leading up to Sethe's escape, the flight itself with Denver's birth, and the death of Denver's older sister shortly afterwards, Morrison removes the narrative from what would have been the central focus of a 19th-century slave narrative or an earlier 20th-century historical narrative. With 1873 as the novel's narrative present, Sethe is—in contrast to Dessa—no longer threatened by recapture. This lack of immediate danger, however, makes the long-term effects of enslavement still more evident, as Dessa's initial mistaken idea of freedom—that "if there was rest for the body there must be peace for the heart" (*DR* 43)—proves even more painfully wrong for Sethe. What is necessary in representing the experience of enslavement is, Morrison's text suggests, a double vision that recognizes not only the importance of physical liberation, but also the difficult processes of psychological recovery.[26]

To shift the narrative focus away from the killing of the child—the one sensational event that most of the existing information on the historical Margaret Garner dwells on—allows Morrison to decenter the attention commonly given to historical "facts," as well as to avoid a reduction of her main character's complexity to being explainable solely by this one crucial moment in her life. Additionally, the novel's temporal set-up reflects the thematic emphasis on the characters' inner lives, by making it necessary to present past experiences as they are seen, recreated and interpreted by those characters for themselves and each other. Obviously, the "facts" of Sethe's and Paul D's pasts can never simply be uncovered and mimetically represented, but are always visual or verbal (re)constructions that depend on the very moments in which they are created. Nevertheless, they are "real" for those engaged in "memory work."[27]

One necessary precondition for this memory work to be successful is the presence of supportive, sympathetic partners in struggle. Whereas Sethe's silent and solitary "work of beating back the past" (*B* 73) results in an emotional paralysis that lasts for over eighteen years, the attempts to share her story with somebody and thus break the silence ultimately assume a healing function. Her isolation—partly brought about by the insistence that she could do it alone—is brought to an end at the very moment in which she can experience herself as a subject-in-relation, because Paul D's gives her the sense of support that she had to do without for too long. In contrast to Dessa, whose talking during the imprisonment is more of a soliloquy despite Nehemiah's presence, Sethe's ability to speak at all crucially depends on a situation in which dialogue is at least wanted and perceivable, even if it cannot always be realized. Only in interaction can she imagine to confront the repressed horrors of her past, and try to express the unspeakable: "Her story was bearable because it was his as well—to tell, to refine and tell again" (B 99). Although this assumption requires modifications later on in the text, at this point in Sethe's life it provides desperately needed reassurance. What is significant is the connection between the need to remember and the need to speak with others, and this is—already at the very beginning of the novel— suggested by different characters, although none is initially able to put this insight into practice. To be able to remember is thus shown to be inextricably linked with the ability to communicate with others and to see oneself as a subject-in-relation.

It thus becomes clear early in the text that none of the characters—Sethe least of all, despite her assertions to the contrary—can bear the burden of their pasts alone. Morrison explores the fundamentally relational nature of each individual's (re)construction of identity by focusing not only on Sethe, but also on Paul D's, Denver's, and Beloved's personal developments: each character's personal story intersects with everybody else's, and creates subtexts that are not as easily noticeable as the three-part surface structure, but nevertheless significant for the effect of the novel as a whole. It is part of Morrison's critique of the humanistic concept of individualism: Sethe is always a subject-in-relation, even in that most solitary of moments when she "[c]ollected every bit of life she had made, all the parts of her that were precious and fine and beautiful, and carried, pushed, dragged them through the veil, out, away, over there where no one could hurt them" (B 163). This makes it necessary to broaden her personal development to include her "significant others"—Paul D, Denver, and Beloved, and (indirectly) Baby Suggs—as well as the community, represented especially through Stamp Paid and Ella.

The relational attitude proposed by the text is further enriched by the notion of "rememory" that is at the center of Sethe's struggle and that she defines as follows:

> Someday you be walking down the road and you hear something or see something going on. So clear. And you think it's you thinking it up. A thought picture. But no. It's when you bump into a rememory that belongs to someone else. (B 36)

As Ashraf Rushdy explains, [t]he term "rememory" ... signif[ies] a magical anamnesis available to one not involved in the originary act." Rememory is thus "never only personal but always interpersonal" ("Rememory" 304). Such a perception of memory as a concrete entity can—depending on the nature of the memory itself—be either positive, because it allows for a knowing of others' experiences without the mediation of language, or extremely threatening, because uninvolved others might experience violence that was not originally directed against them. The latter is the case with Denver: a large part of Sethe's energy goes into the constant protection of her daughter from the horrors of Sweet Home, because ultimately, in Beloved's words, "all of it is now" (B 210). The following section will examine how the unavoidable engagement with the past intersects with the characters' needs to build functional relationships in the present—and how these intersections are reflected in various textual substructures.

Surface Structures

As part of the textual emphasis on the characters' states of mind, a strictly linear, chronological plot is not possible if the narrative structure is to reflect the episte-mological orientation of the text. On the one hand, characters deliberately try to find ways of integrating selective aspects of their slave experience into their present lives; on the other hand, they are also preoccupied with the need to "disremember" those aspects that are too painful to dwell on. Even seemingly forgotten things, however, force their way back to the surface of consciousness and seriously impede daily living.[28] Accordingly, *Beloved* shows a combination of linear and circular narrative patterns: the actual plot—the narrative present—moves through a period of approximately nine months, from late summer 1873 to the spring of 1874. This period of time is framed by two circular movements: the first is Paul D's coming, leaving, and coming back again at the very end, the second is Beloved's appearance and disappearance. Additionally—in correspondence to Sethe's notion that "nothing ever dies" (B 36)—the boundaries between the 1873-present and the past blur constantly through the surfacing of welcome as well as unwelcome memories, which interrupt and further complicate the narrative progression. Consequently, the narrative unfolds with gaps, false starts and repetitions, just as Sethe's attempt to tell Paul D about what happened sends her spinning round the room without her ever being able to get to the point. The varying stages in Sethe's and Paul D's processes of healing, their struggles with painful memories, and their reluctant engagement with those memories determine the pace and the order in which readers learn about their past lives.

As outlined above, Morrison's novel is—like *Jubilee* and *Dessa Rose*—divided into three major parts that are formally set apart from each other and numbered.

Rather than separating historical eras or different narrative perspectives, however, *Beloved*'s division suggests different stages of the characters' confrontations with their pasts that every one of them, but especially Sethe as the novel's main character, has to go through. The three parts' opening sentences create a sense of coherence and parallel structure: "124 was spiteful" (*B* 3), "124 was loud" (*B* 169), and finally "124 was quiet" (*B* 239). These opening sentences also suggest that from the very start, characters are confronted with an active presence— symbolically manifested in Morrison's attributing of emotions and agency to the house—that they can only partly control, but that in turn sets a pattern for them to follow. Whatever they have to confront in the course of the narrative is both larger than they are and yet intimately connected with them: it inhabits the very space they live in.

It has been noted that despite their parallel introductory sentences, the individual parts of *Beloved's* three-part structure appear unbalanced because they vary so much in length.[29] I suggest that part I is necessarily longer because two distinct approaches to the problems of remembrance are outlined here: two different periods of Sethe's former life—personified by Paul D and Beloved— compete with each other for her attention. Initially, Paul D is a lot more important for Sethe: he suddenly and unexpectedly appears on her porch as a material "rememory" of Sweet Home, and his presence triggers both positive and negative memories of the period of time when they both lived on Mr. Garner's Kentucky plantation. In addition—because he also wants to find out what has happened to her since they lost track of each other—he asks Sethe to unlock those parts of her mind in which she buried the time after Sweet Home. At this point in the novel, Sethe does not yet see any connection between the disappearance of the baby's ghost and the appearance of Beloved. The strange young woman is, almost until the end of part I, only an indirect motivating force for Sethe's memory work, mainly through her relationship with Denver. Her presence, connected with Denver's almost immediate certainty that Beloved is her sister returned, signals and anticipates her later significance; as a symbol for Sethe's repressed memories, she is only fully returned when Sethe sees in her the dead daughter come back. However, this does not keep her from exerting influence over Sethe's life and the lives of those around her long before this moment of recognition.

In part I, Sethe gradually constructs new fictions of what it is exactly that she needs to know and remember. Trusting Paul D and relying on his help, she half-consciously avoids reflecting too much on Beloved's identity, so that she does not run the risk of jeopardizing the possibility of a new partnership:

[T]he suspicion that the girl's touch was also exactly like the baby's ghost dissipated. It was only a tiny disturbance anyway—not strong enough to divert her from the ambition welling in her now: she wanted Paul D. No matter what he told and knew, she wanted him in her life. (B 99)

From the beginning of part II, when Sethe finally recognizes Beloved as her daughter and decides to focus all attention on her, Beloved gradually assumes total control. Sethe is forced to confront all those parts of herself and aspects of her past that she had not only forgotten, but repressed: their surfacing—and Beloved's gaining of power over her—is out of her command and becomes so intense that it threatens to overwhelm her completely. During this phase, which is represented in part II (chs. 20-23, pp. 200-217), Sethe does not even have Paul D's support, who at the same time has to confront his own repressed memories. Only in part III is it finally possible for Sethe—with the help of Denver, the women in the community, and Paul D—to escape Beloved's grip, and to become re-initiated into the communal structure in an elaborate rebirth ritual. As the shortest section of the novel, this last one only hints at the possibility of a successful recuperation. It does not complete the process of Sethe's healing—or Paul D's, for that matter—but leaves the next steps to the readers' imagination.

Hidden Patterns

One immediately apparent function of the novel's organization into chapters and parts is to set the pace in which the narrative progresses. Especially the chapter breaks graphically mark shifts in point of view between different characters, and thus provide some orientation in what could otherwise be perceived as a confusing narrative flow. A closer look reveals that the twenty-eight (unnumbered) chapters additionally show hidden patterns—or rhythms—of character development that constantly intersect with and influence the surface structure and strongly support the thematic emphasis that no character can be viewed in isolation, stripped of her or his social context.

Underneath the irregular grouping of chapters into parts, the novel shows at least two sub-divisions into sections of equal length. This symmetry goes largely unnoticed because nothing in the formal presentation of the novel explicitly draws attention to it. Its startling regularity, however, suggests that it is not accidental, and therefore warrants a more detailed examination. It is my suggestion that

Sethe's and Paul D's development follow different paces and rhythmic patterns that make it difficult for them to really make their relationship work before the central confrontation with Beloved has taken place; these patterns exist simultaneously and interdependently within the text, and are inscribed within its formal structure. They are influenced, but not directly caused, by Beloved's presence.

Although it has been remarked that Paul D's coming, going, and coming back again parallels the explicit three-part structure of the text (Finney 22), the surface division is not primarily motivated by Paul D's behavior, but by the way in which Beloved's presence functions at different stages. There is a second, two-part structure that is more directly associated with Paul D and with the psychosocial dynamics that characterize his deepening relationship with Sethe. Paul D's personal narrative reaches its first climax in chapters 13 and 14 (B 125-134)—the exact mid-point of the novel, when Sethe asks him to come back into the house. At this moment, things seem to settle into a possibly permanent arrangement—an arrangement that is, however, broken up immediately afterwards. It is at the very end, in chapter 27 (B 263-273), that Paul D gets a second chance to imagine a lasting relationship with Sethe, but not before he, too, has worked through his traumatic memories and has reconsidered his self-image.

Sethe's development, in comparison, follows a different route that divides the text into three sections of nine chapters each. In chapter 9, she is ready to imagine a partnership with Paul D: "She wanted Paul D. . . . Now it was figured" (B 99). Accustomed to deciding things on her own, however, she does not include Paul D in making this particular decision; she does not even tell him about it. When she later—in chapter 18 (B 159-165)—gets to the point of wanting to explain herself to him, and describe the situation that led her to kill her little daughter, he is in turn not able to "hear" her adequately. He can no longer be the supportive listener that he promised to be earlier; instead of being able to provide the safe space that Sethe needs especially with this most painful of memories, he becomes judgmental and thus precludes understanding: "'You got two feet, Sethe, not four,' he said, and right then a forest sprang up between them; trackless and quiet" (B 165).

Sethe's and Paul D's psychosocial processes of reflection and engagement with themselves and each other are, in part I, so fundamentally out of sync that the apparent moment of repose in chapter 14 (B 133-134) has to prove deceptive. What literally stands between them—in chapters 15 to 18 (B 135-165)—are rememories of the 1855-scene, of the very moment in Sethe's past that both of them have so far been trying to avoid at all costs. This thematic and formal rupture in the narrative is yet another manifestation of the great care with which Morrison constructed this text and synchronized thematic emphases with stylistic and structural considerations.

Conflicting Rhythms: Sethe and Paul D

The different phases of Sethe's and Paul D's relationship often get eclipsed by the attention that is given to Sethe's intense encounter with Beloved in part II. Although part I as a whole delineates the joys and the pains of getting reacquainted, some individual chapters are particularly relevant to illustrate the different psychological rhythms that prevent and postpone Sethe's and Paul D's coming-together until the very end. These are chapters 9 and 18 for Sethe, and chapter 14 for Paul D. In addition, chapters 15 to 18, which circle around the infanticide and thus represent the "return of the repressed," have a significant impact on Sethe's and Paul D's interaction in part I, and function as preparation for part II of the novel.

When Sethe first sees Paul D sitting on her porch at the end of chapter 1, he appears to her as part of a rememory of Sweet Home: "As if to punish her further for her terrible memory, sitting on the porch not forty feet away was Paul D, the last of the Sweet Home men" (B 6). But this spontaneous reaction quickly gives way to a new feeling of safety and support, and after only a short while, Sethe asks herself "Would there be a little space . . . [to t]rust things and remember things because the last of the Sweet Home men was there to catch her if she sank?" (B 18). It is not Paul D's presence alone but his personality that makes Sethe yearn for an end to her stoic self-sufficiency and a chance to share her thoughts: "[H]e had become the kind of man who could walk into a house and cry. . . . There was something blessed in his manner" (B 17). What is significant at this early stage is that both draw great hope and new strength from being together. Although Paul D initially does not expect to be able to stay for long, he "could not account for the pleasure in his surprise at seeing Halle's wife alive" (B 41).

As joyful as this first encounter appears to both Sethe and Paul D, however, it also already anticipates later difficulties. With his good intentions to help Sethe and to become an agent in her development, Paul D creates a role for himself as potential "head of household" that is problematic because it overlooks his own unresolved conflicts. Although he is clearly sincere when he asks her to "[g]o as far inside as [she] need[s] to" (B 46), he does not yet see the need to do the same for himself. Paul D's behavior is motivated by conflicting impulses: he is convinced that he can help others solve their problems without going through similar confrontations himself. He does not realize that his reactions toward Sethe remain inadequate until he follows his own advice to "go inside" while in turn trusting others to hold him. Consequently, the repressed parts of his own past that he keeps locked in the "tobacco tin" in his chest will eventually put as much strain on his ability to interact with Sethe as hers.

Paul D's initial inability to abstract from his own experiences and recognize the experiences of an/other person as equally significant and valid shows in his willingness to accept Sethe's point of view as long as it conforms more or less to his own, but as soon as she talks to him from a specifically female perspective, it beomes too hard for him to follow. This is especially obvious when Sethe tells him what happened to her before she left Sweet Home:

> "After I left you, those boys came in there and took my milk. . . . Schoolteacher made one [of the boys] open my back, and when it closed, it made a tree. It grows there still."
> "They used cowhide on you?"
> "And they took my milk."
> "They beat you and you was pregnant?"
> "And they took my milk!" (B 17)

Paul D is shocked to hear that the pregnant Sethe was flogged; he does not recognize, however, how hurt and humiliated she felt when the white boys took the milk that her baby girl needed so desperately. Sethe's attitude regarding her role as a mother again and again leads to misunderstandings, until Paul D later incautiously goes one step too far and compares her behavior to that of an animal—and thus inadvertently evokes schoolteacher's earlier categorization with his remark that she "got two feet, . . . not four" (B 165). To have both the black and the white man define the black woman in those terms shows that her struggle to find a concept of identity is so different from the men's that it becomes nearly incomprehensible to them.

Despite these signs of impending conflict, Sethe is—in chapter 9—the first of the two to be able to make a decision in favor of a relationship, when she goes to the Clearing to ask for Baby Suggs's advice. After being finally able to accept the loss of her husband, she feels free to turn her attention to Paul D:

> No matter what he told and knew, she wanted him in her life. More than commemorating Halle, that is what she had come to the Clearing

to figure out, and now it *was* figured. Trust and rememory, yes. . . . Her story was bearable because it was his as well." (*B* 99)

At this point, however, Paul D is not yet ready. His own repressed memories—especially about the chain gang in Alfred, Georgia—now emerge forcefully and without prior announcement in chapter 10. Paul D thus is prevented for some time from becoming involved with Sethe because his own rememories claim primary attention.

As an embodiment of the past, it is Beloved who at this moment in Paul D's development demands his full attention. She forces him to confront his own repressed experiences when "she move[s] him" (*B* 114) out of the house and eventually makes him sleep with her in the cold house. Her comment that she regards physical love as separate from spiritual love—"I don't love nobody but her. . . . I want you to touch me on the inside part." (*B* 116)—and their subsequent lovemaking sets forces Paul D's "tobacco tin" open: "She moved closer with a footfall he didn't hear and he didn't hear the whisper that the flakes of rust made either as they fell away from the seams of his tobacco tin. So when the lid gave he didn't know it" (*B* 117). Beloved's demand that he "touch . . . [her] on the inside part" (*B* 116) therefore has a psychological, metaphorical meaning as well as a sexual, literal one. As a part of Paul D, she gives him the chance to confront and accept the repressed feelings and memories which he had locked away for too long: "When he reached the inside part he was saying, 'Red heart. Red heart,' over and over again" (*B* 117).

What is also significant here is the association of sex with power: For Paul D, to have a child with Sethe is to assure himself of a claim he believes to be having; it was "a way to hold on to her" (*B* 128). The irritation that Beloved produces by forcing Paul D into a sexual relationship—exerting power over him that he cannot control—reveals a strong feature of Paul D's self-definition at this moment in time, as part of his sense of manhood lies in having control of a situation. In relation to a woman, this desire for control is expressed through sex. What Paul D has to learn, between chapters 14 and 27, is that his relationship with Sethe has to be based on emotional understanding rather than physical union. In chapters 13 and 14, his personal needs are so much in the foreground that he is unable to recognize Sethe's hesitation when she brings him back into the house. Her offer to take him in quenches the doubts that he might otherwise have had, despite the reluctance he feels coming from Beloved. Significantly, they don't talk, but go to bed together—a deceptive union that hides their basic disagreements.

In chapters 13 and 14, at the formal mid-point of the novel, the text moves toward a moment of repose for Paul D: after picking Sethe up at Sawyer's restaurant and accompanying her home, he "felt as though he had been plucked from the face of a cliff and put down on sure ground" (*B* 131) when she asks him to move back into the house. This very moment in the text thus looks as if it implied a resolution. The tableau we are presented with shows a semblance of "family" that might have the potential to work out: Sethe and Paul D are in the upstairs bedroom—"united" (*B* 134)—whereas Denver and Beloved sit in the downstairs kitchen. Sethe has apparently distanced herself from the "children" in favor of a male partner.

How fragile this attempt to set up a kind of nuclear family is, however, becomes obvious through Sethe's thoughts on the matter. At this point in time she has already moved away from the vision of a life together with Paul D that she had in chapter 9 after going to the Clearing to mourn Halle. In chapter 13, her mood has already changed: Paul D's question whether she wants another baby triggers thoughts and emotions that make Sethe realize some of his intentions— "What did he want her pregnant for? To hold on to her?" (*B* 132)—and to reconsider her own situation: "[S]he had all the children she needed. If her boys came back one day, and Denver and Beloved stayed on—well, it would be the way it was supposed to be, no?" (*B* 132). Paul D does not notice Sethe's doubts; the only disapproval he senses comes from Beloved: "The threads of malice creeping toward him from Beloved's side of the table were held harmless in the warmth of Sethe's smile" (*B* 131).

Chapter 14 describes Beloved's fear of falling apart as a response to Sethe's turning to Paul D, but the chapter's concluding reference to falling snow suggests a temporary halt in events, as the scene in the house turns into an image that appears to freeze the characters in their respective positions: "The couple upstairs, united, didn't hear a sound, but below them, outside, all around 124 the snow went on and on and on. Piling itself. Burying itself. Higher. Deeper" (*B* 134). Besides anticipating the later scene in which Sethe locks herself and the girls into the snow-covered house, the snow suggests another unhealthy point of stasis. The threat to Beloved's existence that is expressed in her fear of completely falling apart signals a disturbing turn of events, although at this very moment she finds temporary solace in Denver's presence, and Sethe and Paul D do not hear her crying.[30]

The following sections in the novel forcefully confirm the impossibility of a "happy ending" at this moment in the text. As I will outline in more detail below, the repressed past erupts in chapters 15 to 18 and forces the characters to respond. Despite his earlier offer to support Sethe's "going inside," Paul D now has to realize that this involves more than he can bear. Instead of bringing them together, Sethe's attempt to explain herself to Paul D in chapter 18 thus results not in a joint effort of finding the words to say it, but in his leave-taking. This in turn initiates Sethe's process of concentrating more and more on Beloved, which in chapters 20 to 23 turns into a severe threat to her life.

The second half of *Beloved* is therefore characterized by two separate developments. Before Sethe and Paul D can finally come together in a new, tender beginning, both have to go through painful and dangerous processes of redefinition: Sethe needs to get away from a concept of self that makes her lose herself in her children's needs, and Paul D has to scrutinize his idea of true manhood, which has already been put to the test so often in the course of his life. When he returns at the very end, his earlier attitudes have been fundamentally changed. Deeply concerned about Sethe's well-being, and considerably further in his own processes of confrontation, Paul D is now able to assume a motherly, caring role. For the first time, he is genuinely able to react to Sethe in a way that privileges her immediate needs over his own; he thus redeems his earlier inattentiveness by "putting Sethe back together again" in a ritualized bathing. During his ruminations in the church basement, Paul D has given up on the urge to control Sethe and her body. His sense of manhood no longer lies in "owning" her, but in their joint effort to counter the dehumanizing treatment of the slave holders:

> Her tenderness about the neck jewelry—. . . [h]ow she never mentioned or looked at it, so he did not have to feel the shame of being collared like a beast. Only this woman Sethe could have left him his manhood like that. (*B* 273)

Paul D finally reaches a point that makes it possible for him to repudiate Garner's definition of black manhood and take on Sixo's, the African "brother's." Sixo, whose pride sprang from his power not to lose his identity even in the face of slavery, becomes Paul D's role model (cf. Krumholz, Ritual and Reconstruction" 23). Consequently, Sixo's respect for "his woman" points the way for Paul D's and Sethe's future relationship. At the final decisive moment, when Paul D is almost overwhelmed by Sethe's pain and his own conflicting emotions, he

> [s]uddenly . . . remembers Sixo trying to describe what he felt about the Thirty-Mile Woman. "She is a friend of my mind. She gather me, man. The pieces I am, she gather them and give them back to me in all the

right order. It's good, you know, when you got a woman who is a friend of your mind." (B 272-273)

And because Sethe is the woman who helped Paul D in a similar way by never really doubting his personal integrity, she will be able to give him enough space to be himself in the future. With the understanding of how much Sethe means to him, Paul D finally realizes that he, too, will have to make room for her and accept her personal experiences: "He wants to put his story *next* to hers" (B 273, emphasis added).

Chapters 15-18: Approaching the "Misery"

The abrupt turn from the final tableau of chapter 14 to the following chapter—Baby Suggs's memories of the 1855 feast and of schoolteacher's arrival—is one of the few temporal shifts into the past that are not directly triggered by anything said or thought immediately before. The four chapters that conclude part I (15 to 18) all deal with the unspeakable core of the novel, Sethe's killing of her baby daughter eighteen years earlier. The abruptness with which this rememory surfaces expresses some of the urgency behind the issue: Sethe still has not adequately dealt with it, but it refuses to be delayed any longer. The event of the killing finally demands immediate attention. It therefore inserts itself into the narrative flow without any more preparation than Beloved's beginning disintegration in chapter 14. And in addition to focusing on possible ways of approaching the repressed past, this set of chapters is also an extended act of contextualization. By including the thoughts and perspectives of many different people, the section describes the killing of the child as a communal responsibility, although Sethe was the one who actually did it. This anticipates the community's later responsibility to help free Sethe out of Beloved's deadly embrace.

There is a short circular plot in chapters 15-18 that initially transports us back into 1855 and then gradually returns to the site of chapter 14—to Sethe and Paul D in 1873. In chapter 15, we first get Baby Suggs's thoughts on the events that led up to the day of schoolteacher's arrival. Chapter 16 then focuses on the slave catchers' and schoolteacher's perspectives, which inherently refer to the text of the newspaper article that Paul D is confronted with by Stamp Paid in chapter 17. Paul D, in turn, shows the article to Sethe and makes her try to explain in chapter 18. This four-chapter intermission is thus again split in two: chapters 15 and 16 shift toward the 1855-present, whereas 17 and 18 are set in 1873. The connection is maintained, however, through Stamp Paid's newspaper article and his memory and love for Baby Suggs, as well as Paul D's memories of the young Sethe. The chapters can also be said to be linked by different manifestations of the master('s) narrative: Baby Suggs's bill of sale in the first chapter, the slave catcher's and schoolteacher's version of events in chapter 16, the newspaper report about Sethe that Stamp Paid gives to Paul D in chapter 17, and finally Sethe's confrontation with the article that neither she nor Paul D can read in chapter 18.

Baby Suggs's section is truly a voice from the past. Consequently, her narrative is not addressed to any of the living characters, but to herself in the form of a monologue. It seems that this passage could well be an expression of what she was preoccupied with when she finally took to her bed: she keeps coming back to the event that finally made her life unbearable, and scrutinizes her own role in what happened.

Baby Suggs rehearses in thought the time span between the celebration of Sethe's and the children's arrival and the arrival of schoolteacher shortly afterwards. Her decision to "do something with the fruit [that Stamp Paid had gathered] worthy of the man's labor and his love" (B 136) leads to the feast that makes the community angry because of its exuberance. They accuse Baby Suggs of undue pride—significantly the same accusation that Sethe will be met with later, although she behaves in exactly the opposite way: instead of reaching out to the community, Sethe retreats into 124 and does not even try to communicate. In their ambivalent reactions to Baby Suggs and the feast, the people of the community are here presented as partly responsible for the events that follow. So before Sethe's desperate act is even mentioned, it is contextualized in a way that takes some of the burden away from her. If the community hadn't reacted as they did, Sethe might not have been forced into the insoluble dilemma of having to decide between the metaphorical death of slavery and literal death. Had the community warned Sethe, the killing of the child might have been prevented.

But not only Sethe's act is contextualized in chapter 15. Baby Suggs's reminiscences about how she got to be "free" provide the necessary background for her joy when she is finally united with parts of her family. Her personal development from the slave "Jenny Whitlow" to the freed woman who is naming herself and extending this newly-won agency to the community traces her steps up to that fateful moment of schoolteacher's arrival. It describes her own process of freeing herself as a deliberate renunciation of a white-authored text that, because it is a bill-of-sale, attempts to fix her identity as property and commodity. Baby Suggs's public identity is defined by this piece of paper, and although she insists that her name is not Jenny Whitlow, even the benevolent Mr. Garner does not accept the alternative naming that shows her kinship relations and represents her own choice. Although the newspaper article that Stamp Paid shows to Paul D later is not a bill-of-sale, it functions similarly in its power to define Sethe according to standards that are not her own. In a way, the article is "selling" her to the readers—defining her in a way that probably has nothing to do with her actual situation.

The next chapter—chapter 16—is especially significant because it contains the only literal depiction of the killing of the child. The cold-blooded descriptions of the scene are given from the perspectives of the four white men who take part in the "hunt" for Sethe and her children, and they express the men's utter lack of understanding for what is happening in front of their eyes. Because they are not emotionally involved, these white men are the only people who can talk about the killing. In the course of this chapter, each of the four gets some space to express his point of view. The slave catcher speaks of Stamp as "the old nigger boy" (B 149); schoolteacher refers to Sethe as "the main one" (B 149) and, once again, compares her to an animal. Only the nephew has not quite learned schoolteacher's lessons: he is still able to compare Sethe's behavior with his own experience of being beaten. Nevertheless, he cannot imagine that her act is not only a reaction to one particular event in the past, but a future-oriented, desperate attempt to prevent her capture.[31] Finally, only the sheriff refers to Sethe, Baby Suggs and Stamp Paid as "people." But although this at least acknowledges their humanity, he still does not recognize them as individuals.

Cummings argues that the scene not only delineates the dehumanizing effects that the ideology of slavery has on the white men, but also forces these characters to confront their own responsibility for what happens in the shed:

> Although the onlookers would prefer to view everything as Sethe's doing, they are menaced by being made to see their own actions spectacularly repeated in hers. Self-recognition here coincides with the return of the Other's gaze. . . . Horrified, the white men recoil from their reflection; they "back out" of the barn and away from the Other's gaze, but not before recognizing their implication in the action or realizing that slavery constitutes the original violence, having always already operated systematically to denature black families and dismember black families. (565)

I doubt that their insights go that far: as long as they cannot even regard black people as human beings, there is no way for them to recognize Sethe's behavior as willful. It can only be interpreted as an instinctive response to previous mistreatment; as schoolteacher says, "you can't just mishandle creatures and expect success" (*B* 151). The slave catcher calls Stamp Paid and Baby Suggs "crazy" (cf. *B* 149); schoolteacher says of Sethe that she has "gone wild" (*B* 149). These are again strategies to renounce responsibility and to maintain one's own sense of identity in contradistinction to the deviant "other," as Hayden White explains:

> The notion of "wildness" . . . belongs to a set of culturally self-authenticating devices which includes, among many others, the ideas of "madness" and "heresy" as well. These terms are used not merely to designate a specific condition or state of being but also to confirm the value of their dialectical antitheses. . . . Thus, they do not so much refer to a specific thing, place, or condition as dictate a particular attitude governing a relationship between a lived reality and some area of problematical existence that cannot be accommodated easily to conventional conceptions of the normal or familiar. ("Forms of Wildness" 151)

According to Cummings, "[n]one of the white men recognize Sethe's murder as a maternal gesture, . . . Instead, they see an unnatural mother severing her child's head" (564). Within the discourse of slavery, the infanticide can only be grasped as subhuman instincts unleashed; as the sheriff phrases it: "All testimony to the results of a little so-called freedom imposed on people who needed every care and guidance into the world to keep them from the cannibal life they preferred" (*B* 151). The mute accusation contained in the eyes of the dead and injured is—if at all—only recognizable for the white men on an irrational/subconscious level. I do not agree with Cummings's assertion that "[s]elf-recognition here coincides with the return of the Other's gaze" (564). The men's unease seems caused not so much by the acknowledgement of their complicity, but by the unexpectedness of Sethe's vehemence. On the whole, her deed is fitted into the ideological frame of schoolteacher's earlier categorizations; this makes it impossible for the men to recognize it as an act that fundamentally destabilizes their very thought system. This lack of understanding stands in strong contrast to the perspective otherwise held in the novel that Sethe's act is one forceful expression of her claim to be responsible for her children's fates, and thus of her re-definition of black motherhood as a space for agency.

What Cummings describes as a threat to the white men's identity rather appears to be the one textual moment in which the characters who serve as focalizers are not included in the effort to achieve self-understanding. Instead, the scene demonstrates their ignorance and their inability to recognize any personal wrongdoings—not, however, without exposing this ignorance to the readers. The threat to the slave catcher's and the slave holder's worldview is obviously there; it is even more effective because the white men are not able to understand it as such.[32]

In chapter 17, Stamp Paid confronts Paul D with an old newspaper article about Sethe. The confidence with which Paul D rejects the description of Sethe in this article and instead trusts his own memories of her is—especially after the points of view presented in the preceding chapter—another important step away from imposed white definitions. However, his assertion that "I didn't just make her acquaintance a few months ago. I been knowing her a long time" (B 158) is not just an isolated expression of self-confidence. It is rather part of the alternative value system that Morrison sets up in order to make it possible for the former slaves to gradually reclaim their freed selves.

One of the most noticeable aspects of the conversation between Stamp Paid and Paul in chapter 17 is the discrepancy between what is thought and what is said by the two men. A combination of the dynamics of the conversation, Paul D's insights into the politics of newspaper articles on black people, and his conviction that the woman depicted in the clipping cannot possibly be Sethe stops Stamp Paid from saying what he came to say:

> He was going to tell him . . . why he and Baby had both missed it. And about the party too, because that explained why nobody ran on ahead; . . . Nobody warned them. . . . He was going to tell him that, but Paul D was laughing, saying, "Uh uh. No way. A little semblance round the forehead maybe, but this ain't her mouth." (B 157)

Instead, he hides behind the white voice of the newspaper, "slowly read[ing] out the words" (B 158) and thus forfeiting the opportunity to really communicate with Paul D. Consequently, Paul D does not have a chance to learn about the difficult role the community played when schoolteacher arrived. The particular context of Sethe's act remains hidden for him. And in his own way, he is right with his evaluation of the article: the woman in the picture is really not the Sethe he knows. It is the image of a Sethe who is filtered through the distortions of the white gaze.

When the narrative finally returns to Sethe and Paul D in chapter 18, the moment of repose represented in the motionless, static image at the end of chapter 14 gets replaced with a highly dynamic, almost compulsive movement: Sethe is "spinning. Round and round the room" (B 160). It is Paul D's present need to understand what happened which prompts her to dig into something that she thought she had finally left behind. With neither him nor her able to bear the consequences of this telling, however, this attempt to find the right "word-shapes" (B 99) ends in disruption and more losses: Sethe loses the man who promised to hold her, and Paul D loses the woman he thought he knew. Both reactions are disappointing for the other person and point to their individual needs to work through their own traumas first, before they can genuinely "hear" the other('s) story.

When Sethe is finally trying to explain to Paul D what happened, the potential for a dialogic exchange is clearly given, first through their smiles, then through their agreement over the connection between freedom and love/desire. It is the definition of love that becomes the problematic issue here. Paul D comes to the conclusion that "more important than what Sethe had done was what she claimed" (B 164). Sethe claimed ownership over her children and responsibility for their fates. On the one hand, as has been repeatedly stated, this is significant in the context of slavery in which an enslaved woman did not "own" herself, let alone her children. On the other hand, it also implicitly relates to Paul D's own secret desires of claiming "ownership" over Sethe by having a child with her. This fundamentally raises the question if love needs to be conceptualized differently—in non-proprietary, non-hierarchical ways—in order to genuinely move out of the behavioral patterns central to slavery.

In conclusion, the four chapters 15 to 18 present different versions of the killing of the child, by all the main characters involved in the scene. Sethe's act is thus placed in a context in which the communal support system fails: Baby Suggs and Stamp Paid feel guilty about not recognizing the signals and about ultimately not caring enough, and the community is also shown to share some of the responsibility. As Lori Askeland says, the community has not been able to internalize Baby Suggs's teaching, to really take it to heart:

> Th[e] refusal of her [Baby Suggs's] love marks Ella and the community as being unable to claim the freedom to love, just as Sethe's marks her as one who has overstepped. Everything depends on knowing how much. . . . [T]he spiritual unity of the town seems to have rested on Baby Suggs's shoulders, and the community refused to go where she was leading them. (798-99)

Baby Suggs's later withdrawal into the keeping room thus becomes understandable as a sign of utter frustration: not only has she failed to protect her daughter and grandchild, but she realizes that all attempts of self-definition are futile as long as even this fragile private space can be invaded from outside: "They came in my yard," (*B* 179) she despairs.[33] The very moment she lets down her guard the illusion of self-determinacy and control is brutally destroyed. She no longer has the strength to hold the community accountable for not reacting; similarly, it takes Stamp Paid years to acknowledge his own inability to protect Sethe.

As part of this four-chapter section, Morrison has Paul D anticipate a relational model of human connection that is related to Baby Suggs's alternative ethics. At this very moment in their respective developments, however, neither he nor Sethe are ready for it; they continue to relate to each other in ways that are still conditioned by slavery. During his confrontation with Sethe, Paul D's thoughts show that he cannot yet accept the changes that "freedom" has brought when he thinks that "[t]his here Sethe was new" (*B* 164). This seemingly contradicts his confidence that he has "been knowing her a long time" (*B* 158)—the sentiment that made him defend Sethe in the encounter with Stamp Paid a little earlier. So for the time being, Paul D is holding on to an image of Sethe that no longer exists, partly because this gives him a sense of stability and acceptance—"Only this woman Sethe could have left him his manhood like that" (*B* 273)—and partly because what he learns about her seems too painful to bear.

Sethe, in turn, has to go through the process of trying to make Paul D understand, before she can work things out with Beloved. In the course of her development, she is going increasingly deeper into herself/her self. Her initial impression that simply being with Paul will help her out of her stasis implies that the initiative comes from his side, an assumption that also corresponds to expectations of "typical" male behavior. In chapter 18, then, his "verbal actions" make her try to explain to him what happened—there is no way to understanding but through talking. The surfacing of the 1855-event in the middle of the text strongly suggests, however, that Sethe is not primarily responsible to Paul D, but to herself. The process of confrontation—represented in all its intensity in part II, chapters 20-23—has to go a lot deeper than defensively trying to justify her actions to an outsider like Paul D.

Chapters 20-23: (Un)speaking Trauma

Following Sethe's resolution that "she had all the children she needed" (*B* 132)—a family complete without Paul D—part II centers on Sethe's crucial encounter with Beloved. This encounter appears, at least at the beginning, to be a deliberate choice on Sethe's part, but it quickly gets out of control and becomes life-threatening. Sethe gives up all contact with the outside world to concentrate entirely on Beloved's needs, wishes and demands: "Whatever is going on outside my door ain't for me. The world is in this room. This here's all there is and all there needs to be" (B 183). However, the symbiotic deadlock between Sethe and Beloved is prevented from being carried out to its last logical consequence by Denver, the second daughter. Denver's importance as an agent of change is worked out thematically in part III of the novel; but this later role is already anticipated by her discursive position in the mother/daughter/daughter triangle of chapters 20 to 23.

The dynamics of the lyrical sequences that form the center of part II have repeatedly been the focus of critical attention (e.g. Wyatt, Schapiro, Mathieson). Critics generally agree that Sethe's feelings of guilt and the resulting urge to explain her behavior to Beloved clash with Beloved's inability to accept any explanation and her insatiable need to come back to "the join" with her mother. What has not been focused on, however, is how this passage is a three-way "conversation" that not only brings the unhealthy merging of Sethe's and Beloved's identities close to completion, but also establishes Denver's important role as the only one who is eventually able to break out of the set patterns and save her mother. What initially seems to be a rather balanced exchange—with all three first expressing their specific points of view, before entering a "trialogue" in chapter 23—quickly reveals different roles for each woman. Although the overall atmosphere of chapters 20 to 23 is one of extreme psychological and emotional closeness, Morrison nevertheless achieves a clear differentiation of each woman's individual needs and desires through subtle shifts in narrative perspective and ambiguous usage of personal pronouns. The significance of this set of chapters is additionally highlighted through Morrison's overall handling of point of view: corresponding to Sethe's closing the house to any outside influences, the third-person narrative voice retreats and gives way to first-person accounts, in which each woman appears to address either herself or one of the two others in the enclosed space that they share only with each other.

The beginning of chapter 20 completes Sethe's retreat into the house, but the process of withdrawal already starts in the preceding chapter when she returns from Sawyer's restaurant for the last time. On her way home she engages in a "conversation" with Beloved that marks the upcoming shift in narrative perspective by introducing the first extended section of first person narration in the book. In addition, Stamp Paid's unsuccessful attempt to come and see Sethe emphasizes both how far beyond the reach of any outside influence she already is, and how dangerous this situation is going to become:

> Stamp Paid abandoned his efforts to see about Sethe, . . . and when he did, 124 was left to its own devices. When Sethe locked the door, the women inside were free at last to be what they liked, see whatever they saw and say what was on their minds.
>
> Almost. Mixed in with the voices surrounding the house, recognizable but undecipherable to Stamp Paid, were the thoughts of the women of 124, unspeakable thoughts, unspoken. (B 199)

This transitional passage lays the ground for what is to come; with the possible double meaning of the very last word "unspoken"[34] it also deliberately leaves the ambiguity whether what we read in the following four chapters are interior monologues or actually spoken words. In addition, at this very moment in the text the narrative voice marks its retreat by stating that the following passages will be presented without the interference of a mediating voice that is located on a different textual plane.

The first sentences of chapter 20, which focuses exclusively on Sethe's perspective, evoke the impression of direct speech: "Beloved, she my daughter. She mine" (B 200). The omission of the verb also effects an unspecificity in regard to time: the initial statements could be both present or past tense. Similarly, Sethe's following statement blurs the boundaries between present and future: "When I explain it she'll understand because she understands everything already" (B 200). Within this temporally ambiguous context, Sethe's mind runs through a host of different memories in her attempt to explain the intersections of various periods of her life, and to apologize for not deciding earlier to focus all her energies on Beloved. How far she has moved away again from her earlier resolve that "she wanted Paul D" (B 99) becomes clear when she attributes the delay in recognizing Beloved to Paul D's interference: "Who in the world is he willing to die for?" (B 203) she asks. Additionally, Sethe conflates the losses of her own mother and Beloved, Beloved's willingness to come back and her own wish to be "a good girl," as to succeed in killing herself and the children would have meant to be able to join her own mother:

> My plan was to take us all to the other side where my own ma'am is. They stopped me from getting us there, but they didn't stop you from getting here. Ha ha. You came right on back like a good girl, like a daughter which is what I wanted to be and would have been if my

ma'am had been able to get out of the rice long enough before they hanged her and let me be one. (B 203)

In addition to the female kinship ties asserted between her mother, herself, and her daughter, Mrs Garner emerges in Sethe's thoughts as another mother figure through subtle shifts in the monologue. "[T]hat woman" (B 201) clearly refers to Mrs. Garner, but immediately afterwards, Sethe describes her reaction to her mother's death. As Karen Field explains,

> [t]he makeshift we see, of Sethe's becoming a daughter, and the daughterless Mrs. Garner's becoming a mother to her, is as important to Sethe as her unrealized relationship with her own mother. Indeed, the two fuse together in her mind. (166)

Sethe's narrative can be described as yet another attempt to position herself anew within the difficult context provided by all that she has had to go through and the emotional needs that result from these experiences.

Initially, the addressed narratee of the chapter could be Sethe herself, or a very sympathetic black private listener. Sethe directly addresses a "you" that could well be her earlier, paralyzed self. Shortly afterwards, however, the focus shifts; she now appears to be directly addressing Beloved, although the reference is still ambiguous: "Think what spring will be for *us*. I'll plant carrots just so *she* can see them, and turnips. Have *you* ever seen one, baby?" (B 201, emphases added). Significantly, Sethe is here doing something that she has been incapable of before: she is making plans by imagining the future, although she herself is not aware of this. Sethe's desires and the unconscious shift away from a focus on the past to a focus on the future on her last return from Sawyer's kitchen is significant because it happens spontaneously at a moment of great relief when she thinks the problems of her past have finally been resolved. The end of the chapter then turns into a kind of prayer and shifts away again from Beloved as narratee for the very last sentence: "She come back to me, my daughter, and she is mine" (B 204).

Because all of Beloved's possible identities lie in the past, however, she cannot outgrow the claims she is making on Sethe. She is always already dead, and can only exist as long as her "presence" is induced by the needs of the living characters.[35] There can be no livable future in that place in which "the peace of winter stars seemed permanent" (B 176); only death makes such stability possible. This is reminiscent of Nel's belief, in Morrison's second novel *Sula*, that "[h]ell ain't things lasting forever. Hell is change" (108): Sethe's only experience of change is the continuous need to "keep[ ] the past at bay" (B 42). Every physical movement thus reinforces her emotional paralysis; paradoxically, every action is aimed at preventing change, because the only changes imaginable are the surfacing of memories that are too painful to bear, and further personal losses that only add to her agony. When her most distressing loss—the loss of her little daughter—is apparently undone through Beloved's return, Sethe no longer needs to spend all her energy forcing herself not to remember.

Denver's section—chapter 21—is almost formal compared to Sethe's. Unlike her mother, Denver uses "Beloved" as a proper name, but as in Sethe's passage, there is a blurring of personalities through the ambiguous use of pronouns:

> I thought she was trying to kill her that day in the Clearing. Kill her back. But then she kissed her neck and I have to warn her about that. Don't love her too much. Don't. Maybe it's still in her the thing that makes it all right to kill her children. I have to tell her. I have to protect her. (B 206)

This can be read as an implicit anticipation of Denver's later insight that it is Sethe, not Beloved, who needs to be protected.

Denver's attention is also not as completely fixed on Beloved as her mother's. This greater emotional distance is stylistically expressed during her monologue through a different narrative perspective: she never addresses her "sister" directly, but talks about her to an unidentified narratee. Sethe's and Denver's different investments in Beloved are thus expressed through different forms of address. The use of a quasi-public narratee in this enclosed (mind-)space expresses the greater emotional distance that will eventually make it easier for Denver to avoid the complete collapse with which Sethe is threatened, and anticipates her turning to the outside community for nurturance. There is nobody inside of 124 whom Denver could easily address: she is afraid of her mother, and Beloved has already told Denver that her attention is only on Sethe. Baby Suggs, who provided wisdom and solace, is long dead.

In Beloved's section—chapter 22—the blurring of boundaries is particularly notable. She never addresses Sethe directly, who is thus not explicitly a private narratee for Beloved's monologue. However, the metaphors of merging identities suggest that because Beloved does not see herself as completely separate from Sethe, a monologue to herself is always also simultaneously a dialogue with Sethe: "now I am her face"—"I want to be the two of us"—she is my face smiling at me"—"now we can join" (B 213).

The first passage of Beloved's chapter corresponds to Sethe's earlier description of leaving the baby in a basket behind the house. The text then shifts to the experience of the Middle Passage, and—most importantly—to the statement that "all of it is now." Consequently, the whole chapter is given in the present tense. Is this a present that is unchangeable, or is it a present in which the life of the mind is so much more real than what is going on outside that it appears as if memories of past experiences are perceived as concrete and real? Are these the perceptions of a mind who does not have the means to distinguish between past and present by way of symbolic substitution? How does memory substantiate itself without the words to describe it as something that has passed? If the only way to distinguish between past and present is to say that memory is an "inner" reality and the actual present an "outer" reality, then even these criteria fail when the boundaries between "inner" and "outer" collapse.

Because Beloved's identity is multiple, she cannot even at this very focused moment in the text be reduced to representing only "the crawling already? girl." Because "all of it is now"—the baby in the basket, the experience of the Middle Passage, the crouching—the different possible "explanations" for Beloved merge into a stream of verbal images which cannot be fixed in meaning. By implication, however—also because "all of it is now"—Sethe can never make up for "leaving" Beloved; the desertion happens again and again, no matter how much Sethe apologizes and explains (cf. Krumholz, "Ghosts of Slavery" 402). When Denver dreams that her head is being cut off every night, she is psychologically acting out what literally does not stop happening to Beloved, who is locked into that very moment of violence. In addition, she is potentially every one of the sixty million who died en route to the Americas and/or to adulthood, on the slave ships and through other violent forms of death, over a period of three centuries. The overriding experience—apart from the physical pain—is a sense of utter displacement and of abandonment, but also a basic, indestructible need to form human relationships.

In the final trialogue in chapter 23, the three different perspectives are still noticeable. The first dialogue is clearly between Sethe and Beloved. They address each other, and thus constitute each other's narratees. Questions go both ways; finally "I" and "you" merge: "Will we smile at me?" (B 215). In the succeeding passage, Denver includes Beloved in a narrative "we." Although Beloved reacts to Denver's prompts, she focuses only on her own need for Sethe, until Denver shifts the topic and talks about Sethe too, trying to convey to Beloved her own sense of her mother's potential violence: "Watch out for her; she can give you dreams" (B 216).

With Sethe's and Denver's attention focused on Beloved, but Beloved only returning Sethe's gaze and call, Denver is being excluded from the progressively narrowing mother-daughter dyad. When all three voices finally merge, this process of exclusion is completed: "you are my sister" and "you are my daughter" are clearly directed toward Beloved, but "you are my face; you are me" is only meant for Sethe. Similarly, in the next passage "I have your milk" and "I have your smile" lock Sethe and Beloved into a dyad, whereas Denver's "I will take care of you" stands partly outside and can, at this moment, be considered as addressing both Beloved and Sethe. Shortly afterwards, Denver is clearly pushed outside the mother-daughter connection. The passage starts with three alternating voices, and although Denver's and Sethe's voices merge, Beloved's responses clearly exclude the sister:

> You forgot to smile [Beloved to Sethe]
>
> I loved you [Sethe and Denver]
>
> You hurt me [Beloved to Sethe]
>
> You came back to me [Sethe and Denver]
>
> You left me [Beloved to Sethe]. (B 217)

This stylistically anticipates the later thematic development, when Denver, at the beginning of part III, recognizes her responsibility to act: "So it was she who had to step off the edge of the world and die because if she didn't, they all would" (B 239).

Within the overall dynamics of the passage, Beloved's disregard for boundaries has achieved its goal. Sethe can no longer recognize Beloved's demands as unreasonable, as she has already been lured into believing that "the join" with her dead daughter is in fact possible. At this stage in her development, Sethe is still incapable of seeing her children as separate from herself. Within the context of this perception, the passages in chapters 20 to 23 assume both a literal and a metaphorical level of meaning. Literally locked into the house with Denver and Beloved, Sethe has—in a figurative sense—an argument with herself: the dead/repressed parts of her life represented by Beloved, the alive parts represented by Denver.

Only in regard to the past can this illusion of "one-ness" be maintained, however, because Sethe's desire to be one with her daughters intersects with and is reinforced by Beloved's infant needs to perceive herself as part of the mother. Mathieson argues that

> Sethe is able to abandon her memories . . . because her past, embodied in Beloved, has forcibly reentered the present. Yet *past* it remains, and Sethe resigns herself ecstatically to the world of the dead child locked within her own room. For Beloved herself, the binding grip of memory

is inescapable. Her psychological development arrested forever at death, she can no more outgrow her dependence on Sethe's smile than she can alter the past. (12)

For Denver, the situation is fundamentally different: in order to survive, she has to establish herself as a person separate from her mother. This need saves her from being pulled into the ever-quickening process of self-absorption and mutual projection in which Sethe and Beloved are engaged. Instead of spiralling inwards, the trajectory of Denver's development therefore leads outwards—first toward the community and eventually toward the rescue not only of herself, but also of Sethe.

Re-entering the Community

Despite the seemingly inescapable pull toward complete separation from any communal structures in chapters 19 to 23, Sethe's actions are nevertheless framed by a context of relationship. Stamp Paid's unsuccessful attempt to "get through" to her—also both literally and metaphorically—signals the beginning of change within the community which Denver later both strenghtens and depends on. Sethe's "world" cannot, despite her efforts, be separated from the world outside, as long as there are people who cannot, or do not want to, accept the boundaries symbolized by the walls of 124. Both structurally, by means of chapter organization, and discursively, by showing the impossibility of reducing the three women in 124 to a single voice, the text counters Beloved's pull toward stasis and death.

The communal rebirth ritual at the end of the novel, in which Beloved disappears and a process of recovery begins for Sethe, has repeatedly been the focus of critical attention (cf. Wyatt; Krumholz, "The Ghosts of Slavery"). Suffice it to say here that the final scenes mark a moment of convergence in the text in which not only Sethe and Paul D's developments intersect at last, but other characters—Denver, Stamp Paid and Ella as the most prominent—have finally reached levels of (self-)knowledge and understanding that allow them to act on Baby Suggs's lessons. This, however, is the result of everybody's confrontation with internalizations of white attitudes—with instances in the past when one's identity was defined by the slaveholder—and a deliberate displacement of these imposed definitions in favor of self-chosen ones.

Paul D, for example, gradually learns to reclaim the African friend Sixo as his male role model, and Sethe can finally acknowledge her mother's behavior as an act of resistance. It also means to recognize alternative ways of communicating and relating to each other and—in a more general sense—caring for others across generational, gendered, and also racial lines.[36] It means to devise ways of interaction that acknowledge individual needs, like Denver's continuing care for Sethe. It also means to acknowledge the losses, even if they are as painful as the death of a child, and not to be overcome by one's own forced complicities in the system and the sense of guilt this produces. Only this makes proper mourning possible, and with the ability to mourn comes the possibility of imagining a future.

All these things would be too painful to bear alone: Morrison's reconstructed community at the end of *Beloved* provides various literal and figurative "holding spaces" so that Sethe can really reach as far inside as she needs in order to recover. The mother/daughter relationship has been resolved in a responsibly connected way: Denver is both there and not-there; she is no longer prevented by her mother from growing up and directing her attention to the outside world, but turns into an adult person both because she cares for her mother and because she has an "outside life."[37] Also, it is partly due to the re-visioned gender relationships that Denver's caring for Sethe is not too much of a burden: Paul D, too, assumes his share of the responsibility and thus relieves Denver of some of the pressure that would be on her if she were the only one looking after Sethe. Paul D, changed after his own painful confrontation with his past, can in turn assume that kind of caring relationship to a woman because he finds support for his attitude within the community. Stamp Paid is another good role model for Paul D in this regard. The tableau scene at the end of chapter 14, fundamentally static in its presentation of family relationships, needs to be replaced with the basically dynamic set-up in the last chapter: there is no exclusive fixation on one particular person—Denver and Paul D both come and go. Sethe can finally mourn the loss of Halle, Howard and Buglar, Baby Suggs, and especially Beloved without being swallowed, devoured by the past.[38]

In the spaces of a renewed communal self-definition at the very end of the novel, then, Baby Suggs's ethic of self-love, caring and personal accountability eventually meets with the conditions in which it can be put into practice and become the privileged mode of behavior. With Sethe's recovery only in its first tentative beginnings, the ending of the novel thus simultaneously carries both a sense of conclusion and the potential for a new beginning. Within an emotionally "safe(r)" space, Sethe might then also be able to mourn her losses in such a way that she can finally accept them.

Text in Context: *Beloved* as Memorial

In her 1993 Nobel Lecture, Morrison clothes her thoughts on literature into a story about the potential and dangers inherent in language and the need for using it "care-fully" and responsibly. Language, she says,

> can never live up to life once and for all. Nor should it. Language can never "pin down" slavery, genocide, war. Nor should it yearn for the arrogance to be able to do so. Its force, its felicity, is in its reach toward the ineffable. (21)

Morrison's attitude toward language, as it is encapsuled in this quotation, is characterized by an extraordinary attention to and concern for its possible effects, both on a textual and a metatextual level. In *Beloved*, the word not only has to be reclaimed, expropriated from the slaveholder and put to use to "unspeak" the silences imposed on enslaved and formerly enslaved African Americans; it has to undergo a cleansing of its own, a re-evaluation of the degree of psychological corruption it carries. As one significant part of the complex reconceptualizations of identity that the characters go through, language needs to be redefined as a means of connection rather than subjugation.

Morrison asks if it can be possible at all to use the language of the slave-holder to express adequately the experiences of the slave, a question that evokes Audre Lorde's remark that "the master's tools will never dismantle the master's house" ("Master's Tools" 112) As Sabine Bröck succinctly puts it, "*Beloved* wrestles with . . . the ethical need to consciously rememory, in order not to be consumed by a past of slavery's horrors, *and* the very impossibility to find a language that will contain that past" (134).[39] My argument is that Morrison is making a strong case against irresponsible, inhumane language use. She does not, however, regard language as inherently oppressive; it only becomes so when it is paired with an abuse of power. Morrison points out the devastating effects that the slaveholders' words have on the psychological and emotional well-being of the slaves, but she also articulates the potential inherent in language to come to a deeper under-standing of self, to engage in dialogue with others, and to be able to mourn the loss of loved ones in appropriate ways. In order to achieve this, Morrison suggests that the currently prevalent (European) theories of language and its usage have to come under critical scrutiny, especially in regard to their applicability in non-western cultural contexts.[40]

The novel is one outstanding example of Morrison's continuous exploration of the intersections of language and thought—of the ways in which a specific epistemological system not only makes knowledge possible, but also always limits our ability to understand. As part of her critique of western ways of thinking, Morrison challenges the claim to centrality that still emanates from the dominant culture's representations and interpretations of a black female "other." In her search for ways "to free up the language" (*Playing in the Dark* xi) and thus to open spaces for the imagination in which whiteness and maleness are not positioned as central, she develops an alternative epistemic framework that shows great affinities to African thought systems.[41] With its critique of dichotomous thinking—its refusal to separate content and form, intellect and emotion, characters', author's and readers' needs—and its emphasis on the power of language to create "reality," I suggest reading *Beloved* in conjunction with *Nommo*, the West African concept of "the life force, which produces all life, which influences 'things' in the shape of the *word*" (*Muntu: Outline* 124) as it has been described by Janheinz Jahn[42]:

> If there were no word, all forces would be frozen, there would be no procreation, no change, no life. 'There is nothing that there is not; whatever we have a name for, that is'; so speaks the wisdom of the Yoruba priests. The proverb signifies that the naming, the enunciation produces what it names. Naming is an incantation, a creative act. What we cannot conceive of is unreal; it does not exist. But every human thought, once expressed, becomes reality. For the word holds the course of things in train and changes and transforms them. And since the word has this power, every word is an effective word, every word is binding. There is no 'harmless', noncommittal word. Every word has consequences. Therefore the word binds the muntu. And the muntu is responsible for his word. (133)[43]

The significance and the potential of an African philosophical frame for Morrison's cultural project lies in its independent history that allows the African American writer to truly decenter the Eurocentric gaze. She can draw from a culturally validated epistemological system that has not developed as a response to western European traditions—which would basically leave the construction of white center versus black margin undisturbed. As part of this larger philosophical context—and this is what makes it especially interesting for the purposes of this study—*Nommo* also addresses questions of authority: the acknowledgement of responsibility and the awareness of the consequences of one's speech acts lead to an interpretation of authority that is fundamentally centered in moral considerations. Additionally, the matter-of-factness with which Morrison integrates the return of the dead child into the narrative context and her emphasis on memory as organizing principle also support the novel's conceptual kinship to West African philosophy (cf. Ray 67).

Chapter 28: Re-Positioning the Reader

Within the context of this refigured conceptual space, in which words are of such crucial significance, Morrison offers *Beloved* as a "site of memory" not only to her fictional characters, but also to her extratextual audience. I have outlined above how the authoritative implied author of the novel's paratexts retreats behind a respectful narrative voice in the main body of the fictional text so that the characters' needs can become the major motivating force for the progression of the plot and its discursive representation. In chapter 28, the very last chapter of the novel, the narrative voice then reasserts its initial authoritative position and comments on the narrative and its implications. Chapter 28 thus assumes the function of an epilogue that frames the narrative by being literally situated in the margin of the textual world.

This overall set-up significantly shapes the position assigned to readers. In the course of the novel, we have been taken deeper and deeper into the world of the black characters, with the expectation that we follow them through all twists and turns of their difficult developments while refraining from undue judgement. Once we have arrived at the end and have accepted the premises laid out in the text, chapter 28 opens the fictional world to invite us in as participants in Morrison's historical project. At the very end readers, too, become part of the community that needs to confront Beloved in order to make her disappear and to allow Sethe to come back into a context of communal recognition and support. So the novel in its entirety moves readers from a position of marginal observers through a process of active participation to a point at which we are asked to extend this work of memory and imagination beyond the fictional text.

To use an inclusive "we" to refer to *Beloved's* extratextual audience is justifiable because the text itself does not give any indication that its primary audience can be specified in regard to race and/or gender. Rather, all readers are asked to enter the text on its own terms. If this makes a decentering of a particular racially inflected or gendered perspective necessary, this is part of the reading process. As Heinze explains:

> By indirection Morrison avoids polarization of black and white humanity—one as inherently good, the other as irrevocably corrupt—

and thus allows all people to vicariously experience a rebirth through the black community. (9)

Morrison takes us on a journey in which it becomes morally and conceptually impossible to support any longer the epistemological and ideological tenets represented by schoolteacher. Instead, Beloved—the black and female child, the casualty of American history, the "disremembered" (B 274) part of the past— becomes the touchstone of historical understanding, both intellectually and emotionally.

Within this context, Morrison's insistence on the importance of memory personalizes the engagement with history, because it becomes impossible to separate the known from the knower(s). Simultaneously, it emphasizes the situatedness of every individual in larger communal contexts. Memory and imagination—two aspects that Morrison describes as fundamental for her own work ("Site of Memory" 111/119)—thus also become crucial components of readers' attempts to understand the implications of historical events. As Bhabha succinctly comments:

> Although Morrison insistently repeats at the close of Beloved, "This is not a story to pass on," she does this only in order to engrave the event in the deepest resources of our amnesia, or our unconsciousness. When historical visibility has faded, when the present tense of testimony loses its power to arrest, then the displacements of memory and the indirections of art offer us the image to our psychic survival. (18)

By thus drawing readers into the fundamental conceptual dynamics of the narrative, the ending of Beloved reiterates the notion that for characters, writers and readers alike, the confrontation with the black American past is a demanding process that is simultaneously necessary, communal, and creative.

Newspapers, Slave Narratives, and The Black Book

In addition to rewriting the original Margaret Garner account, *Beloved* stands in intertextual relationships with a large number of earlier texts.[44] To tell the story of a black woman's enslavement and her gradual liberation situates Morrison most obviously in the African American literary tradition that begun with the slave narratives. Morrison herself has commented extensively on the difficult conditions under which 19th-century African American writers had to work. In a cultural context in which "[a] literate slave was supposed to be a contradiction in terms"

("Site of Memory" 108), the narratives inevitably show signs of the need and the effort to authorize the black writer's public voice in the face of a severely prejudiced but demanding white audience. Within this context, Morrison sets out to "extend, fill in and complement slave autobiographical narratives" (120) from a late 20th-century position that allows her—as I have elaborated above—to displace the dominant culture's expectations, and instead turn her attention to the "interior lives" of her black characters. The initial source for Morrison's "Beloved"-project adds another facet to her work with 19th-century material. To start from a newspaper article about an enslaved black woman brings the question of adequate representation even more to the forefront. Both kinds of documents—black-authored texts addressed to a white audience, and white-authored texts written about African Americans—are limited, albeit in different degrees, because of their interest in meeting dominant expectations.

A second intertextual focus is on other 20th-century projects of historical remembrance and recovery. As integral part of Morrison's reconceptualization of both individual and communal remembrance, she revisions the project of creating spaces for the recognition and documentation of specifically African American historical experience begun in *The Black Book* in the early seventies. It was explicitly part of *The Black Book's* agenda to stress, according to Morrison, "those qualities of resistance, excellence and integrity that were so much a part of [the African American] past," at a time when

> [t]he old verities that made being black and alive in this country the most dynamite existence imaginable—so much of what was satisfying, challenging, and simply more interesting—were being driven under-ground—by blacks. . . . For larger and larger numbers of black people, this sense of loss has grown, and the deeper the conviction that something valuable is slipping away from us, the more necessary it has become to find some way to hold on to the useful past without blocking off the possibilities of the future. ("Rediscovering Black History" 14)

The Black Book meant to provide a concrete space for a recognition of and identifi-cation with "the useful past," and as Morrison's own comments in "Rediscovering Black History" show, it already had exactly this effect on those involved in its making. The book documents, and thus makes publicly visible, information privately preserved and collected within the African American community.[45]

With *Beloved*, Morrison extends the scope of this earlier, largely documentary project. In setting out from one particular item included in *The Black Book*—the newspaper article about "the slave mother who killed her child"—she looks behind the factual surface with the intention to trace her own sense of dismay and to probe more deeply the text's implications for a 20th-century understanding of the past (cf. "Rediscovering Black History" 16). This emphasizes the need to deal with painful experiences and to mourn the losses. As an intertextual engagement with *The Black Book*, *Beloved* thus demonstrates that the concept of a "useful past" cannot be limited to positive moments of identification, but also needs to provide spaces for a confrontation with pain and loss. *The Black Book's* acknowledgments page closes with the editors' "thanks to those millions of people who lived this life and held on"; in turn, Morrison's dedication to the "Sixty Million and more" who did not survive the passages from freedom to enslavement is a deliberate call to extend the basic tenets of cultural remembrance. There need to be spaces not only to recall heroic acts, but also to literally re-member—in the sense of 'reconnecting with'—all those who were forcefully "[d]isremembered and unaccounted for" (B 274) and thus separated from today's historical consciousness.

This process of remembrance, as Morrison's fifth novel shows, cannot be reduced to historical documentation—especially within a discriminatory context in which African Americans' access to public documentation has been so severely limited. To put together a "scrapbook" of "newspaper articles, ... old family photos, trading cards, advertisements, letters, ... stories, ... rumors, dates" (M. Harris, n.p.) is one significant way of presenting the variedness and complexity of African American culture; it is not, however, a transparent representation of black life. In *Beloved*, particularly in regard to textual treatments of historical documents that resemble those given in *The Black Book*, Morrison draws attention to their hidden subjectivities and ideological investments. Marilyn Sanders Mobley's assessment that *Beloved* "shift[s] from lived experience as documented in *The Black Book* to remembered experience as represented in the novel" (190) thus needs to be modified. The items collected in *The Black Book* are not self-explanatory; they are rather material traces of events that are not immediately accessible but require the work of memory and imagination of each reader/viewer to become meaningful. *Beloved* is the elaborate result of such work.

With its thematic emphasis on mourning, *Beloved* extends the focus on historical remembrance even further by exploring the dynamics of the grieving process as one particularly painful but unavoidable aspect. As an extension of the conceptualization of the novel as a "site of memory," then, Morrison also offers *Beloved* as a memorial to the African American presence in America.[46]

I have described above how the gravestone in *Beloved* is inadequate both as expression of Sethe's process of mourning for her dead child and as public documentation of this process for the community. In an extratextual context, however, the tombstone with its one engraved word becomes a metaphor for the conditions of African American women's public expression. Only at the greatest personal cost could the black enslaved woman inscribe herself into historical discourse: one word is all that Sethe is able to "afford." Even in her immediate surroundings, however, this word alone is not enough to explain her actions; as potential historical document, it loses even more of its explanatory force. Sethe's (written) story is reduced, stripped of all context, silenced. The other text in which she appears—the newspaper article—is "unwritten" and delegitimized in the novel as an inadequate representation. As Paul D puts it, "there was no way in hell a black face could appear in a newspaper if the story was about something anybody wanted to hear" (B 155).

Within her fictional text, Morrison thus displaces the factual source that served as her own starting point for the "Beloved"-project. In presenting her own "authentic" evidence of Sethe's existence in the form of a gravestone, she creates an imaginative space in which she can re-vision the account of "the slave mother who killed her child" from a black female perspective in which relationship and connection—encapsuled in the one word "beloved"—are fundamental. Morrison extends the sentiment expressed on the gravestone into an elaborate novelistic text, and thus links her own description of the novel as memorial with the function of the gravestone as memorial that no longer allows adequate remembering because the information that comes with it is too sparse. The 20th-century black female writer has to extend the (almost) silenced story of the 19th-century woman into a detailed narrative in order to make it meaningful in a contemporary context.[47] Morrison displaces the focus on conventional historical documentation—inherent in the original newspaper article, but also in its representation in The Black Book—by emphasizing the significance of an alternative text that would not exist at all without the creative work of memory and imagination.

CONCLUSION

> Be it grand or slender, burrowing, blasting, or
> refusing to sanctify; whether it laughs out loud or is
> a cry without an alphabet, the choice word or the
> chosen silence, unmolested language surges toward
> knowledge, not its destruction.
>
> Toni Morrison, *Nobel Lecture*

Jubilee, *Dessa Rose*, and *Beloved* all negotiate the difficult intersections of historical
thematic focus and 20th-century authorial positionality. In doing so, the three
novels create imaginative spaces to conceptualize the parameters of a culture that
would be able to accommodate the voices of all its members. The point is, as
Morrison so eloquently puts it in a continuation of thought in which *Jubilee* and
Dessa Rose provide important and necessary touchstones, to imagine ways of
thinking and relating to each other that do not replicate the exclusionary,
oppressive structures they critique. At the same time, any revisionist engagement
with slavery and its socio-historical and psychological implications cannot escape a
confrontation with dominant beliefs and attitudes. The inherently intertextual
nature of such a project makes a critical dialogue with "other" voices (in this case
the voices of western historiography and literary history) unavoidable. The
readings of the three novels presented above show, however, that this engagement
with the dominant culture text takes widely different forms and is significantly
shaped by a variety of factors. While Walker, Williams, and Morrison are all
obviously aware of the constant presence of a dominant ideology that still works
with and perpetuates practices of exclusion, their creative responses to this
presence vary greatly.

In a comparison of the three novels, a shift in definition how the text-
context matrix is constituted—especially how the roles of "author," "reader" and
their textual counterparts are defined and endowed with authority and influence—
is particularly noticeable. The novels' historical orientations make it impossible for
the writers to base their authority on personal experience and the notion of
epistemic privilege associated with it.[1] Consequently, other forms of legitimation
have to be considered and employed. While Walker authorizes her narrative
externally by borrowing authority from the dominant culture's accepted literary
forms, Williams legitimizes her black female protagonist's voice from within the

text, thereby by-passing possible extrafictional expectations. Morrison, finally, is no longer looking for this kind of validation. Although she clearly delegitimizes white representations of black lives within the text, her main goal is to explore the psychological rifts within black self-definition, rather than between white and black perceptions (cf. Henderson, "Re-Membering the Body" 63). This gradual shift in focus goes hand in hand with an increasingly critical attitude toward the dominant culture with its inherent claim to being the normative center against which everybody else is measured and defined. It manifests itself in the three writers' distinct estimations of their roles as authors; this includes their differing assessments to whom they feel responsible.

Especially with a subject matter as highly charged as slavery, it seems likely that a first critical or creative engagement would attempt to redress stereotypical assumptions and therefore be outer-directed and didactic. Such an approach places the writer in an authoritative position—a position that Walker clearly claimed for herself. She considered herself possessing privileged information, and felt responsible for passing it on to readers in need of instruction. To safeguard this notion of the author as expert, Walker spent years researching and collecting factual evidence. In contrast, both Williams and Morrison struggled with their material over long periods of time because the unrecorded stories of black enslaved women posed conceptual problems that required a substantial rethinking of literary possibilities. In the course of the literary development after *Jubilee*, the engagement with historical material has therefore shifted toward seeing the writer as learner rather than as privileged knower. In its most expansive sense, it has even become a healing process. In addition, the very subject matter has carried the potential for clarifying fundamental questions about the position of African American women in late 20th-century society. In order to tap those resources for knowledge and understanding, the authors had to find modes of working with the material that were not yet predetermined by potentially hostile or even silencing cultural expectations and literary conventions.

Considerations of genre are therefore another integral part of the three historical projects under discussion here. As the ideological investments of narrative form have become one focus of critical scrutiny, the question of how to synchronize thematic and formal "stories" has been central especially to Williams's and Morrison's projects. In contrast, Walker was much more confident about the adaptability of traditional genres; in her public statements, she presents the 19th-century historical novel as the model most suited to her own literary purposes. I suggest adding Walker's authorial position—her didactic intentions as well as her contested status as a black woman writer in the 1940s and 1950s—as another factor that made the usage of such a recognizable form appealing. Especially realism's inherent claim to stand above ideology, combined with a positivist approach to "reality," seemed to provide an ideal conceptual frame to reach the broad and diverse audience that Walker had in mind. In this context, she could claim a privileged position by asserting that she did not only know all there was to know from history books, but also had—through her great-grandmother's orally transmitted story—additional information that was inaccessible to anybody else. This authoritative position was then additionally bolstered by the high status assigned to the author in the realist tradition.

What is particularly noteworthy about this process of legitimation in regard to *Jubilee* is that Walker is claiming for herself authoritative knowledge that is crucially different from the knowledge her protagonist Vyry possesses. Vyry's authority is based on strong moral integrity that she was able to maintain despite extremely difficult circumstances; it is explicitly not the result of intellectual reflection. Although it can be argued that Walker tries to remain as faithful as possible to what is known about her great-grandmother in her portrayal of Vyry, the discussion also needs to take into account that *Jubilee* is presented primarily as a novel, not as a biography. As fictional(ized) character, Vyry's meaning goes beyond her historical specificity and suggests generalization. In this regard, the image of black womanhood that she represents is worth examining, especially in the context of generic conventions. A comparison to an earlier text like Harriet Jacobs's *Incidents in the Life of a Slave Girl* suggests that the conventions of narrative perspective in a traditional historical novel impede rather than facilitate the assertive representation of a black female subject.

In comparison, *Dessa Rose* and *Beloved* start from a substantially different conceptual position. Because Williams and Morrison's emphases are not primarily on the documentation of evidence, their narratives become exemplary texts in a negotiation of historical representation at large. Matters of knowing oneself and of knowing the past are shown as crucially intertwined, and the dynamics of the fictional characters' engagements in these questions find their counterparts in the authorial approaches toward the material. Although their plots are clearly set in the nineteenth century, the novels' overarching concerns, which link fictional and extrafictional inquiries, add a self-reflexive, metatextual dimension.[2] With *Jubilee* as an important early conceptual stage, then, black women writers' novels of slavery have—like other historically oriented fictional texts—also made the shift from more traditional historical fiction to what Linda Hutcheon calls "historiographic metafiction," in which "the narrativity and the textuality of our knowledge of the past . . . is being stressed" (22).

In *Dessa Rose*, the internal logic of the text fundamentally challenges any alleged neutrality or objectivity of representation. Accordingly, the writer herself can no longer claim authority through the possession of privileged knowledge, but needs to scrutinize the terms on which her own status as author/ity is based. This includes both her conceptual approach to the historical material and her relation to a contemporary audience. Although Williams deliberately employs realistic modes of telling, she prevents her text from evoking the impression of a transparent representation of the past by working very carefully with formal structure and point of view. *Dessa Rose* thus draws explicit attention to the dynamics—and politics—of representation, rather than concealing the mediating role of language. This aspect links Williams's novel with *Beloved*, in which the power of language to create realities is even more forcefully stressed.

Williams and Morrison emphasize in related, yet different ways the intersections of identity-constitution and language, and investigate possible ways of working through, coming to terms with, and finally changing oppressive situations and structures. Despite their 19th-century temporal settings, these projects are intended as constructive dialogues between the writers' 20th-century present and the past—dialogues based on the presumption that what is perceived as "the past" is largely an imaginative construction. If this notion "creates . . . space[s] for new emplotments" of history (Peterson 129), it also implies the need to attend carefully to the possible implications and consequences of one's (hi)stories. These insights into the workings of language result in a strong sense of authorial responsibility. Paired with an increasing confidence that the position of "author" can be undefensively claimed and defined as a space for agency, this notion of responsibility toward the language used, the characters portrayed and the (self-chosen) readers addressed, led Williams and Morrison to conceptualize imaginary spaces in which black women themselves finally set the terms. In so doing, they explicitly try not to replicate the oppressive and silencing structures inherent in a conventional explanatory model of center vs. margin. Rather, with a morally informed approach that recognizes mutual dependencies as unavoidable and differences among people as potentially productive rather than threatening, they use literature as a means of imagining an epistemologically refigured universe.

In regard to their specifically historical orientations, these novels open conceptual spaces in which not only earlier historiographical and literary interpretations of the past can be revisioned and rewritten, but in which necessary acts of individual and communal remembrance can also take shape. In this sense, Holloway's estimation of *Beloved* can be extended to describe a broader cultural phenomenon: "[The novel] underscores how the past (even the literary past) is currently at work as the myth from which we construct the meaning and significance of the present" (*Moorings* 170). Historical narratives by black women writers become "spiritual histor[ies]" (170), taking advantage of the creative potential of literature to provide spaces for identification that are both new and re-membered.[3]

Significantly, the contextual, relational ethics that these novels develop as fundamental to their fictional worlds make them potential "sites of memory" not only for those readers who resemble the protagonists because of their racial and gendered identities. While offering black female readers the greatest imaginative spaces for identification because black female perspectives serve as privileged centers of reference, the novels invite all readers to become engaged in the issues they raise. This obviously requires different steps from different readers. In the spirit of the texts' refigured conceptions of communality, however, the privileging of a black female perspective is not achieved through the exclusion of "others"; it is not, therefore, a mere reversal of the old center vs. margin construction, in which the central position is now merely occupied by a different group. Rather, the texts function as offers that readers can either accept or refuse. "They can touch it if they like" (B 275), the narrative voice in *Beloved's* final chapter states. Just as the characters have to free themselves from externally imposed as well as inter-nalized notions of inferiority, readers are asked to investigate their own involve-ment in structures of thought that continue to privilege some on the basis of seemingly essential categories of identity.

As part of the writers' gradual redefinition of the writer-reader relationship, the three texts' diverse conceptual orientations also have important ramifications for their inclusion in critical/theoretical discussions. Their reception suggests that a writer's self-positioning in relation to society's dominant ideology—including the ways in which this orientation impacts on textual choices—plays a significant role in the critical treatment of her text. How novels are being evaluated seems to depend substantially on the agreement of or disparity between writers' and critics' conceptual premises concerning the possible locactions of black women writers in a larger socio-cultural matrix. Especially *Jubilee* is a poignant example in this respect. Despite its status as the first of an increasing number of African American women's narratives of slavery, Walker's novel has on the whole been given noticeably little critical attention. My analysis of *Jubilee* shows, however, that attention to this particular text can reveal some of the steps necessary to make the later texts, with their more explicit critiques of dominant socio-cultural structures, possible.[4]

Especially in the light of *Jubilee's* sparing critical reception, it is important to come back to Lanser's assertion that "discursive authority . . . is produced interactively" (*Fictions of Authority* 6) and thus subject to historical changes. This notion has informed the conceptual framework for the above analysis of *Jubilee*, especially its authorizing strategies. It includes attention to what was considered "authoritative" at the time of the text's genesis and publication, and how the novel relates to these agreements—being accommodating in some, subversive in other respects. Claudia Tate suggests a similar approach for an adequate treatment of late 19th-century black women's sentimental novels: "[W]e must be mindful that all critical practice arises from specific sets of historical circumstances. Historical time, then, is a central factor in formulating interpretations and making value judgments" ("Allegories of Black Female Desire" 101). This need to historicize both fictional texts and critical practice might be less obvious for *Jubilee* than for the texts that Tate is discussing, as the novel's relatively late publication date suggests a closer conceptual proximity to today's critical emphases. The critical reserve toward *Jubilee* indicates, however, that in today's discussion—with its tendency to focus on novels that more explicitly question and challenge hegemonic traditions and conventions—Walker's novel can no longer generate enough authority to be included in what is emerging as a new canon of representative texts by African American women writers. On the one hand, Walker's strategies to gain understanding and sympathy for her subject matter in a mainstream audience have come under critical scrutiny; on the other hand, however, this overlooks that Walker had to establish authority for her revisionary narrative in the absence of a public support structure that younger writers can now rely on to a much greater degree.

In turn, it does not come as a surprise that much recent criticism—especially in a black feminist context—shows great conceptual affinities to *Dessa Rose* and *Beloved*. Within the parameters of the theoretical model that Henderson develops in her article "Speaking in Tongues," *Dessa Rose* is a fitting choice as one of her fictional examples. Williams's novel supports well Henderson's point that black women's successful self-assertions often happen in the light of massive resistance. Dessa is able to affirm her point of view against the supposedly more powerful interpretations of a white man and a white woman; the discursive struggles that finally lead to the confirmation and authorization of her perspective are central aspects of the novel's plot and formal structure. *Dessa Rose* is thus a main part of the textual basis from which Henderson formulates her theory of "disruption and revision," which is then presented as a comprehensive model for reading black women's texts in general. In a similar vein, Holloway's use of *Beloved* to substantiate her "figurative theory" of black women's writing in *Moorings and Metaphors* is one significant example for the conceptual proximity of much recent black feminist criticism and Morrison's literary and philosophical agenda.

This affinity between contemporary fiction and criticism carries the risk, however, of underestimating the difficulties faced by earlier writers who could not count on similarly empathetic critical responses. When Morrison's conceptual achievement is taken as a critical paradigm that sets new standards, critics have trouble with less explicitly critical or revisionary texts—texts that are more conciliatory and compromising. The question remains how writers whose texts show the impact of the dominant culture more strongly than others can still be included in today's critical discussion and acknowledged for their accomplishments, although some of their thematic and formal choices might appear somewhat outdated in a contemporary critical context.

But even if the attempt of fictional texts to describe social structures in more complex terms than is possible within a model of center vs. margin(s) is recognized, the theoretical potential of such an approach does not yet always translate into the critical discussion. Two of the critical studies that have provided some of the basic questions for the analyses presented here—Henderson's "Speaking in Tongues" and Lanser's *Fictions of Authority*—are cases in point. In their respective attempts to formulate comprehensive theoretical models, both have to employ "strategies of containment" (Henderson, "Response" 162) to keep the projects manageable; however, these strageties are also problematic in setting up new categories of exclusion. For both critics, I would argue, these potential problems are related to their implicit retention of a basic model of white/male center vs. marginal(ized) others, despite their initial theoretical claims to go beyond it.[5]

In *Playing in the Dark*, Morrison states that "[t]he ability of writers to imagine what is not the self, to familiarize the strange and mystify the familiar, is the test of their power" (15). In a continuation of this thought, it becomes the task of readers to learn how to embrace black women's epistemologically reconstructed narratives, even if they do not at first sight offer familiar ways of identification. For this to become possible, black women's voices need to be accepted and validated as central points of reference.[6] If a reader is willing to do that, then the fictional texts provide ways of engagement that can be pursued by readers of all kinds of "identities." Readers are placed in an ethical framework in which respect and authority are granted on the basis on one's willingness to embrace relational paradigms—paradigms based on an ethics of personal accountability and caring. It remains a choice, however, if readers—including critics—enter this imaginative space and take it to be a theoretically as well as epistemologically suggestive way out of binary constructions of white vs. other, and male vs. female—constructions that lock individuals into preconceived notions of identity in which "difference" is constantly reaffirmed as a barrier to communication. The developments in African American women's writing—out of which this study could highlight only one small segment—propose strategies of reading that rely on, but also facilitate, the willingness of readers to submit their strategies of reading and interpreting to critical reflection. Understanding their texts as offers and themselves as participants in a larger communal project, the writers discussed here cannot enforce this willingness. Their novels unfold their liberating potential in the dialogues they initiate and inspire.

NOTES

Introduction

1. It is difficult to decide on a generic term that can do justice to these 20th-century black women's texts, without immediately suggesting their belonging to a specific literary tradition. On the one hand, the term "historical novel" is still largely associated with the 19th-century novels of, e.g., Scott, Tolstoy and Cooper. On the other hand, Bernard Bell's use of "neoslave narrative" suggests too close a connection to the original slave narratives (*Afro-American Novel* 289). I am going to refer to the novels in question either generally as "historical narratives" or, more specifically, "novels (or narratives) of slavery," to indicate their thematic focus without invoking too many genre expectations.

2. Black male writers have also turned to writing historical narratives: the earliest 20th-century novel of slavery is Arna Bontemps *Black Thunder* (1936); this was followed by Ernest Gaines's *The Autobiography of Miss Jane Pittman* (1971), Alex Haley's *Roots* (1976), Ishmael Reed's *Flight to Canada* (1976), David Bradley's *The Chaneysville Incident* (1981), Charles Johnson's *Oxherding Tale* (1982) and *Middle Passage* (1990). A comparative approach between the women's and the men's texts is beyond the intention and the scope of this study. For a detailed treatment of the black male writers' novels, see Benesch.

3. In regard to plot and setting, the novels do not draw explicit attention to their fictionality, but rather expect readers to enter their imaginary worlds in temporary suspensions of disbelief. Correspondingly, characters do not leave the given temporal settings, and the narrators occupy textual planes that are clearly distinguishable from the respective plot levels. These textual characteristics have caused some writers and critics—Charles Johnson and Ishmael Reed among them—to make derisive comments that are, as I hope to show, unwarranted. In contrast to critical reproaches that describe these authorial decisions as theoretically naive, because they supposedly fail to see "history" as a discursive construction, I want to distinguish between a writer's insight into the constructedness of historical knowledge and her deliberate use of certain narrative devices that, at first sight, might appear outdated from a postmodern point of view (cf. Benesch 204-5).

4. To use terms like "experience" and "self" is a precarious thing to do after poststructuralism. The textual analyses will show, however, that they are still necessary and useful, albeit in a sense crucially different from the traditional humanistic discourse of the "autonomous individual." My understanding of "experience" follows Teresa de Lauretis's definition: "[Experience is] a complex of meaning effects, habits, dispositions, associations, and perceptions resulting from the semiotic interaction of self an outer world ... The constellation or configuration of meaning effects which I call experience shifts and is reformed continually, for each subject, with her or his continuous engagement in social reality, a reality that includes—and for women centrally—the social relations of gender" ("Technology of Gender" 18). In this context, see also Friedman, "Post/Poststructuralist Feminist Criticism" and Mohanty, "The Epistemic Status of Cultural Identity."

5. I use "intertextual" in the broad sense of referring not only to other written texts, but also to the general culture text with its various intersecting socio-historical and political discourses.

6. I use the term "signifying" in Henry Louis Gates's definition as "metaphor for textual revision" in an African American context (*Signifying Monkey* 88).

7. Cf. Morrison, "The Site of Memory" and Nora, "Between Memory and History: *Les Lieux de Memoire.*"

8. It is also noteworthy that the rejection of publicly "discredited" material has become an explicit thematic focus in several later novels by black women writers. A recent example is Paule Marshall's *Daughters*, in which the protagonist Ursa McKenzie is not allowed to write her M.A.-thesis on a slave rebellion on the Caribbean island she is from, because this is not considered a relevant topic by her advisor.

9. The phrase is Friedman's ("Weavings" 159).

10. It is difficult to avoid the impression that *Beloved* is often the token black female text in studies that otherwise do not focus explicitly on African American women's writing (see, e.g. Hirsch, *Mother/Daughter Plot*). It has to be examined if Morrison's novel is really integrated into new theoretical developments, or mainly used to make critical studies of women's fiction look more inclusive.

11. Gérard Genette gives the following definition: "A literary work . . . is rarely presented in an unadorned state, unreinforced and unaccompanied by a certain number of verbal or other productions, such as an author's name, a title, a preface, illustrations. . . . These accompanying productions, which vary in extent and appearance, constitute what I have called elsewhere the work's *paratext*. . . . [T]he paratext is what enables the text to become a book and to be offered as such to its readers and, more generally, to the public" (1).

Chapter 1

1. Lanser continues: "Moreover, a fictional text is not usually or centrally a direct statement about the writer's communicative situation, status, or ideology; indeed, a writer may not be consciously aware of the implications of his/her social environment and historical context for the writing act" (*Narrative Act* 103).

2. This approach owes much to Susan Friedman's description of literary texts as consisting of a given "horizontal" narrative as well as of "vertical" narratives that are constituted in the act of reading. Friedman explains: "The horizontal narrative is the sequence of events, whether internal or external, that 'happens' according to the ordering principles of the plot and narrative point of view. . . . [It] is reconstituted in the process of reading. . . .The vertical axis of narrative involves reading 'down into' the text, as we move across it. The vertical does not exist at the level of sequential plot, but rather resides within, dependent on the horizontal narrative as the function that adds multiple resonances to the characters'. movement through space and time" ("Spatialization" 15-16).

3. Henderson's essay first appeared in Cheryl A. Wall's critical anthology *Changing Our Own Words*. Since then, it has been repeatedly anthologized, e.g. in Gates, *Reading Black, Reading Feminist*; S. Jones, *Writing the Woman Artist*; Hein and Korsmeyer, *Aesthetics in Feminist Perspective*.

4. A substantial part of Holloway's theoretical argument was published earlier in "Revision and (Re)membrance."

5. To consider both black and white feminist approaches to African American women's writing broadens the critical framework for the analyses to come. It also raises the question,

however, why a specific focus on strategies of authorization seems less of a critical concern in a black feminist context, whereas it occupies central space in the work of many European American feminists. It is an additional hypothesis that these differences reveal some basic disagreements about the position of women writers in larger socio-cultural contexts. These conceptual disagreements crystallize especially around the issue of authorization.

6. These descriptions are additionally supported by the brief definitions given in the *OED* which subsume "authority" under two categories: the "[p]ower to enforce obedience," and the "[p]ower to influence action, opinion, belief."

7. Hannah Arendt argues that this kind of unquestioned authority *de facto* no longer exists, and that the term "authority" as it is still frequently used in a political context is actually a misnomer (cf. "What Is Authority" 91-95).

8. As Hortense Spillers poignantly puts it: "My country needs me, and if I were not here, I would have to be invented" ("Mama's Baby, Papa's Maybe" 65; see also Collins, *Black Feminist Thought* 68-70).

9. In my use of "hegemonic" and "hegemony," I follow Gramsci's definition as quoted by Ronald Takaki: "[Cultural hegemony is] an order in which a certain way of life and thought is dominant, in which one concept of reality is diffused throughout society and all its institutional and private manifestations, informing with its spirit all taste, morality, customs, religions and political principles, and all social relations, particularly in their intellectual and moral connotations" (*Iron Cages* vi-vii).

10. Morrison comments on the ubiquity of the dominant ideology when she asks: "What happens to the writerly imagination of a black author who is at some level *always* conscious of representing one's own race to, or in spite of, a race of readers that understands itself to be 'universal' or race-free?" (*Playing in the Dark* xii).

11. My use of "ideology" is based on Sacvan Bercovitch's definition: "[I]deology is the system of interlinked ideas, symbols, and beliefs by which a culture—any culture—seeks to justify and perpetuate itself; the web of rhetoric, ritual, and assumption through which society coerces, persuades, and coheres. . . . [I]deology functions best through voluntary acquiescence, when the network of ideas through which the culture justifies itself is internalized rather than imposed, and embraced by a society at large as a system of beliefs" ("Problem of Ideology" 635-36).

12. "Public" is here not to be equated with "dominant," but more generally as referring to all instances in which a writer addresses her or his written or spoken words to an extratextual audience. This usage corresponds to Lanser's explanation that in a literary context, "private voice" is "narration directed toward a narratee who is a fictional character," and "public voice" as "narration directed toward a narratee 'outside' the fiction who is analogous to the historical reader" (*Fictions of Authority* 15). This definition is worth emphasizing, because in her own textual readings, Lanser works with a second "public" versus "private" distinction, in which both terms refer to extratextual audiences. "Public" thus becomes a veiled critical shorthand for "dominant/central," and therefore addresses only part of a text's actual audience. The risk of this inconsistent usage lies in what it suggests: to present a definition in which "public" supposedly refers to all readers, regardless of gender or race, and then to use the term in a way in which it excludes all but readers of the dominant group makes it difficult to perceive readers that are both "public" (i.e. extratextual) and "private" (i.e female/black) as having any part in the process of authorizing a text.

13. I prefer the rather clumsy-looking term '(self-)positioning' to 'standpoint,' because the word itself contains the tension between being positioned and positioning oneself; it also expresses the dynamic, procedural nature of these actions. In addition, 'standpoint' would connote too close an affinity to 'standpoint theories' in which, according to Collins, it is "one implication . . . that the more subordinate the group, the purer the vision of the oppressed group" (*Black Feminist Thought* 207). — For extensive discussions of standpoint theories, see, e.g., Narayan and Harding.

14. For African American critical self-positionings that use a concept of "revision" to establish distinctly black theoretical models, see, e.g., Gates, *Signifying Monkey*; see also Awkward, *Inspiriting Influences*. — Lanser defines "culture text" as the "set of social and cultural norms against which literary discourse is conventionally read" (*Narrative Act* 184).

15. This term was introduced by Rachel Blau DuPlessis to describe white women's situation as both privileged (in terms of race) and oppressed (in terms of gender)—("For the Etruscans" 277).

Chapter 2

1. See, e.g., Kubitschek, *Claiming the Heritage*; Willis, *Specifying*; Holloway, *Moorings and Metaphors*. The one book-length study that includes Margaret Walker is Melissa Walker, *Down from the Mountaintop*.

2. "Most of my life I have been involved with writing this story about my great-grandmother, and even if *Jubilee* were never considered an artistic or commercial success I would still be happy just to have finished it" ("How I Wrote *Jubilee*" 50).

3. Walker makes a point of her exposure to all three historical perspectives: "I was trained as a child in the South to read books at school from the southern viewpoint and books at home from the Negro viewpoint. Once I was out of the South I read more and more from the northern viewpoint" ("How I Wrote *Jubilee*" 52).

4. Levin and Levin explain further: "[The competitive orientation of American society] engages the individual in a competitive struggle to upgrade him or herself and to downgrade others. Respectability demands deviance; good requires evil. As a result, the members of our society must construct and maintain a set of negative stereotypes of minorities, deviants, criminals, and the poor, and attempt to find public methods for stigmatizing such individuals" (205).

5. Elkins's theory of "Sambo personality" denied slaves any degree of agency: "Sambo, the typical plantation slave, was docile but irresponsible, loyal but lazy, humble but chronically given to lying and stealing; his behavior was full of infantile silliness and his talk was inflated by childish exaggeration. His relationship with his master was one of utter dependence and childlike attachment: it was indeed this childlike quality that was the very key to his being" (qtd in Fogel & Engermann 109). How disputed the historical and literary assessments of "slave personality" must have been in the 1950s and 1960s can also be glimpsed from the heated discussion surrounding the publiation of William Styron's *The Confessions of Nat Turner* in 1967. When asked about her attitude toward Styron's novel in a 1973 interview, Walker explained the strong negative reactions with Styron's failure to recognize the importance of Nat Turner as a heroic figure for the African American community: "Styron maligned Nat Turner in every possible way.

Styron attacks his personality. He attacks Nat Turner as a man; he attacks him as a preacher; and he attacks him as a folk hero. He deliberately destroys the image of Nat Turner as hero" (Rowell 11).

6. "[D]ie breite und vielseitige Darstellung des Seins der Epoche kann nur an Hand der Gestaltung des Alltagslebens des Volkes, der Freuden und Leiden, der Krisen und Wirrungen der mittleren Menschen klar an die Oberfläche treten" (*Der historische Roman* 47).

7. "[T]here's nothing wrong with my scholarship. My genius as a writer may be open to question, but my solid foundation of traditional academic education [is not]" (Giovanni and Walker 54).

8. See, e.g., Andrews, "Novelization"; Lanser, *Fictions of Authority* 1-24.

9. The fact that the first complete version of Jubilee was written as a Ph.D.-dissertation raises additional questions in regard to its intended audience. About the role and possible influence of her dissertation committee at the University of Iowa on the final version of the manuscript, Walker was very reserved.

10. For an extensive discussion of such prejudicial assumptions, see DuBois, *Black Reconstruction in America, 1860-1880*, esp. ch. 12, "The Propaganda of History."

11. See, e.g., White, *Ar'n't I a Woman* 70: "Important in understanding why females ran away less frequently than men is that fact that women tended to be more concerned with the welfare of their children, and this limited their mobility." — Hortense Spillers explicates the flight scene, which is described in nightmarish terms, as a key symbolic scene for Vyry's enslavement (cf. "Hateful Passion" 190).

12. In her discussion of Zora Neale Hurston's *Their Eyes Were Watching God*, Hazel Carby identifies a similar tendency in the literary treatment of early 20th-century urban African Americans, whose concrete presence is disregarded in evocations of a rural black folk culture: "One possibility, in fiction, was that 'the people' were represented as a metaphorical 'folk,' which in its rural connotations avoided and ignored the implication of the presence of black city workers" (*Reconstructing Womanhood* 164).

13. After the end of the war, Vyry extends her care to include Lillian and her children; while she is on the road with Innis, looking for a safe place to stay, she shares food with a poor white sharecropping family and delivers a white baby.

14. Not explicitly referring to *Jubilee* but generally to black historical novels she had read as part of the planning for *Dessa Rose*, Sherley Anne Williams has commented on her own decision to make Dessa's resistance the result of deliberate reflection (cf Ross 494-95).

15. On the other hand, Innis is also Minna's "father," and thus has a different kind of authority in the narrative that was passed on to Walker by her grandmother, the real Minna.

16. Asked about Vyry's lack of bitterness, Walker admits that "maybe I have not been as honest as I should be, taking the licence of the imaginative worker, but I have tried to be honest" ("How I Wrote *Jubilee*" 62).

17. Walker herself reconnects her narrative with historical reality by refering to a family "tradition" that supports the veracity of her portrayal of Vyry's character: "The thing that we get from Vyry . . . is that out of outrage and violence and bitterness, she comes up with this Christian love and forgiveness. And you know, I was raised that way. My grandmother was that way. And she was Vyry's child" (Freibert 53).

18. This central part, which proved to be such a challenging and time-consuming task for the author, is hardly ever mentioned in the criticism. It is, however, sometimes suggested as recommended reading in history classes on the Civil War (personal correspondence with Peter Kellogg, University of Wisconsin, Green Bay).

Chapter 3

1. Henderson calls the text a "novella," but Williams herself refers to "Meditations" as a "short story" (Ross 494). I will follow Williams's choice.

2. See, e.g., Harrison's analysis of the southern pastoral and how it relates to *Dessa Rose*; see also Melissa Walker, 13-46. — Comparing the historical circumstances in which *Jubilee* and *Dessa Rose* were published, Melissa Walker identifies the two novels' conceptual orientations with the political climate at the respective moment of publication. This is based on a too narrow cause-and-effect argument that limits the texts to being primarily responses to "public atmosphere" and does not take into account the long writing periods of both novels.

3. In this regard, it is not surprising that *Beloved* comes up repeatedly as a point of reference for comparison, considering the close publication dates of the two novels, and the obvious thematic parallels.

4. Margaret Walker's discussion with Nikki Giovanni, who is about Williams's age, is instructive to see how the older woman defines the differences between herself and the younger writers, whose perspectives are significantly shaped by the events of the 1960s (cf. Giovanni and Walker).

5. There is no emphasis on explaining some of the incidents and circumstances mentioned in the poem; they become better understandable when read in conjunction with "Meditations" and/or *Dessa Rose*. It is clear, however, that Odessa describes being freed by Nathan, Cully and Harker, with Jemima's help; it also becomes clear that Harker, although he is called "father," is not the biological father of Odessa's child. In terms of narrative perspective and thematic focus, the poem differs considerably from the two prose texts: because her son is the private listener for whom the tale is intended, Odessa explains to him the events surrounding his birth. In the novel, in contrast, the birth-scene is not even part of the narrated plot; as part of the flight from the root cellar, it is turned into a representationally liminal space—out of sight and earshot, so to speak. This might be an affirmative reference to slave narrative conventions in which the details of escape were often withheld so that the respective strategy would still be available to other fugitives. — The remainder of the poem gives voice to two more contemporary perspectives who complicate the portrayal of black women initiated by Odessa's son; the four parts together link past and present, describing love and respect as well as violence and danger.

6. In contrast to the novel, the white male scholar remains unnamed in "Meditations"; I will throughout my discussion of both texts refer to this fictional character as "Nehemiah."

7. This is reminiscent of Alice Walker's description of her attitude toward the characters of *The Color Purple*: "Just as the summer was ending, one or more of my characters . . . would come for a visit. We would sit wherever I was sitting, and talk" ("Writing *The Color Purple*" 359). — In her conversation with Gloria Naylor, Toni Morrison also describes the continuing presence of Beloved in similar terms: "Now she comes running when called—walks freely around the house, sits down in a chair" (Naylor and Morrison 593).

8. For a more extensive comparison between "Meditations" and the first part of *Dessa Rose*, see Sievers, "Escaping the Master('s) Narrative."

9. Herbert Aptheker mentions a white woman who helped fugitive slaves in "Slave Guerrilla Warfare": "Arms were found in the place named by Moses 'in possession of a white woman living in a very retired situation—also some meat, hid away & could not be accounted for—a child whom the party [of citizens] found a little way from the house, said that his mamy dressed victuals every for 4 or 5 runaways, & shewed the spot'" (*To Be Free* 25).

10. In "The Lion's History" Williams states: "The histories of slavery available during the late sixties and early seventies were of little help. They focused on issues that could be traced through archival material in which the slave's voice was largely missing, his or her person treated as mute commodity. . . . The Davis article provided me with a model of seeing even the most mundane and trivial aspects of a slave's day-to-day existence in a new light" (252).

11. The passage points to one of the drawbacks of Williams's approach to present Dessa only through her memories and thoughts and through Nehemiah's distorted view: as soon as something needs to be mentioned that is outside of these perceptions, the narrator needs to step in and add information for the reader that is not necessary for the coherence of the narrative itself. This is one manifestation of a personalized narrator who has more insights into the characters' psyches than the characters themselves. This scene in which Dessa's attack on her mistress is described shows a narrative ambiguity similar to the later episode that presents Nathan's experiences; both are not clearly attributable to a fictional character.

12. I owe this thought to Nellie McKay's lecture on *Dessa Rose*, Madison, September 1992.

13. At first, she interprets her dismal situation as individual failure; if Bertie's hadn't disappeared, things would be fine. At this stage, she longs to go back to Charleston: "She hungered for the city of her come-out with a strength she tried guiltily to conceal" (*DR* 117). She does not yet see that introducing young girls into society and marrying them off into invisibility are two sides of the same patriarchal coin. At the end, in contrast, she decides not to go back to her family, but to move out of the South altogether; as Dessa tells it: "We come West and Ruth went East, not back to Charleston; she went on to . . . Philly-me York—some city didn't allow no slaves" (*DR* 259).

14. "Rufel remembered hardly anything of that winter . . . except that she had been miserable. . . . Nothing in the days and weeks since Mammy's death had filled the silence where her voice used to live. Bertie would not return. Rufel never voiced this fear aloud or even phrased it to herself. It had been unthinkable to say when Mammy lived; it was impossible now that Mammy was dead" (*DR* 117-118).

15. Williams intended Ruth's attitude toward the baby as key to her later growth: "[S]he had to have at least that much initial humanity in order for me to even work with her at all. And once she had allowed herself to be human on that level, then she is open to all the other lessons that Dessa and the other runaways had to teach her" (Jordan 293).

16. This is remiscent of Mikhail Baktin's description of the "word in language": "It becomes "one's own" only when the speaker populates it with his own intention, his own accent, when he appropriates the word, adapting it to his own semantic and expressive intention. Prior to this moment of appropriation, the word . . . exists in other people's mouths, in other people's contexts, serving other people's intentions: it is from here that one must take the word, and make it one's own" (Bakhtin 293-94).

17. "Rufel had been lonely, had felt herself ugly and awkward. Mammy talked with her, admired her hair and rather full-lipped smile, showed her how to walk erectly. She praised where Mrs. Carson had criticized, hugged where Rufel's mother had scolded" (*DR* 132). — In *Kindred*, Dana Franklin temporarily assumes a similar role for the white boy Rufus Weylin; Dana is the only person who takes him seriously, and he starts liking her for that (see, e.g., Butler 65f).

18. After Nathan told Ruth about Dessa's ordeal, his mentioning that she has had a hard time, too, sets her off: "It was what her own common sense told her but she was outraged to hear herself compared to the wench. 'I knew that little hellion couldn't be no kin to Mammy,' she said tartly. 'The mistress have to see the welts in the darky's hide, eh?' 'Ye—' His tone implied that her desire for proof was mean and petty and she flushed hotly" (*DR* 147).

19. Dessa says: "[The name] Ruint fit her. Way she was living up there in them two rooms like they was a mansion, making out we was all her slaves. For all the world like we didn't know *who* we was or how *poor* she was. Them rooms was big all right, but it was only two of them, same as any poor buckra; and that stairway didn't lead to no other story" (*DR* 176).

20. In *Woman, Native, Other*, Trinh T. Minh-ha explains: "When we insist on telling over and over again, we insist on repetition in re-creation (and vice versa). On distributing the story into smaller portions that will correspond to the capacity of absorption of our mouths, the capacity of vision of our eyes, and the capacity of bearing out bodies. . . . And the same story has always been changing, for things which do not shift and grow cannot continue to circulate. Dead. Dead times, dead words, dead tongues" (123).

21. Cf. Edwin Ardener's model of "muted cultures"; cf. also Collins, "The Social Construction of Black Feminist Thought." For a critique of concepts of epistimic privilege, see Bar On.

22. Margaret Walker's comments are a case in point here: Question: "What do you think of Styron's novel?" Walker: "I think that what he does to a famous Black hero is unpardonable. The racism in that book is the damage he does to the hero for the Black child. Nat Turner represents to Black people, first of all, a preacher, and that is one of our heroes—you see, folk heroes; and then he represents a leader—a slave leader and a man, an insurrectionist. He was fighting against all of the tyranny and hatred and dominance of the society and of a feudal system that was doomed. Styron maligned Nat Turner in every possible way. Styron attacks his personality. He attacks Nat Turner as a man; he attacks him as a preacher; and he attacks him as a folk hero. He deliberately destroys the image of Nat Turner as a hero. That is unfortunate for Black people. That is why the novel appears to Black people as a racist book and as an anathema. Nat Turner is one of our great heroes" (Rowell 11).

23. Nellie McKay mentioned this aspect in a lecture on *Dessa Rose*, Madison, Sept. 1992.

24. Ralph Ellison's definition of the blues—as "an impulse to keep the painful details and episodes of a brutal experience alive in one's own aching consciousness, to finger its jagged grain, and to transcend it, not by the consolation of philosophy, but by squeezing from it a near-tragic, near-comic lyricism"—is a fitting description here (Gayl Jones 195).

25. Joseph Campbell's description of the "nuclear unit of the monomyth" depends on a concept of the autonomous individual subject: "A hero ventures forth from the world of common day into a region of supernatural wonder: fabulous forces are there encountered and a decisive victory is won: the hero comes back from this mysterious adventure with the power to bestow boons on his fellow man" (*The Hero with a Thousand Faces*).

Chapter 4

1. I borrow the term "unowned" from Patricia J. Williams: "After the Civil War, . . . slaves were unowned—I hesitate to use the word emancipated even yet . . ." (21).

2. In the interview with Nellie McKay, Morrison states: "Obviously, I can force characters to do what I want them to do, but knowing the difference between my forcing them and things coming out of the situation I have imagined is part of knowing what writing is about" (418).

3. The only other critic I know of who explicitly calls *Beloved* "undidactic" is Karen Fields: "*Beloved* is sober yet optimistic, intent yet undidactic" (161).

4. I borrow this alternative spelling from Morrison (cf. *Playing in the Dark* xi).

5. As Morrison herself has repeatedly stated, this has been one of her major concerns ever since *The Bluest Eye*. She has always been trying to encourage "participatory readings" rather than consumerist attitudes that consider the novels as finished products to be enjoyed and then put aside. In the interview with Nellie McKay, Morrison explains how she wants her books to work; the passage anticipates *Beloved* in interesting ways: "I am very happy to hear that my books haunt. That is what I work very hard for, and for me it is an achievement when they haunt readers, as you say. That is important because I think it is a corollary, or a parallel, or an outgrowth of what the oral tradition was, . . . The point was to tell the same story again and again. I can change it if I contribute to it when I tell it. I can emphasize special things. People who are listening comment on it and make it up, too, as it goes along. . . . I don't want to give my readers something to swallow. I want to give them something to feel and think about" (421). Nevertheless I think that *Beloved* reaches a climax in this endeavor that goes beyond her achievements in the earlier texts.

6. Lanser's *Fictions of Authority* has been influential for my approach toward strategies of authorization; Hirsch's *The Mother/Daughter Plot* argues that *Beloved* is one of the first novels in which the "voice of the mother" can be heard. Holloway's *Moorings and Metaphors* finally situates *Beloved* not within a context of (largely) white women's writing, but explores the connections between African American and African women writers' texts. — The frequent appearence of a chapter on *Beloved's* in studies that otherwise focus largely on novels by European American women writers raises the question of how it is meant to function in this context. In ways that require further study, Morrison's fifth novel seems to be considered more and more a prototypical black female text—with all the inherent risks of tokenism that such a usage entails.

7. For "author-studies," see, e.g., Heinze and T. Harris. — For meta-criticism, see Christian, "Fixing Methodologies: *Beloved*"; Diedrich, "Things Fall Apart: The Black Critical Controversy over Toni Morrison's *Beloved*"; Harding and Martin, "Reading at the Cultural Interface: The Corn Symbolism of *Beloved*."

8. For comments on *Beloved*, see especially "A Bench by the Road"; Byatt; Naylor and Morrison; Moyers; Schappell.

9. Heinze engages in related questions when she wonders "if Morrison's novels function in the same way that the ghost Beloved does—to haunt and to torment a guilty conscience in need of absolution and redemption, for in each of her works Morrison launders one American ideal after another, while a huge contingency of Americans—male and female, black and white, rich and poor—wildly cheer her on" (3). In contrast, Michele Wallace comments critically on such public recognition: "[T]he highly visible success of a few black women writers serves to

completely obscure the profound nature of the challenge black feminist creativity might pose to white male cultural hegemony. . . . [T]he media visibility of the black woman provides a symbolic substitute for substantive black female economic and political power, the lack of which is a good deal less visible" ("Variations on Negation" 214-215). — See also Christian, "Fixing Methodologies: *Beloved*." Christian is worried about the novel being appropriated by various critical discourses in ways that result in "the power of this novel as a specifically African American text . . . being blunted" (6).

10. This is reminiscent of Collins's description of how black women's alternative truth claims need to be validated by a black (female) community (cf. *Black Feminist Thought* 202-204).

11. See, e.g., Sara Blackburn's review of *Sula*; see also Morrison's comments on some of Bill Moyers's questions, in the interview conducted by Schappell (119-120).

12. In turn, she expresses appreciation to those critics "for whom the study of Afro-American literature is neither a crash course in neighborliness and tolerance, nor an infant to be carried, instructed or chastised or even whipped like a child, but the serious study of art forms that have much work to do, but are already legitimatized by their own cultural sources and predecessors— in or out of the canon" ("Unspeakable Things" 33).

13. This attitude not only sets her apart from Williams and Walker, but most significantly (especially in regard to *Beloved*) from the original slave narratives whose authors, for reasons of public acceptability, had to pay careful attention to reader expectations so as not to jeopardize their own precarious authority to speak at all. Slave narrators were often locked into modes of explanation that precluded attention to inner-racial needs. For a more detailed discussion of this issue, see Henderson, "Toni Morrison's *Beloved*."

14. Morrison's "spaces" differ from what Wolfgang Iser calls "gaps" in novelistic discourse (*Leerstellen*) in that they are not only rhetorical devices that are necessary to hold readers' interest. They are deliberate thematic and formal challenges to readers' expectations, in order to redefine the creative process as a whole as interactional rather than monologic and authoritarian.

15. So Morrison is, on the one hand, making use of conventional approaches to fiction because this allows her to be experimental in ways that other genres would not; on the other hand, she in a way redeems fiction and returns it to a place where a redefined "truth" is told. This is diametrically opposed to Michele Wallace's evaluation of black women's success in literature and music as highly problematic, because this denies them access to what she considers the really powerful discourses (cf. Wallace, "Negative Images" 244).

16. Such an attitude seems to be suggested by Lanser's statement that "even novelists who challenge this authority [as Western cultures have constructed it] are constrained to adopt the authorizing conventions of narrative voice in order, paradoxically, to mount an authoritative critique of the authority that the text therefore also perpetuates" (*Fictions of Authority* 7).

17. The incident is mentioned, e.g., in Frances E. W. Harper's 1892 novel *Iola Leroy, or Shadows Uplifted*: "My father says the slaves would be very well contented if no one put wrong notions in their heads. . . . I don't know, but I don't think that that slave mother who took her four children, crossed the Ohio river on the ice, killed one of the children and attempted the lives of the other two [sic] was a contented slave" (98). — Harper's poem "The Slave Mother: a Tale of the Ohio" is included in *The Complete Poems of Frances E. W. Harper* 28-30.

18. Cf. the following interpretation of this scene by David Lawrence: "In order to acquire the inscribing power of the white man's chisel, she must transform her body into a commodity; he

will grant the cherished script provided he first be granted the right of sexual inscription. Thus Sethe must temporarily 'kill off' her own body (she lies on a headstone, 'her knees wide open as a grave') to purchase the text that she thinks will buy her peace" (Lawrence 192).

19. Ella's attitude toward Sethe is indicative of the general mood in the community: "She understood Sethe's rage in the shed twenty years ago, but not her reaction to it, which Ella thought was prideful, misdirected, and Sethe herself too complicated. When she got out of jail and made no gesture toward anybody, and lived as though she were alone, Ella junked her and wouldn't give her the time of day" (B 256).

20. In this context, the question needs to be asked if Walker's *Jubilee* has to be considered as a necessary pretext for Morrison. How much positivistically assembled historical information does a reader need to comprehend the quality and scope of Morrison's revisionary act?

21. Sethe's family history—she is born around 1837 to an African mother—contains another implicit comment on 19th-century slave economics: the importation of Africans did not stop with the official ending of the Atlantic slave trade in 1808. The presence of Sixo, who is "in his twenties" around 1850, points to the same issue.

22. "If writing is thinking and discovery and selection and order and meaning, it is also awe and reverence and mystery and magic. I suppose I could dispense with the last four if I were not so deadly serious about fidelity to the milieu out of which I write and in which my ancestors actually lived. Infidelity to that milieu—the absence of the interior life, the deliberate excising of it from the records that the slaves themselves told—is precisely the problem in the discourse that preceded without us. How I gain access to that interior life is what drives me" ("Site of Memory" 111).

23. Morrison's treatment of the Middle Passage could be said to parallel Sethe's inability to talk about her daughter's death because putting it in language would mean to accept the loss—an aspect I will examine in detail later. For a detailed explication of Sethe's attitude toward language, see Wyatt.

24. Wyatt is drawing from Hortense Spillers's article "Mama's Baby, Papa's Maybe." Spillers writes: "Those African persons in 'Middle Passage' were literally suspended in the 'oceanic,' if we think of the latter in its Freudian orientation as an analogy for undifferentiated identity: removed from the indigenous land and culture, and not-yet 'American' either, these captive persons, without names that their captors would recognize, were in movement across the Atlantic, but they were also *nowhere* at all. Inasmuch as, on any given day, we might imagine, the captive personality did not know were s/he was, we could say that they were culturally 'unmade', thrown in the midst of a figurative darkness that 'exposed' their destinies to an unknown course" (72).

25. Cummings analyzes Sixo's behavior as follows: "Although the white men's punishment is intended to set an example for would-be runaways, Sixo will wrest another meaning from the masters' text, jamming the circuits of their disciplinary apparatus by withholding the pain that would become the other's "power" were it voiced. Sixo never screams nor cries out while burning; instead, he chooses silence and thereafter laughter .... Nearby, Paul discovers his friend's laughter to be contagious; in it he hears the voice of resistance and the self-proclaimed manhood of his race" (566).

26. Elisabeth Mermann, in her analysis how Morrison signifies on *Bildungsroman*-conventions, even speaks of *Beloved* having a double plot: "First, the analeptic stories of Sethe's escape from slavery and life in the Cincinnati community depict a process of *physical* (re)construction of the

subject after slavery has disassembled it. In the process, it revises the *Bildungsroman*'s assumptions by emphasizing the primacy of physicality. Second, the 1873 narrative focuses on the process of psychological recovery, specifically Sethe's healing from the repressed memory of her killing of her two-year old child" (78).

27. I adopt the term "memory work" from Mitscherlich's study *Erinnerungsarbeit*.

28. This is not to imply that Morrison relies exclusively on psychoanalytic theory; her outspoken interest in the "inner lives" of her characters suggests, however, a deep knowledge of and interest in psychoanalysis. Morrison expands and modifies this model—that I call "psychoanalytical" here for lack of a better term—by combining it with aspects that come out of African and African American culture. The existence of the ghost at the very beginning, the sudden mysterious appearance of Beloved, the ritual of healing, and especially Sethe's attitude toward time and history question basic Western concepts of what constitutes "reality"—both material and psychological, outer and inner—and how it is perceived. It will be the focus of a later section of this chapter how Morrison rewrites both Freud and Lacan by contextualizing her characters' psychological developments.

29. Brian Finney refers to Paul D's movements as an alternative way to describe the three-part structure: "Part One covers the half a year (from summer to winter) during which Paul D comes to live with Sethe until he leaves her. . . . Part Two covers the period from Paul D's departure . . . to Stamp Paid's discovery of Paul D at the church when he explains Sethe's actions in murdering her daughter. . . . Part Three moves from winter to spring, from the deterioration at 124, climaxing in Sethe's mistaken attack Mr. Bodwin [sic], to Beloved's disappearance and Paul D's return and reconciliation with Sethe" (30-31). Despite Paul D's obvious importance for the text, however, to subdivide the text mainly in relation to him appears to grant him too much influence. – Note that Part I is 18 chapters long, Part II 7 chapters, and Part III 3 chapters; lined up next to each other, these three numbers make up 1873, the novel's present. I owe this insight to Heike Hartrath, private conversation, April 8, 1994.

30. Beloved's role as instigator of complications in the Sethe/Paul D relationship is not explicitly spelled out in part I, but the intensity with which she claims Sethe's attention in part II suggests that she is not simply unhappy about certain turns of events in part I but actively tries to undermine Sethe's attempts to enter a new relationship. After Sethe's decision that "she wanted Paul D," Beloved fundamentally threatens his newly-found sense of stability and self-confidence by moving him out of the house and making him sleep with her. Although this ultimately has the positive effect of allowing Paul D to confront his own "ghosts of the past," it is also an expression of Beloved's envy and her desire to keep Sethe and Paul D separate.

31. The fact that he is shaking indicates that he has not yet totally internalized schoolteacher's lessons; the older man's authority is so binding, however, that the nephew is forced to distrust his own emotional, physical reactions. Only the sheriff shows some signs of being emotionally affected in his behavior toward Sethe; he treats her with some degree of civility.

32. The repeated references to eyes staring at the white men signify not only the "Other's gaze"; for a brief moment, roles are reversed, as the white men find themselves under the scrutiny of black people's open observation; they cannot return the gaze, but avert their eyes. They are forced into a position of defeat. Schoolteacher can only explain Sethe's staring at him by saying "she'd gone wild"—only a crazy black woman would dare to confront a white man like that; the scene clearly shows, however, that Sethe has shed all pretense to submissiveness.

Her looking back has the same effect as Sixo's talking back: neither of them any longer accepts schoolteacher's claims to authority.

33. For Baby Suggs, as for Sethe, schoolteacher's arrival marks a literal "return of the repressed"—it shows that "self-love" is hard to achieve as long as the system that insists on fragmentation and denial of self literally still exists. Geographical displacement alone is not enough.

34. In *Webster's New Collegiate Dictionary*, "unspeak" is given as a synonym of "unsay," which is explained as "to make as if not said: recant, retract."

35. Beloved can never really constitute herself as a subject in her own right; in a variety of ways, she needs to remain—as symbol for and embodiment of the past—an object; an object everybody else, including us as readers, can project our desires and fears onto. Cf. Wyatt's final comment that Beloved's story "continues to haunt the borders of a symbolic order that excludes it" (484).

36. See, for example, the black men's "talking" to each other through the chain in the chain gang (cf. *B* 110-111); see also the metaphorical baptism in sound in the final ritual: "[T]he voices of women searched for the right combination, the key, the code, the sound that broke the back of words. . . . It broke over Sethe and she trembled like the baptized in its wash" (*B* 261).

37. What is important to note here is that the mother—even the mother in extremely difficult circumstances—is not necessarily an impediment for the development of the child, but provides opportunities to grow.

38. Moving through several stages of Sethe's and Paul D's wish to become a family, and finally arriving at an alternative model in the last scene, Morrison revises the Lacanian notion of what constitutes a "typical" family configuration. She challenges Lacan's (decontextualized) stages of psycho-linguistic development from a position in which race and gender figure as important components. She also critiques the strict distinction between presymbolic relationships that are usually associated with the mother, and the child's later "entry into the symbolic," which is commonly associated with the father. What Morrison suggests instead is that what is important about these developmental stages is not gender, but power, and that a revised power structure—out of necessity—offers alternative means of maturation. If a healthy development of adult identity depends on on identification with as well as separation from one's parents or elders, slavery forcefully disrupted these processes. The black child could not enter into the "law of the father" and establish a secure sense of self, because the language of the powerful (white) "father"/master was meant to prevent just this (cf. also Wyatt and Spillers).

39. Margaret Homans expresses a similar idea: "*Beloved* . . . challenges narrative to accommodate the non-narrative space of memory. . . . [T]he novel presents the limits of storytelling as much as its powers. . . . [It casts a doubt] over its own allegiance to storytelling" ("Feminist Fictions" 10-11).

40. Morrison thus clearly distances herself from some of the tenets of French feminism, especially Hélène Cixous's contention that there is no place for women in "phallogocentric" language (cf. Cixous "Laugh of the Medusa").

41. Barbara Christian explicitly draws attention to Morrison's use of African cosmology and the need for critics to take this into consideration: "The [critical] perspective I am proposing is one that acknowledges the existence of an African cosmology, examines how that cosmology

has been consistently denigrated in the West, and explores its appropriateness for texts that are clearly derived from it" ("Fixing Methodologies" 7).

42. Morrison herself refers to the concept of *Nommo* in "Unspeakable Things" 33. Holloway picks up the notion of the word as creative force when she asserts that "[i]t is as if Sethe's telling, her voice, has assured Beloved her essence. Death loses its permanence in such a voiced universe. The essence of Beloved's presence is Sethe's remembrance of her" (*Moorings* 185); Rigney also refers to *Nommo* as "the creative potential" (231). Finally, there is a reference to *Nommo* in Kimberly Benston, "I yam what I am: The Topos of (Un)naming in Afro-American Literature." Benston does not make it explicit anywhere in his discussion, however, that parts of his text are directly quoted from Jahn.

43. "Wäre das Wort nicht, würden die Kräfte erstarren, wäre kein Zeugen, kein Wandel, kein Leben. 'Es gibt nichts, was es nicht gibt; wofür wir einen Namen haben, das gibt es,' lautet die Weisheit alter Yoruba-Priester. Der Spruch besagt, daß die Nennung, das Aussprechen das Genannte erzeugt. Die Nennung ist Beschwoerung, ist Schöpfungsakt. Was wir uns nicht vorstellen können, ist irreal, ist nicht existent. Jeder menschliche Gedanke aber wird, sobald ausgesprochen, zu Realität. Denn das Wort hält den Lauf der Dinge in Gang und verändert die Dinge, verwandelt sie. Und da das Wort diese Macht hat, ist jedes Wort ein Wirkwort, ist jedes Wort verbindlich. Es gibt kein 'harmloses,' kein unverbindliches Wort. Jedes Wort hat Folgen. Daher verpflichtet das Wort den Muntu. Und der Muntu ist verantwortlich für sein Wort" (*Muntu: Umrisse* 137-38)

44. Several critical articles on *Beloved* investigate the novel's acts of signifying on white-authored 19th-century texts that cannot be my explicit focus here; see, e.g., Mayer; Askeland; Castronovo.

45. Although Morrison herself is not explicitly mentioned in *The Black Book's*, she was the editor at Random House in charge of the project. Her personal involvement is nevertheless apparent, if only in an indirect way: both her parents are listed as contributors in the acknowledgments: "Ramah Wofford, George Carl Wofford." (This is also mentioned by Mobley 198 n.3.)

46. Morrison thus implicitly answers the call formulated by Mary Helen Washington in her introduction to the anthology *Any Woman's Blues*: "In all the great capitals—. . .—there are hundreds of monuments to them [white men], bronzed busts of immense proportions, statues of figures in ceremonial robes, documents and signatures on display in museums, all witnessing the historic power of men to mythologize themselves, to remake history, and to cast themselves eternally in heroic form. There is hardly any trace of women's lives. We have been erased from history" (xiii).

47. This also links *Beloved* with Paule Marshall's *The Chosen Place, the Timeless People* (1969) and *Daughters* (1991). Both novels are seeking ways for remembering and honoring African American and African Caribbean historical experience with a carnival procession, the statue of Will Cudjoe ad Congo Jane, and Ursa Mackenzie's wish to write her master's thesis about the slave rebellion on her home island.

Conclusion

1. To claim the "authority of experience" is both understandable and problematic. On the one hand, as Bar On explains, it justifies the claims "of members of socially marginalized groups to . . . produce their own self-defined descriptions of themselves and the world." On the other hand, "by claiming an authority based in epistemic privilege the group reinscribes the values and practices used to socially marginalize it by excluding its voice, silencing it and commanding its obedience to the voice of the dominant group" (95-97).

2. Especially in studies that compare historically oriented fiction by black women and black men, these critical dimensions are sometimes overlooked, and the women writers' novels are presented as lacking in theoretical insight into the discursive construction of "the past." Such an evaluation is unfounded. — See, e.g., Charles Johnson's evaluation of Morrison's writing in *Being and Race* (101); see also Benesch's brief reference to black women writers' historical fiction in *The Threat of History* (205).

3. One poignant example is Julie Dash's feature film *Daughters of the Dust*. As Dash herself states, her film is often compared to *Beloved*, although the shooting of the movie started before the novel went into print ("Dialogue" 36). If the film and the novel are therefore not explicitly referring to each other, the similarities in approach in these two works of art by African American women—despite the different media they chose—suggest that their revisionary projects are expressions of a more widespread concern within a black female cultural community. Like *Beloved*, *Daughters* invites its audience to let themselves be drawn into the black and female perspectives that are privileged in its narrative, although this identification does not necessarily work through a recognition of racial and gendered similarities. "The challenge for the audience," bell hooks states, "is to be able to see and see again this film until they require the apparatus to embrace it" (Dash, "Dialogue" 40). The same can certainly be said for novels like *Dessa Rose* and *Beloved*.

4. Barbara Christian explicitly situates *Jubilee* in a context of the historically possible when she writes that "[d]espite the many historical details about which she informs her readers, her characters have little internal life, perhaps because Walker, who is writing her historical novel in the forties and fifties before the rise of the black culture movements of the sixties, could not give slaves the right to claim those events they do not want to remember—not only what was done to them but what they might have had to do, given their precarious context. So Vyry is not complex in the way that Sethe and Dessa Rose are" ("Somebody Forgot to Tell" 334).

5. In regard to the critical discussion, I suggest that critics' needs to position themselves within academic contexts and to claim authoritative spaces for their own work also impacts on the theoretical frameworks with which they approach literary texts. This would recognize critics as a "receiving community" that also interacts with writers and texts in complex negotiations of critique, approval, and authority.

6. In a black feminist critical context, this has also already been attended to. For an investigation of black men's responses to African American women's writing, see Deborah McDowell, "Reading Family Matters"; for a study of black women as interpretive community, see Bobo.

Abel, Elizabeth. "Black Writing, White Reading: Race and the Politics of Feminist Interpretation." *Critical Inquiry* 19 (Spring 1993): 470-98.

-----. "Race, Class, and Psychoanalysis?" *Conflicts in Feminism*. Ed. Marianne Hirsch and Evelyn Fox Keller. New York: Routledge, 1990. 184-204.

Alcoff, Linda. "The Problem of Speaking for Others." *Cultural Critique* 20 (Winter 1991-92): 5-32.

-----, and Elizabeth Potter. "Introduction: When Feminism Intersects Epistemology." *Feminist Epistemologies*. Ed. Alcoff and Potter. New York: Routledge, 1993. 1-14.

Anderson, Linda. "The Re-Imagining of History in Contemporary Women's Fiction." *Plotting Change: Contemporary Women's Fiction*. Ed. Linda Anderson. London: Edward Arnold, 1990. 129-41.

Andrews, William. "The Novelization of Voice in Early African American Narrative." *PMLA* (January 1990): 23-34.

-----. "The Representation of Slavery and the Rise of Afro-American Literary Realism 1865-1920." *Slavery and the Literary Imagination*. Ed. Deborah McDowell and Arnold Rampersad. Baltimore: Johns Hopkins UP, 1989. 62-80.

-----. *To Tell a Free Story: The First Century of Afro-American Autobiography, 1760-1865*. Urbana: U of Illinois P, 1986.

Angelo, Bonnie. "The Pain of Being Black." Interview with Toni Morrison. *Time* 22 May 1989: 120-22.

Aptheker, Herbert. "Slave Guerilla Warfare." *To Be Free*. New York: Citadel, 1991 [[1]1948]. 11-30.

Ardener, Edwin. "The 'Problem' Revisited." *Perceiving Women*. Ed. Shirley Ardener. London: Malaby, 1975. 19-28.

Arendt, Hannah. "What Is Authority?" *Between Past and Future: Six Exercises in Political Thought*. New York: Viking, 1961. 91-141.

Askeland, Lori. "Remodeling the Model Home in *Uncle Tom's Cabin* and *Beloved*." *American Literature* 64.4 (December 1992): 785-805.

Atwood, Margaret. "Haunted by Their Nightmares." Rev. of *Beloved*. *New York Times Book Review* 13 Sept. 1987: 1, 49-50.

Awkward, Michael. *Inspiriting Influences: Tradition, Revision, and Afro-American Women's Novels*. New York: Columbia UP, 1989.

-----. "Negotiations of Power: White Critics, Black Texts, and the Self-Referential Impulse." *American Literary History* 2 (Winter 1990): 581-606.

Baker-Fletcher, Karen. "Fierce Love Comes to Haunt." Rev. of *Beloved*. *Commonweal* 6 Nov. 1987: 631-33.

Bakerman, Jane. "The Seams Can't Show." Interview with Toni Morrison. *Black American Literature Forum* 12 (Summer 1978): 56-60.

Bakhtin, Mikhail. "Discourse in the Novel." *The Dialogic Imagination*. Ed. Michael Holquist. Austin: U of Texas P, 1981. 259-422.

Bar On, Bat-Ami. "Marginality and Epistemic Privilege." *Feminist Epistemologies.* Ed. Linda Alcoff and Elizabeth Potter. New York: Routledge, 1993. 83-100.

Barksdale, Richard K. "Margaret Walker: Folk Orature and Historical Prophecy." *Black American Poets Between Worlds, 1940-1960.* Ed. R. Baxter Miller. Knoxville: U of Tennessee P, 1986. 104-17.

Basel, Marilyn K. "Walker, Margaret Abigail." *Contemporary Authors.* New Revision Series. Vol. 26. Detroit: Gale, 1989. 451-54.

-----. "Williams, Sherley Anne." *Contemporary Authors.* New Revision Series. Vol. 25. Detroit: Gale, 1989. 492-94.

Bassett, P. S. "A Visit to the Slave Mother Who Killed Her Child." *The Black Book.* Ed. Middleton Harris et al. New York: Random House, 1974. 10.

Bauer, Dale. *Feminist Dialogics: A Theory of Failed Community.* Albany: State U of New York P, 1986.

Belenky, Mary, Blythe Clinchy, Nancy Goldberger, and Jill Tarule. *Women's Ways of Knowing: The Development of Self, Voice, and Mind.* New York: Basic, 1986.

Bell, Bernard. *The Afro-American Novel and Its Tradition.* Amherst: U of Massachusetts P, 1987.

-----. "*Beloved*: A Womanist Neo-Slave Narrative; or Multivocal Remembrances of Things Past." *African American Review* 26.1 (Spring 1992): 7-15.

Belsey, Catherine. *Critical Practice.* London: Routledge, 1980.

Benesch, Klaus. *The Threat of History: Geschichte und Erzählung im afro-amerikanischen Roman der Gegenwart.* Essen: Die Blaue Eule, 1990.

Benston, Kimberly. "I yam what I am: The Topos of (Un)naming in Afro-American Literature." *Black Literature and Literary Theory.* Ed. Henry Louis Gates, Jr. New York: Methuen, 1984. 151-74.

Bercovitch, Sacvan. "The Problem of Ideology in American Literary History." *Critical Inquiry* 12 (1986): 631-53.

Bhabha, Homi. "Introduction: Locations of Culture." *The Location of Culture.* New York: Routledge, 1994. 1-18.

Blackburn, Sara. Rev. of *Sula. NY Times Book Review* 30 Dec 1973: 3.

Blake, Susan L. "Toni Morrison." *Dictionary of Literary Biography, Vol 33: Afro-American Fiction Writers after 1955.* Ed. Thadious Davis and Trudier Harris. Detroit: Gale, 1984. 187-99.

Blassingame, John W. "Using the Testimony of Ex-Slaves: Approaches and Problems." *The Slave's Narrative.* Ed. Charles T. Davis and Henry Louis Gates, Jr. Oxford: Oxford UP, 1985. 78-97.

Bobo, Jacqueline. *Black Women as Cultural Readers.* New York: Columbia UP, 1995.

Bontemps, Arna. *Black Thunder.* Boston: Beacon, 1992 [[1]1936].

Bowers, Susan. "*Beloved* and the New Apocalypse." *Journal of Ethnic Studies* 18.1 (Spring 1990): 59-76.

Bradley, David. "On the Lam From Race and Gender." Rev. of *Dessa Rose. New York Times* 3 Aug. 1986: vii, 7.

Bradley, David. *The Chaneysville Incident.* New York: Avon Books, 1981.

Braxton, Joanne M., and Andrée Nicola McLaughlin, eds. *Wild Women in the Whirlwind: Afra-American Culture and the Contemporary Literary Renaissance.* New Brunswick: Rutgers UP, 1990.

Broad, Robert L. "Giving Blood to the Scraps: Haints, History, and Hosea in *Beloved*." *African American Review* 28.2 (Summer 1994): 189-96.

Bröck, Sabine. "A Trace of Body Writing." *"Beloved, she's mine." Essais sur* Beloved *de Toni Morrison*. Ed. Geneviève Fabre and Claudine Raynaud. Paris: Cetanla, 1993. 133-38.

Bröck-Sallah, Sabine. "Plots to a Happy Ending: Re-Reading Closure." *Feminist Critical Negotiations*. Ed. Alice Parker and Elizabeth Meese. Amsterdam: John Benjamin, 1992. 59-81.

-----. "Women Writing: Plotting Against HIStory." *Reconstructing American Literary and Historical Studies*. Ed. Günter Lenz et al. Frankfurt: Campus, 1990. 225-37.

Brown, Elsa Barkley. "African-American Women's Quilting: A Framework for Conceptualizing and Teaching African-American Women's History." *Signs* 14.4 (Summer 1989): 921-29.

Buckmaster, Henrietta. "The Other Side of the Plantation." Rev. of *Jubilee*. *Christian Science Monitor* 29 Sept. 1966: 11.

Busia, Abena P.B. "Words Whispered over Voids: A Context for Black Women's Rebellious Voices in the Novel of the African Diaspora." *Studies in Black American Literature, vol III: Black Feminist Criticism and Critical Theory*. Ed. Joe Weixlmann and Houston A. Baker, Jr. Greenwood: Penkevill, 1988. 1-42.

Butler, Octavia. *Kindred*. Boston: Beacon, 1988 [¹1979].

Byatt, A.S. Interview with Toni Morrison. Video. Dir. Fenella Greenfield. ICA Videos, 1989.

-----. Rev. of *Beloved*. *Passions of the Mind: Selected Essays*. New York: Random, 1993. 230-32.

Campbell, Joseph. *The Hero with a Thousand Faces*. Princeton: Princeton UP, 1968 [¹1949].

Campbell, Stanley W. *The Slave Catchers: Enforcement of the Fugititve Slave Law, 1850-1860*. Chapel Hill: U of North Carolina P, 1970.

Carby, Hazel V. "Ideologies of Black Folk: The Historical Novel of Slavery." *Slavery and the Literary Imagination*. Ed. Deborah McDowell and Arnold Rampersad. Baltimore: Johns Hopkins UP, 1989. 125-43.

-----. *Reconstructing Womanhood: The Emergence of the Afro-American Woman Novelist*. New York: Oxford UP, 1987.

Caruth, Cathy. "Unclaimed Experience: Trauma and the Possibility of History." *Yale French Studies* 79 (1991): 181-92.

Castronovo, Russ. "*Beloved* as Political Rememory: Towards a Transvaluation of American Freedom." *"Beloved, she's mine." Essais sur* Beloved *de Toni Morrison*. Ed. Geneviève Fabre and Claudine Raynaud. Paris: Cetanla, 1993. 35-44.

Chambers, Ross. *Story and Situation: Narrative Seduction and the Power of Fiction*. Minneapolis: U of Minnesota P, 1984.

Chase-Riboud, Barbara. *Sally Hemings*. New York: Seaver-Viking, 1979.

Christian, Barbara T. *Black Feminist Criticism: Perspectives on Black Women Writers*. New York: Pergamon P, 1985.

-----. *Black Women Novelists: The Development of a Tradition, 1892-1976*. Westport: Greenwood, 1980.

-----. "Fixing Methodologies: *Beloved*." *Cultural Critique* 24 (Spring 1993): 5-15.

-----. "Layered Rhythms: Virginia Woolf and Toni Morrison." *Modern Fiction Studies* 39.3/4 (Fall/Winter 1993): 483-500.

-----. "The Race for Theory." *Feminist Studies* 14.1 (1988): 67-79.

-----. "'Somebody Forgot to Tell Somebody Something': African-American Women's Historical Novels." *Wild Women in the Whirlwind.* Ed. Joanne M. Braxton and Andrée Nicola McLaughlin. New Brunswick: Rutgers UP, 1990. 326-41.

Cixous, Hélène. "The Laugh of the Medusa." *New French Feminisms.* Ed. Elaine Marks and Isabelle de Courtivron. New York: Schocken Books, 1981. 245-64.

Clarke, John Henrik. "African-American Historians and the Reclaiming of African History." *African Culture: The Rhythms of Unity.* Ed. Molefi Asante and Kariamu Asante. Westport: Greenwood, 1985. 157-71.

-----, ed. *William Styron's Nat Turner: Ten Black Writers Respond.* Boston: Beacon, 1968.

Clayton, Jay. "The Narrative Turn in Recent Minority Fiction." *American Literary History* 2.3 (Fall 1990): 375-93.

Clemons, Walter. "A Gravestone of Memories." Rev. of *Beloved. Newsweek* 28 Sept. 1987: 74-5.

Collins, Patricia Hill. *Black Feminist Thought.* Boston: Unwin Hyman, 1990.

-----. "The Social Construction of Black Feminist Thought." *Signs* 14.4 (Summer 1989): 745-73.

Cooper, J. California. *Family.* New York: Doubleday, 1991.

Cornwell-Giles. JoAnne. "Afro-American Criticism and Western Consciousness: The Politics of Knowing." *Black American Literature Forum* 24.1 (Spring 1990): 85-98.

Crouch, Stanley. "'Aunt Medea': *Beloved* by Toni Morrison." Rev. of *Beloved. The New Republic* 19 Oct. 1987: 38-41.

Cummings, Kate. "Reclaiming the Mother('s) Tongue: *Beloved, Ceremony, Mothers and Shadows.*" *College English* 52.5 (September 1990): 552-69.

Darling, Marsha. "In the Realm of Responsibility: A Conversation with Toni Morrison." *Women's Review of Books* 5.6 (March 1988): 5-6.

-----. "Ties that Bind." Rev. of *Beloved. The Women's Review of Books* 5.6 (March 1988): 4-5.

Dash, Julie, dir. *Daughters of the Dust.* Geechee Girls/American Playhouse, 1991.

Dash, Julie. "Dialogue between bell hooks and Julie Dash." *Daughters of the Dust: The Making of an African American Woman's Film.* New York: New Press, 1992. 27-67.

Davenport, Doris. Rev. of *Dessa Rose. Black American Literature Forum* 20 (Fall 1986): 335-40.

Davies, Carole Boyce. "Mother Right/Write Revisited: *Beloved* and *Dessa Rose* and the Construction of Motherhood in Black Women's Fiction." *Narrating Mothers: Theorizing Material Subjectivities.* Ed. Brenda O. Daly and Maureen T. Reddy. Knoxville: U of Tennessee P, 1991. 44-57.

Davis, Angela. "Reflections on the Black Woman's Role in the Community of Slaves." *Black Scholar* (December 1971): 2-15.

Davis, Mary Kemp. "Everybody Knows Her Name: The Recovery of the Past in Sherley Anne Williams's *Dessa Rose.*" *Callaloo* 12.3 (Summer 1989): 544-57.

Dehay, Terry. "Narrating Memory." *Memory, Narrative and Identity.* Ed. Amritjit Singh et al. Boston: Northeastern UP, 1994. 26-44.

de Lauretis, Teresa. "The Technology of Gender." *Technologies of Gender: Essays on Theory, Film, and Fiction.* Basingstoke: Macmillan, 1987. 1-30.

Demetrakopoulos, Stephanie A. "Maternal Bonds as Devourers of Women's Individuation in Toni Morrison's *Beloved.*" *African American Review* 26.1 (Spring 1992): 51-59.

Diedrich, Maria. "Sherley Anne Williams: 'Meditations on History.'" *The African American Short Story*. Ed. Wolfgang Karrer and Barbara Puschmann-Nalenz. Trier: Wiss. Buchverlag Trier, 1993. 133-44.

-----. "Things Fall Apart: The Black Critical Controversy over Toni Morrison's *Beloved.*" *Amerikastudien* 34.2 (1989): 175-86.

DuBois, W.E.B. *Black Reconstruction in America, 1860-1880*. New York: Atheneum, 1979 [¹1935].

duCille, Ann. "The (Oc)cult of True Black Womanhood: Critical Demeanor and Black Feminist Studies." *Signs* 19.3 (Spring 1994): 591-629.

DuPlessis, Rachel Blau. "For the Etruscans." *The New Feminist Criticism*. Ed. Elaine Showalter. New York: Pantheon, 1985. 271-291.

-----. *Writing beyond the Ending: Narrative Strategies of Twentieth-Century Women Writers*. Bloomington: Indiana UP, 1985.

Egejuru, Phanuel, and Robert Elliot Fox. "An Interview with Margaret Walker." *Callaloo* 2.2 (May 1979): 29-35.

Elkins, Stanley. *Slavery: A Problem in American Institutional and Intellectual Life*. Chicago: U of Chicago P, 1968 [¹1959].

Ensslen, Klaus. "Fictionalizing History: David Bradley's *The Chaneysville Incident.*" *Callaloo* 11.2 (1988): 280-295.

Felman, Shoshona. *Jacques Lacan and the Adventure of Insight: Psychoanalysis in Contemporary Culture*. Cambridge: Harvard UP, 1987.

Ferguson, Rebecca. "History, Memory and Language in Toni Morrison's *Beloved.*" *Feminist Criticism: Theory and Practice*. Ed. Susan Sellers and Linda Hutcheon. Toronto: U of Toronto P, 1991. 109-127.

Fields, Karen. "To Embrace Dead Strangers." *Mother Puzzles: Daughters and Mothers in Contemporary American Literature*. Ed. Mickey Pearlman. Westport, CT: Greenwood, 1989. 159-169.

Finney, Brian. "Temporal Defamiliarization in Toni Morrison's *Beloved.*" *Obsidian II: Black Literature in Review* 5.1 (Spring 1990): 20-36.

Flax, Jane. *Thinking Fragments: Psychoanalysis, Feminism, and Postmodernism in the Contemporary West*. Berkeley: U of California P, 1990.

Fogel, Robert, and Stanley Engermann. *Time on the Cross: The Economics of American Negro Slavery*. Boston: Little, Brown, 1974.

Foley, Barbara. "History, Fiction, and the Ground Between: The Uses of the Documentary Mode in Black Literature." *PMLA* 95 (1980): 389-403.

-----. *Telling the Truth: The Theory and Practice of Documentary Fiction*. Ithaca: Cornell UP, 1986.

Foster, Frances Smith. *Witnessing Slavery: The Development of Ante-Bellum Slave Narratives*. Westport: Greenwood, 1979.

Fox-Genovese, Elizabeth. "Strategies and Forms of Resistance: Focus on Slave Women in the United States." *In Resistance: Studies in African, Caribbean, and Afro-American History*. Ed. Gary Okihiro. Amherst: U of Massachusetts P, 1986. 143-165.

-----. *Within the Plantation Household: Black and White Women of the Old South*. Chapel Hill: U of North Carolina P, 1988.

Freibert, Lucy. "Southern Song: An Interview with Margaret Walker." *Frontiers* 9.3 (1987): 50-6.

Friedman, Richard B. "On the Concept of Authority in Political Philosophy." *Concepts in Social and Political Philosophy*. Ed. Richard Flathman. New York: Macmillan, 1973.

Friedman, Susan Stanford. "Beyond White and Other: Relationality and Narratives of Race in Feminist Discourse." *Signs* 21.1 (Autumn 1995): 1-49.

-----. "Post/Poststructuralist Feminist Criticism." *New Literary History* 22 (1991): 467-492.

-----. "Spatialization: A Strategy for Reading Narrative." *Narrative* 1.1 (January 1993): 12-23.

-----. "Weavings: Intertextuality and the (Re)birth of the Author." *Influence and Intertextuality in Literary History*. Ed. Eric Rothstein and Jay Clayton. Madison: U of Wisconsin P, 1992. 146-80.

Frye, Joanne. *Living Stories, Telling Lives: Women and the Novel in Contemporary Experience*. Ann Arbor: U of Michigan P, 1986.

Fultz, Lucie. "Images of Motherhood in Toni Morrison's *Beloved*." *Double Stitch: Black Women Write about Mothers and Daughters*. Ed. Patricia Bell-Scott. New York: Beacon, 1991. 32-41.

Gable, Mona. "Understanding the Impossible." Rev. of *Dessa Rose*. *Los Angeles Times Magazine* 7 Dec. 1986: 22, 24, 27-28.

Gaines, Ernest. *The Autobiography of Miss Jane Pittman*. New York: Bantam Books, 1972 [[1]1971].

Gates, Henry Louis, Jr. *The Signifying Monkey: A Theory of African American Literary Criticism*. New York: Oxford UP, 1988.

-----. "'What's Love Got To Do with It?' Critical Theory, Integrity, and the Black Idiom." *New Literary History* 18.2 (Winter 1986): 345-362.

-----, ed. *Reading Black, Reading Feminist: A Critical Anthology*. New York: Meridian, 1990.

Genette, Gérard. *Paratexts: Thresholds of Interpretation*. Transl. Jane E. Lewin. Cambridge: Cambridge UP, 1997.

Genovese, Eugene D. *Roll, Jordan, Roll: The World the Slaves Made*. New York: Pantheon, 1974.

-----. "William Styron before the People's Court." *Critical Essays on William Styron*. Ed. Arthur D. Casciato and James L.W. West. Boston: G.K. Hall, 1982. 201-212.

Giddings, Paula. *When and Where I Enter: The Impact of Black Women on Race and Sex in America*. New York: Bantam, 1984.

Giovanni, Nikki, and Margaret Walker. *A Poetic Equation: Conversations between Nikki Giovanni and Margaret Walker*. Washington: Howard UP, 1974.

Goldman, Anne E. "'I made the ink': (Literary) Production and Reproduction in *Dessa Rose* and *Beloved*." *Feminist Studies* 16.2 (Summer 1990): 313-330.

Gomez, Jewelle. *The Gilda Stories*. New York: Firebrand Books, 1991.

Goodman, Charlotte. "From *Uncle Tom's Cabin* to Vyry's Kitchen: The Black Female Folk Tradition in Margaret Walker's *Jubilee*." *Traditions and the Talents of Women*. Ed. Florence Howe. Urbana: U of Illinois P, 1991. 328-337.

Graham, Maryemma. "The Fusion of Ideas: An Interview with Margaret Walker Alexander." *African American Review* 27.2 (Summer 1993): 279-287.

-----. "Margaret Walker and the Vision of Afro-American Life." *Langston Hughes Review* 7.2 (Fall 1988): 22-27.

Greene, Gayle. "Feminist Fiction and the Uses of Memory." *Signs* 16.2 (Winter 1991): 290-321.

Greenlee, Marcia. Interview with Margaret Walker. *The Black Women Oral History Project*. Vol. II. Ed. Ruth Edmonds Hill. Westport: Meckler, 1991. 3-65.

Gwin, Minrose G. "*Jubilee*: The Black Woman's Celebration of Human Community." *Conjuring: Black Women, Fiction, and Literary Tradition*. Ed. Marjorie Pryse and Hortense Spillers. Bloomington: Indiana UP, 1985. 132-150.

Haley, Alex. *Roots*. New York: Dell, 1977 [¹1976].

Hall, Cheryl. "Beyond the 'Literary Habit': Oral Tradition and Jazz in *Beloved*." *MELUS* 19.1 (Spring 1994): 89-95.

Harding, Sandra. "Rethinking Standpoint Epistemology." *Feminist Epistemologies*. Ed. Linda Alcoff and Elizabeth Potter. New York: Routledge, 1993. 49-82.

Harding, Wendy, and Jacky Martin. "Reading at the Cultural Interface: The Corn Symbolism of *Beloved*." *MELUS* 19.2 (Summer 1994): 85-97.

Harper, Frances E. W. *Iola Leroy, or Shadows Uplifted*. New York: Oxford UP, 1988 [¹1892].

-----. "The Slave Mother: a Tale of the Ohio" (1874). *The Complete Poems of Frances E. W. Harper*. Ed. Maryemma Graham. New York: Oxford UP, 1988. 28-30.

Harris, Middleton, et al., eds. *The Black Book*. New York: Random, 1974.

Harris, Trudier. *Fiction and Folklore: The Novels of Toni Morrison*. Knoxville: U of Tennessee P, 1991.

Harrison, Jane. "Sherley Williams's Post-Pastoral Vision: *Dessa Rose*." *Female Pastoral: Women Writers Re-Visioning the American South*. Knoxville: U of Tennessee P, 1991. 117-31.

Hein, Hilde, and Carolyn Korsmeyer, eds. *Aesthetics in Feminist Perspective*. Bloomington: Indiana UP, 1993.

Heinze, Denise. *The Dilemma of "Double-Consciousness": Toni Morrison's Novels*. Athens: U of Georgia P, 1993.

Henderson, Mae Gwendolyn. "Response" [to Houston A. Baker. "There Is No More Beautiful Way: Theory and the Poetics of Afro-American Women's Writing"]. *Afro-American Literary Study in the 1900s*. Ed. Houston A. Baker and Patricia Redmond. Chicago: U of Chicago P, 1989. 155-163.

-----. "Speaking in Tongues: Dialogics, Dialectics, and the Black Woman Writer's Literary Tradition." *Changing Our Own Words: Essays on Criticism, Theory, and Writing by Black Women*. Ed. Cheryl Wall. New Brunswick: Rutgers UP, 1989. 16-37.

-----. "Toni Morrison's *Beloved*: Re-Membering the Body as Historical Text." *Comparative American Identities: Race, Sex, and Nationality in the Modern Text*. Ed. Hortense Spillers. New York: Routledge, 1991. 62-86.

-----. "(W)Riting *The Work* and Working the Rites." *Black American Literature Forum* 23.4 (Winter 1989): 631-60.

Heron, Liz. "It Won't Let Go." Rev. of *Beloved*. *The Listener* 29 Oct. 1987: 28.

Higginbotham, Evelyn Brooks. "Beyond the Sound of Silence: Afro-American Women in History." *Gender and History* 1.1 (Spring 1989): 50-67.

Hirsch, Marianne. *The Mother/Daughter Plot: Narrative, Psychoanalysis, Feminism*. Bloomington: Indiana UP, 1989.

Hof, Renate. "Engendering Authority: Zum Verhältnis von Autorität und Autorschaft." *Die Grammatik der Geschlechter: Gender als Analysekategorie der Literaturwissenschaft.* Frankfurt: Campus, 1995. 145-66.

Holloway, Karla. "*Beloved*: A Spiritual." *Callaloo: A Journal of Afro-American Arts and Letters* 13 (1990): 516-25.

-----. *Moorings and Metaphors: Figures of Culture and Gender in Black Women's Literature.* New Brunswick: Rutgers UP, 1992.

-----. Rev. of *Beloved. Black American Literature Forum* 23.1 (Spring 1989): 179-82.

-----. "Revision and (Re)membrance: A Theory of Literary Structures in Literature by African-American Women Writers." *Black American Literature Forum* 24.4 (Winter 1990): 617-31.

Homans, Margaret. "Feminist Fictions and Feminist Theories of Narrative." *Narrative* 2.1 (January 1994): 13-16.

-----. "'Women of Color' Writers and Feminist Theory." *New Literary History* 25 (Winter 1994): 73-94.

hooks, bell. "Choosing the Margin as a Space of Radical Openness." *Yearning: Race, Gender, and Cultural Politics.* Boston: South End Press, 1990. 145-54.

-----. "Feminist Scholarship: Ethical Issues." *Talking Back: Thinking Feminist, Thinking Black.* Boston: South End Press, 1989. 42-48.

-----. "Revolutionary Black Women: Making Ourselves Subject." *Black Looks: Race and Representation.* Boston: South End Press, 1992. 41-60.

Horvitz, Deborah. "Nameless Ghosts: Possession and Dispossession in *Beloved.*" *Studies in American Fiction* 17.2 (Autumn 1989): 157-67.

House, Elizabeth B. "Toni Morrison's Ghost: The Beloved Who Is Not Beloved." *Studies in American Fiction* 18.1 (Spring 1990): 17-26.

Huggins, Nathan Irvin. *Black Odyssey: The Afro-American Ordeal in Slavery.* New York: Vintage, 1979.

Hutcheon, Linda. "Historiographic Metafiction: Parody and the Intertextuality of History." *Intertextuality and Contemporary American Fiction.* Ed. Patrick O'Donnell and Robert Con Davis. Baltimore: Johns Hopkins UP, 1989. 3-34.

Inscoe, John. "Slave Rebellion in the First Person: The Literary 'Confessions' of Nat Turner and Dessa Rose." *The Virginia Magazine of History and Biography* 97.4 (Oct. 89): 419-36.

Irele, Abiola. "Narrative, History, and the African Imagination." *Narrative* 1.2 (May 1993): 156-72.

Iser, Wolfgang. *Der Akt des Lesens.* München: Fink, 1976.

Jablon, Madelyn. "Rememory, Dream Memory, and Revision in Toni Morrison's *Beloved* and Alice Walker's *The Temple of My Familiar.*" *CLA Journal* 37.2 (Dec 1993): 136-44.

Jacobs, Harriet. *Incidents in the Life of a Slave Girl.* Ed. Jean Fagan Yellin. Cambridge: Harvard UP, 1987 [¹1861].

Jahn, Janheinz. *Muntu: An Outline of the New African Culture.* Transl. Marjorie Grene. New York: Grove, 1961.

-----. *Muntu: Umrisse der neoafrikanschen Kultur.* Düsseldorf: Diederichs, 1958.

Jessee, Sharon. "'Tell me your earrings': Time and the Marvelous in Toni Morrison's *Beloved*." *Memory, Narrative and Identity*. Ed. Amritjit Singh et al. Boston: Northeastern UP, 1994. 198-211.

Johnson, Charles. *Being and Race: Black Writing since 1970*. Bloomington: Indiana UP, 1990.

-----. *Middle Passage*. New York: Plume, 1991.

-----. *Oxherding Tale*. Bloomington: Indiana UP, 1982.

Johnson, James Weldon, and J. Rosamond Johnson. *The Book of American Negro Spirituals*. New York: Da Capo, 1977.

Jones, Bessie. "An Interview with Toni Morrison." *The World of Toni Morrison: Explorations in Literary Criticism*. Dubuque: Kendall/Hunt, 1985. 127-51.

Jones, Gayl. *Corregidora*. Boston: Beacon, 1975.

-----. "Multiple Voiced Blues: Sherley A. Williams's 'Someone Sweet Angel Chile." *Liberating Voices*. New York: Penguin, 1992. 38-43.

Jones, Jacqueline. *Labor of Love, Labor of Sorrow: Black Women, Work, and the Family from Slavery to the Present*. New York: Basic Books, 1985.

Jones, Kathleen B. "On Authority: Or, Why Women Are Not Entitled to Speak." *Feminism and Foucault: Reflections on Resistance*. Ed. Irene Diamond and Lee Quinby. Boston: Northeastern UP, 1988. 119-34.

Jones, Suzanne W., ed. *Writing the Woman Artist: Essays on Poetics, Politics, and Portraiture*. Philadelphia: U of Pennsylvania P, 1991.

Jordan, Shirley M. "Sherley Anne Williams."*Broken Silences: Interviews with Black and White Women Writers*. New Brunswick: Rutgers UP, 1993. 285-301.

Joyce, Joyce A. "The Black Canon: Reconstructing Black American Literary Criticism." *New Literary Criticism* 18.2 (Winter 1986): 335-44.

Katz, Bernard, ed. *The Social Implications of Early Negro Music in the United States*. New York: Arno, 1969.

Kekeh, Andrée-Anne. "Sherley Anne Williams's *Dessa Rose*: History and the Disruptive Power of Memory." *History and Memory in African-American Culture*. Ed. Geneviève Fabre and Robert O'Meally. New York: Oxford UP, 1994. 119-27.

Kellner, Hans. *Language and Historical Representation: Getting the Story Crooked*. Madison: U of Wisconsin P, 1989.

Killens, John Oliver. "To Margaret Walker Alexander." *The Zora Neale Hurston Forum* 1.2 (Spring 1987): 19-21.

King, Nicole R. "Meditations and Mediations: Issues of History and Fiction in *Dessa Rose*." *Soundings* 76.2-3 (Summer/Fall 1993): 351-68.

Klotman, Phyllis Rauch. "'Oh Freedom'--Women and History in Margaret Walker's *Jubilee*." *Black American Literature Forum* 11.4 (Winter 1977): 139-45.

Koenen, Anne. "'Women out of Sequence': An Interview with Toni Morrison." *History and Tradition in Afro-American Culture*. Ed. Günter H. Lenz. Frankfurt: Campus, 1984. 207-21.

Kolodny, Annette. "A Map for Rereading: Gender and the Interpretation of Literary Texts." *The New Feminist Criticism*. Ed. Elaine Showalter. New York: Pantheon, 1985. 46-62.

Krumholz, Linda. "The Ghosts of Slavery: Historical Recovery in Toni Morrison's *Beloved*." *African American Review* 26.3 (Fall 1992): 395-408.

-----. "Ritual and Reconstruction: Toni Morrison's *Beloved* and the Making of History." Unpublished manuscript. Madison, 1989.

-----. "Ritual, Reader, and Narrative in the Works of Leslie Marmon Silko and Toni Morrison." U of Wisconsin-Madison Diss., 1991.

Kubitschek, Missy Dehn. *Claiming the Heritage: African-American Women Novelists and History.* Jackson: UP of Mississippi, 1991.

Lanser, Susan Sniader. *Fictions of Authority: Women Writers and Narrative Voice.* Ithaca/London: Cornell UP, 1992.

-----. *The Narrative Act: Point of View in Prose Fiction.* Princeton: Princeton UP, 1981.

-----. "Toward a Feminist Narratology." *Feminisms.* Ed. Robyn R. Warhol and Diane Price Herndl. New Brunswick: Rutgers UP, 1991. 610-29.

Lawrence, David. "Fleshly Ghosts and Ghostly Flesh." *Studies in American Fiction* 19.2 (Autumn 1992): 189-201.

Lee, Hermione. "The Women's Gloom." Rev. of *Beloved. The Observer* 11 Oct. 1987: 27.

Lehmann-Haupt, Christopher. "Friendship in Chains." Rev. of *Dessa Rose. New York Times* 12 July 1986: i, 12.

Lerner, Gerda, ed. "The Case of Margaret Garner." *Black Women in White America: A Documentary History.* New York: Vintage, 1973. 60-63.

Levin, Jack, and William Levin. *The Functions of Discrimination and Prejudice.* New York: Harper and Row, 1982.

Levine, Lawrence W. *Black Culture and Black Consciousness: Afro-American Folk Thought from Salvery to Freedom.* Oxford: Oxford UP, 1977.

Lidinsky, April. "Prophesying Bodies: Calling for a Politics of Collectivity in Toni Morrison's *Beloved.*" *The Discourse of Slavery: Aphra Behn to Toni Morrison.* Ed. Carl Plasa and Betty J. Ring. London: Routledge, 1994. 191-216.

Liscio, Lorraine. "*Beloved*'s Narrative: Writing Mother's Milk." *Tulsa Studies in Women's Literature* 11.1 (Spring 1992): 31-46.

Little, Jonathan. "Charles Johnson's Revolutionary *Oxherding Tale.*" *Studies in American Fiction* 19.2 (Autumn 1991): 141-52.

Lorde, Audre. "Age, Race, Class, and Sex: Women Redefining Difference." *Sister Outsider.* Freedom, CA: The Crossing Press, 1984. 114-123.

-----. "Eye to Eye: Black Women, Hatred, and Anger." *Sister Outsider.* Freedom, CA: The Crossing Press, 1984. 145-75.

-----. "Foreword." *Wild Women in the Whirlwind: Afra-American Culture and the Contemporary Literary Renaissance.* Ed. Joanne M. Braxton and Andrée Nicola McLaughlin. New Brunswick: Rutgers UP, 1990. xi-xiii.

-----. "The Master's Tools Will Never Dismantle the Master's House." *Sister Outsider.* Freedom, CA: The Crossing Press, 1984. 110-13.

-----. "The Uses of Anger: Women Responding to Racism." *Sister Outsider.* Freedom, CA: The Crossing Press, 1984. 124-33.

-----. *Zami: A New Spelling of My Name.* London: Sheba, 1984.

Lukács, Georg. *The Historical Novel.* Translated by Hannah and Stanley Mitchell. Lincoln: U of Nebraska P, 1983.

Lukács, Georg. *Probleme des Realismus III: Der historische Roman.* Neuwied/Berlin: Luchterhand, 1965.

Maroney, Sheila. "New View of the Plantation." Rev. of *Jubilee. The Crisis* 73.9 (Nov 1966): 493.

Marshall, Paule. *The Chosen Place, the Timeless People.* New York: Vintage, 1992 [¹1969].

-----. *Daughters.* New York: Atheneum, 1991.

Martin, Wallace. *Recent Theories of Narrative.* Ithaca: Cornell UP, 1986.

Mathieson, Barbara Offutt. "Memory and Mother Love in Morrison's *Beloved.*" *American Imago* 47.1 (Spring 1990): 1-21.

Mayer, Sylvia. "'You Like Huckleberries?' Toni Morrison's *Beloved* and Mark Twain's *Adventures of Huckleberry Finn.*" *The Black Columbiad: Defining Moments in African American Literature and Culture.* Ed. Werner Sollers and Maria Diedrich. Cambridge: Harvard UP, 1994. 337-46.

Mbiti, John. *African Religions and Philosophy.* London: Heinemann, 1969.

McDowell, Deborah E. "'The Changing Same': Generational Connections and Black Women Novelists." *Reading Feminist, Reading Black: A Critical Anthology.* Ed. Henry Louis Gates, Jr. New York: Meridan, 1990. 91-115.

-----. "Negotiating between Tenses: Witnessing Slavery after Freedom--*Dessa Rose.*" *Slavery and the Literary Imagination.* Ed. Arnold Rampersad and Deborah McDowell. Baltimore: Johns Hopkins UP, 1989. 144-64.

-----. "New Directions for Black Feminist Criticism." *The New Feminist Criticism.* Ed. Elaine Showalter. New York: Pantheon, 1985. 186-99.

-----. "Reading Family Matters." *Changing Our Own Words.* Ed. Cheryl A. Wall. New Brunswick: Rutgers UP, 1989. 75-97.

McDowell, Margaret. "The Black Woman as Artist and Critic: Four Versions." *Kentucky Review* 7.1 (Spring 1987): 19-41.

McKay, Nellie. "An Interview with Toni Morrison." *Contemporary Literature* 24.4 (Winter 1983): 413-30.

McKible, Adam. "'These are the facts of the darky's history': Thinking History and Reading Names in Four African American Texts." *African American Review* 28.2 (Summer 1994): 223-35.

Meese, Elizabeth. "(Trans)Forming the Grammar of Racism in Sherley Anne Williams's *Dessa Rose.*" *(Ex)Tensions: Re-Figuring Feminist Criticism.* Urbana: U of Illinois Press, 1990. 129-54.

Mermann, Elisabeth. "A New Cultural Politics: Women Writers and Postmodernism." Diss., U of Wisconsin-Madison, 1993.

Meyer, Laure. *Black Africa: Masks, Sculpture, Jewelry.* Paris: Terrail, 1992.

Miller, Jane. "Understanding Slavery." Rev. of *Beloved. London Review of Books* 12 Nov. 1987: 8.

Miller, R. Baxter. "The 'Intricate Design' of Margaret Walker: Literary and Biblical Re-Creation in Southern History." *Black American Poets Between Worlds, 1940-1960.* Ed. R. Baxter Miller. Knoxville: U of Tennessee P, 1986. 118-35.

Min-Ha, Trinh. *Woman, Native, Other.* Bloomington: Indiana UP, 1989.

Mitchell, G. Duncan. "Authority." *A New Dictionary of Sociology.* London: Routlegde & Kegan Paul, 1979.

Mitscherlich, Margarete. *Erinnerungsarbeit: Zur Psychoanalyse der Unfähigkeit zu trauern.* Frankfurt: Fischer, 1993.

Mobley, Marilyn Sanders. "A Different Remembering: Memory, History and Meaning in Toni Morrison's *Beloved*." *Toni Morrison*. Ed. Harold Bloom. New York: Chelsea, 1990. 189-99.

Moglen, Helene. "Redeeming History: Toni Morrison's *Beloved*." *Cultural Critique* 24 (Spring 1993): 17-40.

Mohanty, Satya P. "The Epistemic Status of Cultural Identity: On *Beloved* and the Postcolonial Condition." *Cultural Critique* (Spring 1993): 41-80.

Moody, Joycelyn K. "Ripping Away the Veil of Slavery: Literacy, Communal Love, and Self-Esteem in Three Slave Women's Narratives." *Black American Literature Forum* 24.4 (Winter 1990): 633-48.

Morrison, Toni. *Beloved*. London. Triad Granada, 1988 [[1]1987].

-----. "A Bench by the Road: *Beloved*." *The World* (January/February 1989): 4, 5, 37-41.

-----. "Introduction: Friday on the Potomac." *Race-ing Justice, En-gendering Power*. New York: Pantheon, 1992. vii-xxx.

-----. "Memory, Creation, and Writing." *Thought* 59 (Dec. 1984): 385-90.

-----. *The Nobel Lecture in Literature, 1993*. New York: Knopf, 1994.

-----. *Playing in the Dark: Whiteness and the Literary Imagination*. Cambridge: Harvard UP, 1992.

-----. "Rediscovering Black History." *New York Times Magazine* 11 Aug. 1974: 14-24.

-----. "Rootedness: The Ancestor as Foundation." *Black Women Writers: Arguments and Interviews*. Ed. Mari Evans. London: Pluto, 1985. 339-45.

-----. "The Site of Memory." *Inventing the Truth: The Art and Craft of Memoir*. Ed. William Zinsser. Boston: Houghton Mifflin, 1987. 103-24.

-----. *Sula*. New York: Plume, 1982 [[1]1973].

-----. "Unspeakable Things Unspoken: The Afro-American Presence in American Literature." *Michigan Quarterly Review* 28.1 (Winter 1989): 1-34.

-----. "Writers Together." *The Nation* 24 Oct. 1981: 396-97, 412.

Morton, Patricia. *Disfigured Images: The Historical Assault on Afro-American Women*. New York: Praeger, 1991.

Moyers, Bill. "Toni Morrison: Novelist." *A World of Ideas, II: Public Opinions from Private Citizens*. New York: Doubleday, 1990. 54-63.

Moynihan, Daniel P. *The Negro Family: the Case for National Action*. Washington, D.C.: United States Department of Labor, Office of Policy Planning and Research, 1965.

Narayan, Uma. "The Project of Feminist Epistemology." *Gender/Body/Knowledge*. Ed. Alison Jaggar and Susan Bordo. New Brunswick: Rutgers UP, 1989. 256-69.

Naylor, Gloria, and Toni Morrison. "A Conversation." *The Southern Review* 21 (1985): 567-92.

Nielsen, Aldon L. "Of Slave Girls and Women: Two Epilogues." *Writing between the Lines: Race and Intertextuality*. Athens: U of Georgia P, 1994. 253-82.

Nora, Pierre. "Between Memory and History: *Les Lieux de Memoire*." *History and Memory in African-American Culture*. Ed. Geneviéve Fabre and Robert O'Meally. New York: Oxford UP, 1994. 284-300.

Ong, Walter. *Orality and Literacy: The Technologizing of the Word*. New York: Routledge, 1982.

Orr, Linda. "The Revenge of Literature: A History of History." *New Literary History* 18.1 (Autumn 1986): 1-22.

Otten, Terri. *The Crime of Innocence in the Fiction of Toni Morrison.* Columbia: U of Missouri P, 1989.

Page, Philip. "Circularity in Toni Morrison's *Beloved.*" *African American Review* 26.1 (Spring 1992): 31-39.

Patterson, Orlando. *Slavery and Social Death: A Comparative Study.* Cambridge: Harvard UP, 1982.

Pennington, Dorthy L. "Time in African Culture." *African Culture: The Rhythms of Unity.* Ed. Molefi Asante and Kariamu Asante. Westport: Greenwood, 1985. 123-39.

Peterson, Nancy. "The Politics of Language: Feminist Theory and Contemporary Works by Women of Color." Diss., U of Wisconsin-Madison, 1991.

Pettis, Joyce. "The Historical Novel as Best Seller." *Kentucky Folklore Record* 25.3 (1979): 51-59.

-----. "Margaret Walker: Black Woman Writer of the South." *Southern Women Writers: The New Generation.* Ed. Tonette Bond Inge. Tuscaloosa: U of Alabama P, 1990. 9-19.

Phelan, James. "Narrative Discourse, Literary Character, and Ideology." *Reading Narrative: Form, Ethics, Ideology.* Ed. James Phelan. Ohio State UP, 1989. 132-46.

-----. "Toward a Rhetorical Reader-Response Criticism: The Difficult, the Stubborn, and the Ending of *Beloved.*" *Modern Fiction Studies* 39.3/4 (Fall/Winter 1993): 710-28.

Porter, Nancy. "Women's Interracial Friendships and Visions of Community in *Meridian, The Salt Eaters, Civil Wars,* and *Dessa Rose.*" *Tradition and the Talents of Women.* Urbana: U of Illinois P, 1991. 251-67.

Poussaint, Alvin F. "*The Confessions of Nat Turner* and the Dilemma of William Styron." *William Styron's Nat Turner: Ten Black Writers Respond.* Boston: Beacon, 1968: 17-22.

Prettyman, Quandra. "Visibility and Difference: Black Women in History and Literature--Pieces of a Paper and Some Ruminations." *The Future of Difference.* Ed. Hester Eisenstein and Alice Jardine. New Brunswick: Rutgers UP, 1985. 239-46.

Rainwater, Lee, and William L. Yancey. *The Moynihan Report and the Politics of Controversy.* Cambridge: M.I.T. Press, 1967.

Ray, Benjamin C. "African Religions: An Overview." *Encyclopedia of World Religions.* Vol. 1. Ed. Mircea Eliade. New York: Macmillan, 1987. 60-69.

Reed, Ishmael. *Flight to Canada.* New York: Random, 1976.

Rev. of *Jubilee. Publishers Weekly* 21 Aug. 1967: 76.

Rich, Adrienne. "When We Dead Awaken: Writing as Re-Vision." *On Lies, Secrets, and Silence.* London: Virago, 1980. 33-49.

Rigney, Barbara Hill. "'A Story to Pass On': Ghosts and the Significance of History in Toni Morrison's *Beloved.*" *Haunting the House of Fiction: Feminist Perspectives on Ghost Stories by American Women.* Ed. Lynette Carpenter and Wendy L. Kolmar. Knoxville: U of Tennessee P, 1991. 229-35.

Rimmon-Kenan, Shlomith. *Narrative Fiction: Contemporary Poetics.* Lon-don/New York: Methuen, 1983.

Rodrigues, Eusebio. "The Telling of *Beloved.*" *Journal of Narrative Technique* 21.2 (Spring 1991): 153-69.

Ross, Jean W. "*CA* Interview: Sherley Anne Williams." *Contemporary Authors.* New Revision Series, vol. 25. Detroit: Gale, 1989. 494-96.

Rothstein, Mervyn. "Toni Morrison, in Her New Novel, Defends Women." Rev. of *Beloved*. *New York Times* 26 Aug. 1987: C17.

Rowell, Charles. "Poetry, History, and Humanism: An Interview with Margaret Walker." *Black World* (Dec. 1975): 4-17.

Rubenstein, Roberta. *Boundaries of the Self: Gender, Culture, Fiction*. Urbana: U of Illinois P, 1987.

Rumens, Carol. "Shades of the Prison-House." Rev. of *Beloved*. *Times Literary Supplement* 16 Oct. 1987: 1135.

Rushdy, Ashraf. "Daughters Signifyin(g) History: The Example of Toni Morrison's *Beloved*." *American Literature* 64.3 (Sept 1992): 567-97.

-----. "'I Write in Tongues': The Supplement of Voice in Barbara Chase-Riboud's *Sally Hemings*." *Contemporary Literature* 35.1 (Spring 1994): 101-35.

-----. "The Phenomenology of the Allmuseri: Charles Johnson and the Subject of the Narrative of Slavery." *African American Review* 26.3 (Fall 1992): 373-93.

-----. "'Reading Mammy': The Subject of Relation in Sherley Anne Williams' *Dessa Rose*." *African American Review* 27.3 (Fall 1993): 365-90.

-----. "'Rememory': Primal Scenes and Constructions in Toni Morrison's Novels." *Contemporary Literature* 31 (1990): 300-23.

Sale, Maggie. "Call and Response as Critical Method: African-American Oral Traditions and *Beloved*." *African American Review* 26.1 (Spring 1992): 41-50.

Sale, Roger. "Toni Morrison's *Beloved*." *Toni Morrison*. Ed. Harold Bloom. New York: Chelsea House, 1990. 165-70.

Samuels, Wilfried, and Clenora Hudson-Weems. "'Ripping the Veil': Meaning through Rememory in *Beloved*." *Toni Morrison*. Boston: Twayne, 1990. 94-138.

Schappell, Elissa. "Toni Morrison: The Art of Fiction." *Paris Review* 128 (Fall 1993): 83-125.

Schwartz, Amy. "*Beloved*: It's Not a Question of Who Suffered More." *The Washington Post* 3 April 1988: B7.

Schweickart, Patrocinio. "Reading Ourselves: Toward a Feminist Theory of Reading." *Feminisms: An Anthology of Literary Theory and Criticism*. Ed. Robyn R. Warhol and Diane Price Herndl. New Brunswick: Rutgers UP, 1991. 525-50.

Shapiro, Herbert. "Historiography and Slave Revolt and Rebelliousness in the United States: A Class Approach." *In Resistance: Studies in African, Caribbean, and Afro-American History*. Ed. Gary Okihiro. Amherst: U of Massachusetts P, 1986. 133-41.

Showalter, Elaine. "Feminism in the Wilderness." *The New Feminist Criticism*. Ed. Elaine Showalter. New York: Pantheon, 1985. 243-70.

Sievers, Stefanie. "Escaping the Master('s) Narrative? Sherley Anne Williams's Rethinking of Historical Representation in 'Meditations on History.'" *Re-Visioning the Past: Historical Self-Reflexivity in American Short Fiction*. Ed. Bernd Engler and Oliver Scheiding. Trier: Wissenschaftlicher Verlag Trier, 1998. 365-81.

-----. "Rethinking Feminist Fictions of Authority." Workshop "Gender and Genre." German Association for American Studies Convention/Jahrestagung der Deutschen Gesellschaft für Amerikastudien. Hamburg, June 7, 1995.

Sitter, Deborah Ayer. "The Making of a Man: Dialogic Meaning in *Beloved*." *African American Review* 26.1 (Spring 1992): 17-29.

222

Smart, Barry. *Michel Foucault.* London: Tavistock, 1985.

Smith, Amanda. "Toni Morrison." *Publishers Weekly* 21 Aug. 1987: 50-51.

Smith, Barbara. "Introduction." *Home Girls: A Black Feminist Anthology.* Ed. Barbara Smith. New York: Kitchen Table/Women of Color Press, 1983. xix-lvi.

-----. "Toward a Black Feminist Criticism." *The New Feminist Criticism.* Ed. Elaine Showalter. New York: Pantheon, 1985. 168-85.

Smith, Valerie. "Black Feminist Theory and the Representation of the 'Other.'" *Changing Our Own Words: Essays on Criticism, Theory, and Writing by Black Women.* Ed. Cheryl Wall. New Brunswick: Rutgers UP, 1989. 38-57.

Smith-Wright, Geraldine. "In Spite of the Klan: Ghosts in the Fictions of Black Women Writers." *Haunting the House of Fiction: Feminist Perspectives on Ghost Stories by American Women.* Ed. Lynette Carpenter and Wendy Kolmar. Knoxville: U of Tennessee P, 1991. 142-65.

Snitow, Ann. "Death Duties: Toni Morrison Looks Back in Sorrow." Rev. of *Beloved. Village Voice Literary Supplement* 58 (September 1987): 25-26.

Spears, James. "Black Folk Elements in Margaret Walker's *Jubilee.*" *Mississippi Folklore Register* 14 (1980): 13-19.

Spelman, Elizabeth. "Now You See Her, Now You Don't." *The Inessential Woman.* Boston: Beacon, 1988. 160-88.

Spillers, Hortense J. "Afterword: Cross-Currents, Discontinuities: Black Women's Fiction." *Conjuring: Black Women, Fiction, and Literary Tradition.* Ed. Marjorie Pryse and Hortense J. Spillers. Bloomington: Indiana UP, 1985. 249-61.

-----. "A Hateful Passion, a Lost Love." *Feminist Issues in Literary Scholarship.* Ed. Shari Benstock. Bloomington: Indiana UP, 1987. 181-207.

-----. "Mama's Baby, Papa's Maybe: An American Grammar Book." *Diacritics* (Summer 1987): 65-81.

Spivak, Gayatri Chakravorty. "Subaltern Studies: Deconstructing Historiography." *In Other Worlds: Essays in Cultural Politics.* New York: Methuen, 1987. 197-221.

Stepto, Robert B. *From Behind the Veil.* Urbana: U of Illinois P, 1979.

-----. "'Intimate Things in Place.'" Interview with Toni Morrison. *Massachusetts Review* 18.3 (Autumn 1977): 473-89.

-----. "I Rose and Found My Voice: Narration, Authentication, and Authorial Control in Four Slave Narratives." *The Slave's Narrative.* Ed. Charles T. Davis and Henry Louis Gates, Jr. Oxford: Oxford UP, 1985. 225-41.

Stuart, Andrea. "Telling Our Story." Interview with Toni Morrison. *Spare Rib* 189 (April 1988): 12-15.

Styron, William. *The Confessions of Nat Turner.* London: Panther Books, 1968 [¹1967].

-----. "Nat Turner Revisited." *American Heritage* 43.6 (October 1992): 64-73.

-----. "This Quiet Dust." *This Quiet Dust and Other Writings.* New York: Random, 1982. 9-20.

Takaki, Ronald. *Iron Cages: Race and Culture in 19th-Century America.* New York: Oxford UP, 1990.

Tate, Claudia. "Allegories of Black Female Desire; or, Rereading Nineteenth-Century Sentimental Narratives of Black Female Authority." *Changing Our Own Words.* Ed. Cheryl A. Wall. New Brunswick: Rutgers UP, 1989. 98-126.

-----. "Gayl Jones." *Black Women Writers at Work.* New York: Continuum, 1983. 90-99.

-----. "Margaret Walker." *Black Women Writers at Work*. New York: Continuum, 1983. 188-204.

-----. "Sherley Anne Williams." *Black Women Writers at Work*. New York: Continuum, 1983. 205-13.

Thelwell, Mike. "Back With the Wind: Mr. Styron and the Reverend Turner." *William Styron's Nat Turner: Ten Black Writers Respond*. Ed. John H. Clarke. Boston: Beacon, 1968. 79-91.

"Toni Morrison: *Beloved* - Pulitzer Prize: Fiction." *Contemporary Literary Criticism*, Vol. 55: *Yearbook 1988*. Ed. Roger Matuz. Detroit: Gale, 1989. 194-213.

Traylor, Eleanor. "Music as Theme: The Blues Mode in the Works of Margaret Walker." *Black Women Writers, 1950-1980*. Ed. Mari Evans. London: Pluto, 1985. 511-25.

Walker, Alice. *The Color Purple*. London: The Women's Press, 1983.

-----. *The Temple of My Familiar*. New York: Harcourt Brace, 1989.

-----. "Writing *The Color Purple*." *In Search of Our Mothers' Gardens*. London: The Women's Press, 1984. 355-60.

Walker, Margaret. "How I Wrote *Jubilee*" [11972]. *How I Wrote Jubilee and Other Essays on Life and Literature*. Ed. Maryemma Graham. New York: Feminist Press, 1990. 50-65.

-----. "The Humanistic Tradition of Afro-American Literature." *How I Wrote Jubilee and Other Essays on Life and Literature*. Ed. Maryemma Graham. New York: Feminist Press, 1990. 121-133.

-----. *Jubilee*. Toronto/New York: Bantam, 1967 [11966].

-----. "On Being Female, Black, and Free." *The Writer on Her Work*. Ed. Janet Sternburg. New York: Norton, 1980. 95-106.

-----. "Religion, Poetry, and History: Foundations for a New Educational System." *The Black Seventies*. Ed. Floyd Barbour. Boston: Horizon, 1970. 284-95.

-----. *Richard Wright: Daemonic Genius*. New York: Amistad, 1988.

-----. *This Is My Century: New and Collected Poems*. Athens: U of Georgia P, 1989.

-----. "Willing to Pay the Price." *How I Wrote Jubilee and Other Essays on Life and Literature*. Ed. Maryemma Graham. New York: Feminist Press, 1990. 15-25.

Walker, Melissa. "Slavery and Reconstruction." *Down from the Mountaintop: Black Women's Novels in the Wake of the Civil Rights Movement, 1966-1989*. New Haven: Yale UP, 1991. 13-46.

Wall, Cheryl. "Introduction: Taking Positions and Changing Words." *Changing Our Own Words: Essays on Criticism, Theory, and Writing by Black Women*. New Brunswick: Rutgers UP, 1989. 1-15.

Wallace, Michele. "Negative Images: Towards a Black Female Cultural Criticism." *Invisibility Blues: From Pop to Theory*. New York: Verso, 1990. 241-56.

-----. "Slaves of History." *Invisibility Blues: From Pop to Theory*. New York: Verso, 1990. 137-45. [first published in *The Women's Review of Books* 4.1 (Oct 1986): 1, 3-4.]

-----. "Variations on Negation and the Heresies of Black Female Creativity." *Invisibility Blues: From Pop to Theory*. New York: Verso, 1990. 213-40.

Ward, Jerry W. "A Writer for Her People: An Interview with Dr. Margaret Walker Alexander." *Mississippi Quarterly* 41.4 (Fall 1988): 515-27.

Washington, Mary Helen. "In Pursuit of Our Own History." *Any Woman's Blues: Stories by Contemporary Black Women Writers*. London: Virago, 1986. xiii-xxv.

-----. "Sherley Anne Williams." *Any Woman's Blues*. London: Virago, 1986. 198-99.

White, Deborah Gray. *Ar'n't I a Woman? Female Slaves in the Plantation South*. New York: Norton, 1985.

White, Hayden. "The Forms of Wildness: Archaeology of an Idea." *Tropics of Discourse: Essays in Cultural Criticism*. Baltimore: Johns Hopkins UP, 1978. 150-82.

-----. "The Value of Narrativity in the Representation of Reality." *Critical Inquiry* 7 (1980): 5-28.

Williams, Delores S. "Black Women's Literature and the Task of Feminist Theology." *Immaculate and Powerful: The Female in Sacred Image and Social Reality*. Ed. Clarissa W. Atkinson et al. Boston: Beacon, 1985. 88-109.

Williams, Patricia J. *The Alchemy of Race and Rights*. Cambridge: Harvard UP, 1991.

Williams, Sherley Anne. "The Blues Roots of Afro-American Poetry." *Chant of Saints*. Ed. Michael Harper and Robert Stepto. Urbana: U of Illinois P, 1979. 123-35.

-----. "Cultural and Interpersonal Aspects of Black Male/Female Relationships: Comment on the Curb." *The Black Scholar* (May-June 1979): 49-51.

-----. *Dessa Rose*. New York: Berkley Books, 1987 [¹1986].

-----. *Give Birth to Brightness: A Thematic Study in Neo-Black Literature*. New York: Dial Press, 1972.

-----. "The Lion's History: The Ghetto Writes B[l]ack." *Soundings* 76.2-3 (Summer/Fall 1993): 245-60.

-----. "Meditations on History." *Any Woman's Blues: Stories by Contemporary Black Women Writers*. Ed. Mary Helen Washington. London: Virago, 1986. 200-48.

-----. "Some Implications of Womanist Theory." *Reading Black, Reading Feminist*. Ed. Henry Louis Gates, Jr. New York: Meridian, 1990. 68-75.

Williams, Shirley [sic]. *The Peacock Poems*. Middletown, CT: Wesleyan UP, 1975.

Willis, Susan. *Specifying: Black Women Writing the American Experience*. Madison: U of Wisconsin P, 1987.

Witt, Judith. "Black Maternity: 'A Need for Someone to Want the Black Baby to Live.'" *Abortion, Choice, and Contemporary Fiction: The Armageddon of the Maternal Instinct*. Chicago: U of Chicago P, 1990. 132-66.

Wolff, Cynthia Griffin. "'Margaret Garner': A Cincinnati Story." *The Massachusetts Review* 32.2 (Fall 1991): 417-40.

Wyatt, Jean. "Giving Body to the Word: The Maternal Symbolic in Toni Morrison's *Beloved*." *PMLA* 108.3 (May 1993): 474-88.

Young, James E. "The Texture of Memory: Holocaust Memorials and Meaning." *Writing and Rewriting the Holocaust*. Bloomington: Indiana UP, 1988. 172-89.

Young, Melvina Johnson. "Exploring the WPA Narratives: Finding the Voices of Black Women and Men." *Theorizing Black Feminisms: The Visionary Pragmatism of Black Women*. Ed. Stanlie M. James and Abena P.A. Busia. New York: Routledge, 1993. 55-74.

FORECAAST

(Forum for European Contributions
to African American Studies)

Maria Diedrich; Carl Pedersen;
Justine Tally (eds.)
Mapping African America
History, Narrative Formation, and the
Production of Knowledge
The world of African America extends throughout
the northern, central, southern and insular parts of
the American continent. The essays included in
this volume take the creation of that world as a
single object of study, tracing significant routes and
contacts, building comparisons and contrasts. They
thus participate in the reworking of traditional
approaches to the study of history, the critique
of literature and culture, and the production of
knowledge. All are engaged in an effort to locate
the African American experience within a wider
pan-African vision that links the colonial with the
postcolonial, the past with the present, the African
with the Western.
Mapping African America sketches lines that,
far from limiting our geography, extend our
knowledge of the Africanist influence on and their
participation in what is generally called "Western"
culture. This creative challenge to traditional
disciplines will not only enhance the reader's
understanding of African American Studies but
will also help forge links with other academic
fields of inquiry.
Bd. 1, 1999, 256 S., 59,80 DM*, br., ISBN 3-8258-3328-3

Justine Tally
Toni Morrison's (Hi)stories and Truths
Toni Morison's *Paradise* (1998) arrived on
the scene amid vociferous acclaim and much
consternation. Third in the trilogy begun with
Beloved and *Jazz,* this fascinating yet complicated
the novel has sown as much confusion as
admiration. How does it work? How does the
novel close the trilogy? Indeed, a major complaint
amog reviewers, why does Morrison overload us
with so many characters and stories?
In this first book-length study of *Paradise*, Justin
Tally securely links the work to Morrison's entire
oeuvre and effectively argues that while all of
the novels of the trilogy are deeply analytical of
the relationship of memory, story and history,
the historical narrative: memory is fickle, story is
unreliable, and history is subject to manipulation.
A master narrative of the past is again dictated by
the dominant discourse, but this time the control
exerted is black und male, not white and male.
Though this stranglehold threatens to deaden life
and put the future on hold, Morrison's narrative
disruptions challenge the very nature of this
"paradise" on earth.
With these considerations, *"Paradise"*
Reconsidered locates the author at the center

of the on-going literary and cultural debates of
the late 20th century: the postmodern discussion
of history, particularly Afro-centrist history, the
production of knowledge, the class divisions that
are shattering the black community, and questions
of "race" and essentialism. What does ist mean to
be "black"? And who is the white girl anyway?
Bd. 3, 1999, 112 S., 34,80 DM*, br., ISBN 3-8258-4204-5

Anglophone Literaturen
Anglophone Literatures
Hamburger Beiträge zur Erforschung neuerer
englischsprachiger Literaturen
Hamburg Studies in the New Literatures in English
Herausgeber/General Editors:
Gerd Dose und Bettina Keil

Gerd Dose; Bettina Keil (Eds.)
Writing in Australia
Perceptions of Australian Literature in Its
Historical and Cultural Context
A Series of Lectures Given at Hamburg
University on the Occasion of the 1st Festival
of Australian Literature in Hamburg 1995
Bd. 1, 1999, 248 S., 38,80 DM*, br., ISBN 3-8258-2796-8

Susanne Braun-Bau
Natur und Psyche
Landschafts- und Bewußtseinsdarstellung in
australischen Romanen des 20. Jahrhunderts
Die Untersuchung australischer Romane lädt zu
einer Reise durch literarische Landschaften ein. Sie
beginnt zur Jahrhundertwende mit Joseph Furphy
als frühem Vertreter des modernen Romans und
zeigt eine Entwicklung auf, die schließlich in der
Auflösung realer Landschaften in eine *Psychogeo-*
graphie bei Gerald Murnanc gipfelt.
Mentale Prozesse sind Filterinstanzen, die zwischen die Landschaft und ihre literarische Umsetzung treten. Die literarische Umsetzung die-
ser 'Filter' wird analysiert, um ein umfassendes
Erklärungsmodell für die kominierende Busch-
bildlichkeit in der Literatur Australiens, die bis
heute fortwirkt, zu entwerfen. Das Stereotyp des
menschenfeindlichen *Outback* erweist sich als
Frustration der perzipierenden Figur, die eine an
britische Konventionen geprägte Bewußtseins-
haltung auf die Natur projiziert. Diese mentale
Haltung ist den Naturgegebenheiten Australiens
unangemessen.
Dabei ermöglicht die breite Auswahl von Romanen die Ableitung einer historische Stufenfolge,
bei der sich im Verhältnis von Protagonist und
Landschaft eine zunehmende Bewußtseinsdomi-
nanz herauskristallisiert. Die Untersuchung liefert
daher einen wichtigen Beitrag zur australischen
Literaturgeschichte und stellt ein Stufenmodell als

LIT Verlag Münster – Hamburg – London
Bestellungen über: Grevener Str. 179 48159 Münster Tel.: 0251 – 23 50 91 Fax: 0251 – 23 19 72
∗ unverbindliche Preisempfehlung

)moderne Romanent-

, ISBN 3-8258-2824-7

Horst Priebnitz; Marion Spies (Hrsg.)
**Neuere Informationsmittel zur Literatur
Australiens**
Ein bibliographischer Essay
Der bibliographische Essay richtet sich an litera-
...schaftliche Intersssenten auf der Suche
...ormationen zur Literatur- und Kul-
...des 5. Kontinents. Gleichzeitig ist
...im Aufbau einer Spezialabteilung
...srelevanten Informationsmittel in
...konzipiert.
..., 19,80 DM*, br., ISBN 3-8258-31

...ser Studien zur Anglist
...und Amerikanistik
...eben am Institut für Anglistik
...nistik (Martin-Luther-Univers
Halle-Wittenberg)

Martin Meyer; Gabriele Spengemann;
Wolf Kindermann (Hrsg.)
Tangenten: Literatur & Geschichte
Die Hallenser Studien zur Anglistik und A
kanistik wollen an die Tradition des Dialog
den inzwischen vielfältig verzweigten Teilg
eines einstmals einheitlichen Faches anknü
wie sie durch den Hallenser Anglisten Han
und seine Kollegen gepflegt wurde.
Der vorliegende erste Band der Reihe ist d
Weyhe-Schüler Martin Schulze gewidmet,
sen Werdegang und Tätigkeit als Hochschu
die vielschichtigen Entwicklungen des Fac
Schatten des Ost-West-Konfliktes spiegelt,
sen Initiative die Hallenser Anglistik die C
eines Neubeginns verdankt.
Die hier versammelten Beiträge zur englise
amerikanischen Literatur, zu Geschichte, S
wissenschaft und Bildungspolitik eint trotz
Vielfalt der Blick auf die Wechselbeziehun
zwischen europäischer und amerikanischer
turtradition sowie das Bemühen um den D
zwischen den philologischen und den histo
sozialwissenschaftlichen Disziplinen.
Bd. 1, 1996, 278 S., 48,80 DM*, br., ISBN 3-8258-

Wolf Kindermann (Hrsg.)
**Entwicklungslinien: 120 Jahre Angl
Halle**
Das Institut für Anglistik und Amerikanist
Martin-Luther-Universität in Halle und Wi
feierte im Jahr 1996 sein 120jähriges Best
erstes rein englisches Seminar in deutsche
kann es auf eine lange Tradition der angli
Forschung und Lehre, vor allem auf dem
von Sprachwissenschaft und Sprachgeschi

zurückblicken. Namhafte Fachgelehrte, unter ihnen
Friedrich E. Elze, Max Förster, Max Deutschbein,
Hans Weyhe und Otto Ritter, haben die Geschichte
der Hallenser Anglistik mit geprägt. Heute steht
das Institut vor einem Neubeginn, der sich aber
auch den Entwicklungslinien der Hallenser Anglistik verpflichtet fühlen muß.
Der vorliegende Band soll durch Forschungs-
ergebnisse und Arbeitsproben von Mitarbeitern
und Gästen des Instituts die thematische Vielfalt
des Neubeginns dokumentieren. Er umfaßt neben
einem kurzen Überblick zur Institutsgeschichte
Beiträge zur Realismusproblematik in der engli-

DATE DUE

Demco, Inc. 38-293

LIT Verlag Münster – Hamburg – London
Bestellungen über: Grevener Str. 179 48159 Münster Tel.: 0251 – 23 50 91 Fax: 0251 – 23 19 72
* unverbindliche Preisempfehlung